CHURCH AND POLITICS TODAY

CHURCH AND POLITICS TODAY

ESSAYS ON THE ROLE OF THE CHURCH OF ENGLAND IN CONTEMPORARY POLITICS

EDITED BY

GEORGE MOYSER

T. & T. CLARK LIMITED
59 GEORGE STREET, EDINBURGH

Copyright © T. & T. Clark Ltd, 1985
Index compiled by Pennart Publishing Services
Typeset by Pennart Publishing Services, Edinburgh, Scotland
printed and bound by Page Brothers (Norwich) Ltd., England

for

T. & T. CLARK LTD, EDINBURGH

FIRST PRINTED 1985

British Library Cataloguing in Publication Data

Church and Politics Today: essays on the role of the Church of England in
contemporary politics.
1. Church of England 2. Church and State – Church of England
I. Moyser, George
261.7   BX5157

ISBN: 0 567 29350 5

FOREWORD

Church–State relationships in England are passing through an uneasy period. Parliamentary rebuffs, criticism of Church involvement in politics, uncertainty and division within the Church of England itself about its role in public life, these are only a few of the symptoms pointing to much deeper unresolved problems of theological understanding. The essays in this book do not provide any solutions. They do, however, provide a clear articulation of some of the questions, and a wealth of useful information with which to tackle them. I see it as an important contribution to a long-standing debate. Those who speak in easy generalities about religion and politics now have no excuse for their ignorance.

As one who has participated in much of what the book describes, I can vouch for its general accuracy. I detect a slightly false note in Frank Field's essay on the Church of England and Parliament largely, I suspect, because he has a politician's tendency to attribute a greater measure of political foresight and cunning to the leadership of the Church than, in my experience, it actually possesses. I am conscious, too, that John Elford's essay on the Church and Nuclear Defence Policy lacks an important dimension through concentrating on public documents and public debate. The huge personal contribution made by people like Robert Stopford when he was Bishop of London, in promoting informed discussion among Christians with widely different views on defence matters, is one of those hidden factors which those who are dependent on the literature can easily overlook.

But these are marginal comments on a work which for the most part I find convincing. The Church of England continues to have an extraordinary fascination as an object of public scrutiny. This book will appeal, not only to hardened church-watchers, but to all who care about the quality of Christian public life and especially, I hope, to those who bear the responsibilities of leadership in both Church and State.

JOHN HABGOOD

2nd August 1984

v

CONTRIBUTORS

George Moyser, Lecturer in Government, University of Manchester.

Peter Cornwell, Vicar of the University Church of St. Mary The Virgin, Oxford.

Frank Field, Member of Parliament for Birkenhead.

Kenneth Medhurst, Professor of Political Studies, University of Stirling.

Giles Ecclestone, currently Tutor at Westcott House, Cambridge, formerly Secretary of the Board for Social Responsibility, Church House, Westminster.

Ronald Bowlby, Bishop of Southwark.

Gerald Wheale, Area Dean of Hulme, Manchester Diocese and Lecturer in Community Development, University of Manchester.

John Elford, Lecturer in Social Ethics, University of Manchester.

Kenneth Leech, Race Relations Field Officer, Board for Social Responsibility, Church House, Westminster.

Robert Waddington, Dean of Manchester and formerly General Secretary, Board of Education, Church House, Westminster.

John Sleeman, formerly Senior Lecturer in Political Economy, University of Glasgow.

Anthony Dyson, Samuel Ferguson Professor of Social and Pastoral Theology, University of Manchester.

Raymond Plant, Professor of Politics, University of Southampton.

CONTENTS

PREFACE

This volume contains a collection of essays concerned with evaluating, from different vantage points, the political role of the Church of England. Amongst the contributors are a diocesan bishop and cathedral dean, a parish priest, a Member of Parliament, individuals who have served in the Church's central bureacracy, professional theologians and political scientists. To all of them I wish to extend my grateful thanks for the time and effort they took in putting their thoughts on paper about a subject which has attracted wide attention within England, has provoked renewed and serious thinking amongst the Church's leadership and is again becoming a matter of considerable importance to the Church's local membership up and down the country. It is to this general ecclesiastical audience, as well as to those outside the Church who have an interest in the contribution of the Church of England to English society and politics, that the volume is addressed. What is offered is a set of varied and independent perspectives collectively and individually concerned with the political dimension of the Church of England's work, a belief in its potential theological and social significance and a desire to offer some carefully considered assessments and judgements based on wide personal and practical experience, research and reflection over many years. Needless to say, however, any imperfections of the volume as a whole is entirely the responsibility of myself.

The collection is divided into three broad areas prefaced by an introductory essay which examines some of the more general characteristics of the Anglican Church's political and social engagement. Further more specific and brief introductions are then provided at the beginning of each of these parts. The first contains papers that examine the various institutional linkages between the Church and politics, and some of the characteristics of the individuals who are involved. The subject matter ranges across the historical legacy of Church–State ties, the role of the diocese and parish in local politics, and the contribution made by the Church's archiepiscopal and episcopal leadership. The second section examines the contribution the Anglican Church has made in a number of important areas of national public policy, including defence, economic affairs and race relations. The final part of the book then examines the thinking and ideas that have underpinned the Church's relationship with the State and with politics in recent times, thus providing an essential basis for understanding the relevant issues as they have arisen in the recent past and as they may develop in the future.

GEORGE MOYSER

Chapter 1

THE CHURCH OF ENGLAND AND POLITICS: PATTERNS AND TRENDS

George Moyser

1.1: Introduction

A classic study of politics and religion written over 30 years ago characterized their relationship as 'very complex, confusing and changing'.[1] The writer also claimed the subject to be a long-standing issue of perennial perplexity, an enduring problem 'through all the Christian centuries'.[2] The present volume, therefore, reasonably sets its sight on covering only part of that potentially huge overlap between these two great spheres of social life and human understanding, namely the Anglican Church's contribution to politics and public life in England. That contribution, however, has been substantial in earlier centuries and even in modern times there are grounds for suggesting it is far from insignificant.

Indeed, the importance of the Church of England's impact on current social and political affairs is indicated by a renewed debate about how the Church should be so involved – if at all. It is equally underscored by the extent to which the whole matter has been aired in the national mass media. Not least has this arisen because, in a number of very public examples, the Church has demonstrated a considerable departure in important respects from traditional understandings of its relationship with society and the state. This, in turn, has caused considerable tension and argument to arise between those who are in the vanguard of such changes and those who see the Church as moving down the

[1]H.R. Niebuhr, *Christ and Culture* (London: Faber, 1952), p. l.
[2]Niebuhr, *op. cit.*, p. 2.

1

wrong path and regret the disturbance of time-honoured assumptions and practices.[3]

To focus upon the conflictual aspects of the Church-State relationship is, for the media, perhaps understandable. And, insofar as it highlights the sometimes difficult choices the Church's members and leaders now face, this attention might even be welcomed. But, important though the more visual and dramatic aspects may be, they are by no means the whole story.

To give one brief example, it is well known that the Archbishop of Canterbury, by virtue of his office, attracts enormous attention from press and television when he makes observations (as he frequently does) on national and international affairs. Television coverage of his sermon in St. Paul's Cathedral, London, at the Service of Reconciliation following the Falklands' War, is a graphic illustration. But the Archbishop is only one, albeit overall the most important one, of a considerable number of influential and senior Church figures who constitute the Church's leadership. In other words, though the Archbishop speaks with considerable authority, and possibly with more than any other individual Anglican, it is simply untrue to take his politial views and statements as an adequate or fair representation of of the Church's leadership as a whole. Still less are they to be taken as a summation of the views of the Church of England. In this regard, the real weight of the Church's presence is not to be found in Lambeth Palace, nor even in London, but in the 'grass-roots' up and down the length and breadth of England. This 'army' of over 10,000 clergymen, and around two million active lay members[4] in literally every parish in the Kingdom are arguably far more decisive so far as the Church's total contribution to English society and politics is

---

[3]Two recent and specific illustrations that come to mind are the intervention by the Archbishop of York in the Coal Miners' Strike and the Bishop of Liverpool's 1984 Richard Dimbleby Lecture on BBC Television. For the former, see "The Company They Keep", *The Times*, April 28, 1984, p. 9 and the Archbishop's letter of reply on May 2nd. For the latter, see "God, Mammon and Liverpool", *The Times*, April 17, 1984 and subsequent associated correspondence, e.g. "Balance of Dues to God and Mammon", April 27.

[4]See the *Statistical Supplement to the Church of England Yearbook* (London: CIO Publishing, annually), Table 1. See also *Prospects for the 80s* (London: Bible Society, 1980), p. 23.

concerned. On top of that, however, there is another still larger but more diffuse and tenuously linked diaspora, constituting perhaps a third to a half of all adults in England, who claim at least a minimal sense of Anglican identity.[5] Individuals in this category must certainly find a place in any balanced assessment of the Church's public presence in the life of the country.

It is clear, therefore, that any valid enquiry must look beyond those particular facets of the relationship highlighted by the mass media. But, in attempting to do so, inevitably problems and constraints arise. In the first place, potentially relevant information is sometimes just not available and one has perforce to focus on some matters leaving others, that might give a somewhat different or at least more elaborate impression, untouched. It is remarkable in this context how large are the gaps in our knowledge of the workings of what is, by any standards, one of England's most important social institutions. For example, there is no study equivalent to that of the Roman Catholic Church which sets out in any detail the patterns of beliefs, attitudes and activities of the Anglican laity.[6] Apart from some superficial and narrow indications of how they vote, or how they feel on specific and transient issues, derived from relevant opinion polls, it is virtually a blank field. Necessarily, therefore, analysis of the political engagement of the Church at this private level must be somewhat impressionistic and limited. In similar vein, we have virtually no knowledge on a comprehensive national basis of how rank and file Anglican clergymen see themselves and the parishes in relation to the political realm.[7] So in this way, too,

[5]The Gallup Omnibus Survey, 1978, reported in Hornsby-Smith and Lee (see footnote 6) has a figure for Anglican adherence amongst the English (and Welsh) population of 65%. In the British Election Survey of October, 1974 and in 1979 (University of Essex, ESRC Data Archive) the figures were 41.6% and 31.2% respectively.

[6]See M.P. Hornsby-Smith and R.M. Lee, *Roman Catholic Opinion: A Study of Roman Catholics in England and Wales in the 1970s* (University of Surrey, Department of Sociology, 1979).

[7]See, however, S. Ranson *et al.*, *Clergy, Ministers and Priests* (London: Routledge and Kegan Paul, 1977) for a sociological study. For some political data, see the survey, *Attitudes of the Church of England Clergy*, commissioned by the Credo Programme at London Weekend Television from Opinion Research Centre (Richmond, Surrey, September 1982).

the picture cannot be as complete as would be preferable.

In this situation, we have to focus more on the Church's official activities as a corporate organization than the Church as a composite of countless individual Christians. Equally, more can be said about the Church's engagement in public life at the national level than at the local level although the latter rightly finds a place in this volume.

Those aspects that do receive detailed attention and emphasis are, however, seemingly the most politically significant features of the Church. For England's political arrangements are, certainly compared with the United States, for example, relatively centralized, and perhaps are becoming more so. As Thomas has noted, 'penetration', or the effective capacity of the national state to 'reach into' the constituent parts of society, may not be a wholly modern phenomenon. But the late Twentieth Century certainly represents in this country, as in many others, a high point in the extent to which national governmental and political institutions dominate the society.[8] In most important areas of public life, in education or the management of the economy, or even the personal living standards of ordinary citizens, the decisions of the central Government in Whitehall, and the political preferences of the national party leadership in Westminster and Downing Street, undoubtedly play a very large part. For this reason, it is singularly appropriate to look at how the Church relates to the State, and associated political institutions, at the national level. This is not to say, of course, that local factors are unimportant or that some individuals would prefer a different balance between the two. But it is to suggest that, in present-day England, one must accord a senior role to 'the centre' in its dealings with 'the periphery'. That seems to have been the conclusion of the extensive debates over devolution in the 1960s and 1970s, and equally seems to be the mood of the present Government in its dealings with the European Community.

[8]See K. Thomas, "The United Kingdom", in R. Grew (ed.), *Crises of Political Development in Europe and the United States* (Princeton: Princeton University Press, 1978), Ch. 2.

1.2: Defining The Relationship Between Religion And Politics In England

In using terms like 'government', 'state' or 'church', one must, of course, be wary of tacit assumptions that may be entailed about 'politics' and 'religion'. Most fundamentally, one might wish to be guarded about a too-easy acceptance of a distinction between the two. In writing on this issue, Pannikar has accused Western writers of adopting an historically false dualism about the two spheres.[9] Instead, he prefers to see them as distinctive but totally interdependent phenomena; not two realities but two elements of the same reality. In some respects there is merit in such a view. Certainly the Christendom model as inaugurated by Constantine could be seen as a non-dualistic, or at least closely integrated, relationship between the Catholic Church and the Roman Empire. The Henrician Reformation (as will be seen in Chapter 2) was an attempt in England to recast such an arrangement along lines more acceptable to the monarch. However, in present-day England, it would be difficult to argue that close interdependence remains an appropriate characterization. At the same time though, Pannikar is correct in pointing out the continued existence of forces operating to bring them into contact. Indeed, it is interesting to speculate as to whether in very recent times the strength of these forces has increased, thus possibly counteracting longer term historical trends running in the opposite direction. This is a point which will be returned to later in the essay.

While it seems quite clear then that 'religion' and 'politics' are broadly distinct, if overlapping, spheres in England, delimitation of their individual reference points is more difficult and contentious. Yet some attempt of this sort must be undertaken if only to indicate the variety of ways in which the two might come together. Equally, it is important in understanding the particular position of the Church of England not only as a

[9]R. Pannikar, "Religion or Politics: The Western Dilemma", in P.H. Merkl and N. Smart (eds), *Religion and Politics in the Modern World* (New York: New York University Press, 1983). See also, K. Medhurst, "Religion and Politics: A Typology", in the *Scottish Journal of Religious Studies*, Vol. 2 (1981), pp. 115-134.

political institution of some sort but also as an ecclesiastical body within English religion.

1.2.1:   Religion in England

So far as the latter point is concerned, it is obvious that the Anglican Church is nowadays only one manifestation of organized religion in English society. Four centuries ago, one no doubt could have virtually equated Anglican adherence with the totality of formalized religious activity – though even then England was not completely homogeneous. But since that time, first religious toleration and then the growth through immigration of significant non-Christian minorities have considerably altered the picture. *De facto*, England is now religiously pluralistic. No one single church can claim to be dominant, although arguably the Christian churches are in this position, if taken as a whole. However, this variegated present-day reality is only imperfectly reflected in the public life and institutional arrangements of the country. To an extent perhaps not entirely supported by actual adherence, the Church of England still commands a position of unique saliency, a saliency reflected in English cultural assumptions, and underpinned by now largely antiquated formal institutional arrangements.

One area where this Anglican legacy can be found reflected is in the still considerable amount of privatized or unorganized religion within the English social culture. There is, in this respect, a very large segment of the population who still feel some residual connection with the Christian community even though they themselves may have few or no formal ties as individuals with any specific religious institution. This 'folk' or 'implicit' religion within English society and culture expresses itself in a variety of ways.[10] For many in this category 'rites of passage' – birth, adolescence, marriage and death – are celebrated through Christian rituals, even though these may be the only occasions in which such individuals have specific contacts with the churches. In addition, and lying behind these social

[10]For a brief, if rather dated, review, see D.Martin, *A Sociology of English Religion* (London: Heinemann, 1967).

patterns, there is a continuing cultural linkage between English identity and Christianity. Many Englishmen and women still think of England as a 'Christian country' and themselves as Christian, albeit in a possibly very diffuse sense.[11] Hence, it is no surprise that national opinion polls conducted in Britain continue to find large numbers of people who assent to various aspects of the Christian faith – the existence of God, life after death, the divinity of Christ. Only a minority, in fact, would, on these grounds, put themselves totally outside the Christian pale.

This cultural and social saliency of religion has, in turn, some modest political significance. For politicians, both national and local, are likely to share in, and be influenced by, the unspoken assumptions that sustain this prominence. These assumptions, in other words, are indicative of a reservoir of goodwill amongst such secular leaders towards religious institutions, and instil amongst them a greater readiness to listen to, and possibly to be moved by, religious arguments than might otherwise be the case. In short, there is an expectation on their part that religion in general has an important part to play in English public life.

Within this culture, the Church of England has a unique role. For it is the Anglican Church, as 'the most exclusively English of all our major institutions',[12] which principally embodies the religious aspects of English identity and seems to command the greatest general prestige in local and national affairs. Not least, it is the principal participant amongst religious institutions in state occasions, and the Church to which political leaders most naturally turn when moments of national crisis arise. The Falklands Service in St. Pauls, the Remembrance Day Service in Whitehall and the Coronation in Westminster Abbey are all particular illustrations of this. Hence, while it remains true that the Anglican Church by itself cannot adequately represent or delimit 'religion' in England, it has a unique significance in that regard, and especially where the place of religion in public life is concerned.

[11]See D. Jenkins, *The British: Their Identity and Their Religion* (London: SCM Press, 1975).

[12]D. Jenkins, *op. cit.*, p. 65.

1.2.2: Politics in England

It is equally important to consider the political side of the relationship, bearing in mind the enormous importance of government in everyday life. This is not to say that politics or government in England is all-pervasive as it is both in style and in substance 'liberal democratic' reflecting a generally held belief that government should be to some degree restrained and limited. But those areas that would be considered 'off-limits' to political influence and governmental or Parliamentary control are, by and large, diminishing. The recognition and acceptance by British Governments of their responsibilities for the management of the economy in the 1930s, the creation of a substantial public sector of government-owned industry in the late 1940s and the development of a welfare state intended to support minimum standards of living, all these were the foundations on which post-war British government was built and to which all major parties subscribed.[13]

Now it is true that in very recent years the Conservative Party under Mrs. Thatcher has put something of a question mark against this level of state intervention and has, in consequence, 'privatised' significant portions of the public sector economy, reduced civil service staffing levels, and encouraged private initiatives in health care, education, mass communications and the like. Nevertheless, from a historical perspective, these moves probably amount to little more than relatively marginal shifts towards more 'limited government', shifts which leave the general level of state intervention in society largely untouched and mass expectations of government responsibility unchanged. As the Federal Government has found in the United States, where the concept of limited government has been an even more entrenched part of the political culture, it is impossible for government significantly to modify and curtail the scope of its responsibilities in present day social life.

So what constitutes this broad political realm? As has been implied, its core and most obvious manifestation, lies in the

[13]For a brief review, see A. Sked and C. Cook, *Post-War Britain: A Political History* (Harmondsworth: Penguin, 1979).

national institutions of government – Whitehall, Westminster and the major parties who provide the political leadership. But politics and government obviously involves far more than this. The whole machinery of government and party political organization at *local* level must certainly be included even if many of the 'politicians' concerned regard themselves and/or the decisions they take as somehow 'independent' or outside of party politics *per se* and, therefore, as 'unpolitical'.

Another direction in which 'politics' must be expanded is indicated by the trend toward a so-called 'corporate state'.[14] This emphasizes the degree to which, in the context of broad governmental responsibilities in modern society, actual policy-making is shared by the Government of the day with major non-governmental groups and organizations within one organic or corporate framework. A major illustration of this in Britain is the 'collaboration' between Government, the Confederation of British Industry (CBI) and the Trades Union Congress (TUC) in the establishment of broad agreement over the directions of economic policy within the National Economic Development Council (NEDC). The effect of such arrangements is to politicize groups and organizations whose principal activities or interests might well lie outside formal and narrowly conceived boundaries of government.

Recent events, and not least the withdrawal of the TUC from the NEDC, and CBI protestations about the indifference of the Government to their views, have to some extent undermined this corporatist vision. Nevertheless, it remains true that, both formally and informally, governmental bodies at all levels are linked to a very diverse range of groups and organisations in society for the purpose of mutual influence in the development of public policy and the making of political decisions. In other words, the boundaries between governmental and non-

[14]See, for example, J.K. Galbraith, *The New Industrial State* (Harmondsworth: Pelican Books, 1969); R.J. Harrison, *Pluralism and Corporatism: The Political Evolution of Modern Democracies* (London: George Allen and Unwin, 1980) and, particularly on Britain's experience, K. Middlemas, *Politics and Industrial Society: The Experience of the British System Since 1911* (London: Andre Deutsch, 1979).

governmental, between public institutions and private institutions, and even between partisan and non-partisan bodies are often very difficult to locate. Not least is this the case with the Church of England. As this present volume illustrates in virtually all the contributions, the Church is linked to government at many levels and in many diverse ways. So although principally a 'religious' body, it is also almost inevitably a 'political' body well illustrating in a specific way the distinctive but interdependent quality of the broader relationship between religion and politics to which Pannikar drew attention.

As with religion, however, the political realm is not demarcated simply by those institutions which are centrally or peripherally involved in government. For underpinning those institutions are a 'system of tacit understandings',[15] conventions, unspoken assumptions, and personal values that comprise what can be called England's 'political culture'. It is these beliefs about the legitimacy of governmental authority, the appropriate scope of governmental responsibilities, the obligations of citizenship and so forth which are equally a part of 'politics' even if they are less tangible and more latent.

Included in this, of course, are the perceptions surrounding the relationship between Church and State - the question of establishment, for example. For even though the established position of the Church of England may be seen by many as one of those 'permanent elements in the inalienable given order of the universe',[16] they are all, in fact, expressions of, and dependent upon, certain particular political decisions often taken in much earlier historical eras. As the same can also be said in general terms of other qualities of English public life – the sustaining of 'liberal democracy', the relative importance of

[15]The phrase is from Sydney Low's *The Governance of England*, Revised edition (London: Ernest Benn, 1914) and is quoted in R. Rose, *Politics in England: An Interpretation for the 1980s*, 3rd edition (Boston: Little, Brown and Co., 1980), Ch. 4, in which an up-to-date account of England's political culture is provided. See also D. Kavanagh, "Political Culture in Great Britain: The Decline of the Civic Culture", in G.A. Almond and S. Verba (eds.), *The Civic Culture Revisited* (Boston: Little, Brown and Co., 1980), Ch. 5.

[16]Jenkins, *op. cit.*, p. 62.

liberty and equality, the protection of human rights, etc. – so these too form a fundamental part of politics. Perhaps the reality of this can be seen in the perception by some writers of a gradual erosion of consensus about what should be the general directions of British governmental policy and even some of the basic qualities to be encouraged in British society.[17]

So what is the essence of politics when all these different aspects are taken into account? Definitions abound in the writings on this subject (as also is the case with 'religion'). For Pannikar, politics is about 'the realization of the common good' in society, 'the art of the means and ways for the realization of a human order'.[18] Religion, on the other hand, he sees as being more about the 'means and ways for the realization of the ultimate order'.[19]

But to define what is concretely meant by 'the common good' and to bring it about by appropriate actions of government, requires an exercise of power and this to many, if not most, writers is the essence of what much of politics is about.

However, the exercise of power is, or can be, an extremely subtle and difficult matter to unravel.[20] So far, I have spoken of power as exercised through governmental decision-making or, more indirectly, through processes of mutual influence between political authorities and groups in society. But this is only 'one face' of power, the power manifested in choosing a particular course of action or policy to follow. It takes no account of the power to decide which problems are to be considered appropriate for governmental attention, which grievances should be heard, what alternatives should be considered and whether any action or decision should be taken at all. For many, the power not to listen and not to decide represents another face of power, but a face perhaps more real and more compelling than that of

[17]See, for example, S.E. Finer, *Adversary Politics and Electoral Reform* (London: Wigram, 1975) and by the same author, *The Changing British Party System 1945-1979* (Washington, D.C.: American Enterprise Institute, 1980).

[18]See Panikkar, *op. cit.*, p. 45.

[19]*Ibid.*.

[20]See, for example, S. Lukes, *Power: A Radical View* (London: Macmillan, 1974).

decision taking. In other words, there is, in some sense, another world of politics, a world of negative power, in which the 'political problem' starts much further back in the decision-making process, and is arguably much more fundamental. Furthermore, there are those who go on to argue that the whole complex of social institutions, including trade unions, the military, political parties and the churches themselves are inextricably involved in sustaining particular manifestations of power. In this view, to decide not to take action is itself a decision or choice in favour of current arrangements of power and rewards. To opt out is, in fact, merely a way of opting in; it is itself a political decision, a part of politics and a contribution of some sort to political outcomes. This is, of course, one of the problems those who argue that churches should stay out of politics must come to terms with. For it would seem that it is not in the final analysis an available option.

1.3. Should the Church Get Into Politics?

Whether or not one has, in fact, a choice, from a religious perspective the issue certainly remains unresolved. Indeed, it is a debate that has intensified in recent years to no as yet definitive conclusion. It is also an issue that is now more salient within the Church's leadership.[21] The possible causes and consequences of this heightened awareness will be examined later in this essay. The immediate and preliminary need is to examine some of the alternative views about this relationship that are on offer.

They range, it seems, from the 'extreme' of calling for total withdrawal to an advocacy of total involvement, with various more 'moderate' alternatives in between. The first is represented by Norman, Powell and Worsthorne, amongst others, as well as by a significant part of lay opinion within the Church.[22] Various

[21]See, for example, the Archbishop of York's (John Habgood) recent book, *Church and Nation in a Secular Age* (London: Darton, Longman and Todd, 1983).

[22]A full statement of supporting arguments can be found in E. Norman, *Christianity and the World Order: The BBC Reith Lectures, 1978* (London: Oxford University Press, 1979). See also his "Four Wrong Roads to God", *The Times*, February 24, 1984.

arguments are adduced to sustain this position. Their general tenor is that the Church should be concerned above all else with 'the sacred', the private spiritual life of individuals, the seemingly absolute and uncontingent principles of personal morality. Only through these means should the Church attempt to move society for it is in that area alone that it can claim a unique authority and hold on truth. Ventures into mundane politics, on the other hand, are seen as demeaning to the Church's sacred and supernatural character and entail alliances with corrupting secular ideologies (often liberal-bourgeois) that are inherently partial, relative and ephemeral. Political action also requires special expertise that the Church's membership probably lacks and, in any event (as with all human-based affairs), cannot create any worthwhile or lasting achievements.

In stark contrast is the view that the realization of the true nature and mission of Christianity entails a total identification with society and a total involvement in the political institutions and processes that are part of that society. Such a complete immersion of religious bodies (both Christian and non-Christian) in politics has been approximated at many times in history. One notable example, according to John Baker, Bishop of Salisbury, is represented in the Old Testament. As he put it in a recent address:

'The prophets and sages of the Old Testament were constantly concerned with political and social issues. Because they saw God as having, by his own free choice, a special relationship with the nation Israel − as having, indeed, given her nationhood in the first place − the life and destiny of that nation were primary material for their understanding of God. To them international affairs were central to revelation and ethics, and the right conduct of rulers was at the heart of religious teaching and reflection.'[23]

[23]J. Baker, "Morality, Power and Government", the 1983 Hetherington Lecture, University of Manchester. A revised version is to appear in *The Modern Churchman*. See also H. Kung, *On Being a Christian* (London: Fount, 1978), pp. 178-9.

In the Christian tradition, the European Christendom model is a further historical illustration of this dedication of the church to the affairs of the state. Though institutionally distinct, church and state were totally interlocked in a mutually dependent symbiotic relationship. In this, the church tried to ensure the privileged recognition of its particular vision of society and the State, in turn, received the potent reward of religious legitimation and quasi-sanctification.[24] This was, in fact, very much the style of the Church of England's own relationship with the secular authorities in the pre-Reformation and immediate post-Reformation period. But equally, it is one that has long since lost any real substance even though its institutional embodiment may still linger albeit in attenuated form.

The modern Christian version of a politicized church does not, of course, any longer aspire to exclusive access to the levers of power but rather recognizes and even welcomes the pluralistic nature of society. Yet it is this particular quality which seems to deter many from continuing to advocate a thorough-going and corporate political witness by the Church. Even Temple, who was in his day a highly politicized Archbishop of Canterbury, drew a distinction between individual Christian political action and corporate Church engagement.[25] The difficulty seems to be the creation of a political theology to which all Church members would assent and yet which is specific enough to provide a basis on which the Church could collectively act. Attempts have been made to develop parts of such a programme in the form of 'middle axioms', most notably in recent times in the sphere of nuclear weaponry.[26] The outcome of that particular venture, however, seems merely to underscore the difficulties which need to be overcome if corporate action by the Church of England on specific political issues of the day is to command wide support.[27]

[24]See K. Medhurst, op. cit., p. 118.

[25]See W. Temple, Christianity and the Social Order (London: SPCK, 1976), p. 41.   [26]See Chapter 8.

[27]The Credo poll cited above showed that 45% of clergymen thought that the Church of England should 'as a body take a public position on policy issues facing the Government and the nation'. Of these 66% had in mind economic and defence issues and not just 'traditional' moral issues. This is considerable support but still obviously leaves many unwilling to underwrite this type of political involvement.

Between these two polarized positions, there is a broad middle ground inhabited, it would seem, by the bulk of the Church of England's present leadership. For example, John Habgood, the present Archbishop of York, holds to what he admits is, by the standards of some fellow Christians, a rather 'timid' and 'conservative' position.[28] In his view, and in contradistinction to Edward Norman's, engagement in public debates is a necessary part of the Christian task. As he puts it:

'In short, a Gospel which belongs to the world of public discourse, which it must if it is to be credible, cannot fail to have relevance to public life as well as private life. To this extent a high degree of social awareness in Christianity is unavoidable.'[29]

But he goes on to argue that to avoid the dangers of divisiveness, loss of distinctiveness and the 'absolutizing' of political conflict, the Church as a corporate entity, including its leadership, ought to eschew involvement in political action *per se*. The Church's role should be to 'keep the discussion of morals firmly within the public framework, looking for new points of contact and agreement, and trying to reinforce such Christian values as are already widely shared'.[30] This entails supporting the values which undergird society' and hence which sustain 'social cohesion and national unity'. The challenging prophetic task, necessarily inducing conflict and tension, should be left to individual Christians. But these should, it is argued, receive the support and encouragement of the Church and its leadership.

Many other writers also take this view.[31] But, as was hinted earlier, for the Church corporately to reinforce values, however subterranean and consensual, is itself a form of political engagement. This, in turn, would seem to necessitate a political theology similar to, though possibly less specific than, that

[28]See his *Church and Nation*, *op. cit.*, pp. 172, 175.
[29]*Ibid.*, p. 60.
[30]*Ibid.*, p. 62.
[31]See, for example, R. Gill, *Prophecy and Praxis* (London: Marshall, Morgan and Scott, 1981) and P. Hinchliff, *Holiness and Politics* (London: Darton, Longman and Todd, 1982).

required for the form of prophecy he reserves to individuals. In other words, merely to rely on broad agreement as a basis for action would seem theologically inadequate. Even so, in practical terms, it is clearly a more eirenic and less divisive form of engagement than that entailing more direct action on social and political issues of the day. In this way, some of the problems involved in grappling with the relationship of the Church of England and politics in a pluralistic society may be solved but possibly at the expense of postponing or neglecting others.

The main focus of this volume, however, is not what this Church-politics nexus *ought* to be but what it is *in fact*, and how it is changing.[32] It is to this question and the possible causes and consequences associated with it that the remainder of this essay is addressed.

1.4: Church and Politics in Practice:

As I have already mentioned, there is an increased awareness of the relationship between religion and politics within the Church of England. Some would even suggest that the two spheres have moved more closely together. Pannikar, for example, believes this is happening on a very broad front:

'....we are approaching the close of the modern Western dichotomy between religion and politics, and we are coming nearer to a non-dualistic relation between the two. All the burning religious issues are at the same time political, as the examples of Ireland, Lebanon, Israel, Iran, Latin America, etc., sufficiently show. Likewise, all the important political questions are at the same time religious, as the examples of Marxism, liberalism, capitalism, socialism, etc., make sufficiently clear. Religion without politics becomes uninteresting, just as politics without religion turns irrelevant.'[33]

---

[32]It should be noted, however, that both papers in Part III are concerned with the normative questions raised briefly here.

[33]See Pannikar, *op. cit.*, p. 46.

On the other hand, there are historians and sociologists of religion in England and on the Continent who strongly argue the opposite. From a situation of very close engagement, they identify processes of secularization that have, they claim, removed religious issues from the political agenda, sharply curtailed the effective influence of religious institutions in political affairs and left politicians largely indifferent to religious claims.[34] Can these contradictory analyses be reconciled in some way?

To take the latter view first, there are obvious and indisputable indicators of a general loss of prominence of religion in English society. Church attendance and Christian celebration of rites of passage have steeply declined, and the proportion of English adults thinking of themselves as at least nominal adherents of particular religious institutions has also fallen sharply. In political terms, few nowadays ascribe to the churches any substantial influence or control over events.

Yet there are definite question marks to be placed against the assumption that this process of marginalization is a uniform, unrelenting and irreversible trend in English society. In the first place, it is evident that there is still a substantial persistence of religious beliefs and values in English society. To that extent, the process of erosion or secularization is perhaps one that has affected the support of institutional religion more sharply than its implicit and cultural presence.[35] Secondly, to the extent that religion has been displaced, the new values and institutions are not those of a militant atheism hostile to religion but rather of a liberal humanism to some degree indebted to and arising out of earlier Christian perspectives.

This latter point has been developed by Gill into the status of wholly different interpretation of the relationship between religion and politics from that provided by the more conven-

[34]See, for example, A.H. Birch, *The British System of Government*, 4th edition (London: George Allen and Unwin, 1980), pp. 6-7.

[35]This may be connected with the 'privatization' of religion discussed in J. Habgood, *op. cit.*, Ch. 3.

tional secularization model.[36] Rather than seeing 'Christianity within contemporary Western society (as) not generally politically significant', he argues that that society was so thoroughly Christianized and suffused by Christian values that it is scarcely possible now to detect or differentiate those social and political values of Christian provenance from those deriving from wholly non-Christian sources. Thus, the apparent lack of a large-scale religious intrusion into present-day politics by way of politicized religious conflicts and issues, is not an indication of the lack of a relationship between religion and politics, but the reflection of a religio-political consensus so complete and successful as to be virtually invisible. Now without accepting this view in its entirety, it does seem to have some merit. For there is some substance to the claim that many of the economic, social and political values that stand behind English society do owe a considerable debt to Christianity.[37] To this degree, there is indeed a continuing latent religious presence at the heart of English society and politics but a presence that is not always made explicit or that is easy to detect. Equally, it is a presence that, for this reason, may be under-estimated.

There is yet a third basis for questioning the assumption of an apparently relentless marginalization of religious institutions. Thus, the establishment of a permanently secularized society is itself predicated on the continuing validity of the view that the world is susceptible to systematic improvement by human endeavour and that a social and political order can be sustained on the basis of human rational calculation. To the extent that man can create for himself a stable and satisfying environment and self-definition, appeals to supernatural or religious understandings tend to lose their relevance and power. However, medical breakthroughs notwithstanding, 'death remains the great inescapable reminder of human powerlessness and insecurity' thereby setting 'firm limits on secularization'.[38] Furth-

---

[36]See R. Gill, *Prophecy and Praxis* (London: Marshall, Morgan and Scott, 1981), Ch. 3.

[37]For the details, see R. Gill, *op. cit.*.

[38]See A.D. Gilbert, *The Making of Post-Christian Britain* (London: Longman, 1980), pp. 61-2.

ermore, in the midst of a crisis of international security, an increasing sense of the finiteness of resources and a growing perception of the ultimate vacuity of materialism,[39] there is a growing potential for the reassessment of the place of religion in setting society's agenda and in contributing to the terms in which that agenda is debated. Even within intellectual circles, amongst mathematicians, scientists and social scientists, religious or supernatural explanations are not as readily dismissed as was once possibly the case.

It is out of considerations such as these that Pannikar's view may not be wholly fanciful, if possibly somewhat over-stated. In addition, there may well be other factors from within Christianity itself working more directly and explicitly to 'close the gap' between the two spheres, to draw the Church of England in particular more into the centre of public and political debate. One of these is undoubtedly the shift in the centre of gravity of the Anglican Communion, away from Britain and towards the 'Third World'. As will be indicated at various points in the present volume, the impact of this world-wide movement upon the Church of England is more immediate and profound than ever it was. The change in the balance of membership (the rise of Anglican adherence outside Britain coupled with a decline within this country), the growth of an indigenous local ecclesiastical leadership together with the general facility of modern travel have made the Church of England more aware than ever before of the limitations of its own particular horizons. A concomitant of all this has been an increased awareness of gross injustices, violations of basic rights, economic inequality and extreme deprivation present in other parts of the world. Such a situation challenges all churches, and not least the Anglican Church, to think of how they might respond through appropriate representations to their own national governments.

A greater openness to views of fellow Christians from outside England has had a further impact in making the Church of England think much more critically about its own inherited

[39]See C.A. Reich, *The Greening of America* (New York: Random House, 1970).

arrangements, the quality of its engagement with society and the extent to which it may have been too complacent about injustice and inequality in its own back-yard.[40] All of this has, in turn, been reinforced by the advent in recent times of a so-called 'liberation theology' which was developed out of the experiences of Christians primarily in Latin America.[41] And although the issues that gave rise to such a response were and are far more sharply drawn than is the case in England, there is sufficient common ground to make this theology both relevant and potentially compelling.

Finally, one might mention two factors tending to 'politicize' the Church of England that are essentially of internal provenance. The first concerns the changing character of its leadership. This is a matter that the author has already written about elsewhere.[42] But the essence of the argument is that there has been a shift from a 'prince-bishop' to a 'pastoral-bishop' model over recent decades. The consequence of this shift in political terms has been for the emergence of an episcopal bench to some degree more at odds with traditional social and political arrangements and more disposed to take critical or even radical political stands or to be favourably disposed towards those in their immediate pastoral care who might do so. This is not to say that the overall level of political involvement of the Church has necessarily increased much as a result. But it is to say that the style and content is shifting in ways which certainly give the impression, through their historical novelty, of a greater degree of political concern and activism.

This change in the type of episcopal leadership of the Church of England is, in fact, part of a broader set of changes brought about, consciously or unconsciously, as a response to the perceived marginalization of religion in English society. The

[40]An important recent contribution on this is David Shephard's (Bishop of Liverpool) *Bias to the Poor* (London: Hodder and Stoughton, 1983). For the impact of 'outsiders' on the Church's internal arrangements, see *To a Rebellious House?* (London: CIO Publishing, 1981).

[41]See, for example, G. Gutierrez, *A Theology of Liberation* (London: SCM Press, 1974).

[42]See K. Medhurst and G. Moyser, "From Princes to Pastors: The Changing Position of the Anglican Episcopate in English Society and Politics", *West European Politics*, Vol. 5 (April 1982), pp. 172-191.

basíc issue here, as Gilbert, Habgood and others have put it, is the basis on which the Church should conceive its relationship with society (and therefore politics). One possiblility Neibuhr referred to as 'Christ against culture', emphasizing the fundamental differences of values and goals between Church and secular society.[43] In this view, men must make a choice between their respective claims. Those who heed the call of the Church would then form 'little groups of with-drawing Christians' or, for 'mainstream' churches to whom a sect-like posture would be unattractive let alone organizationally untenable, members would maintain an 'uncompromising attitude towards the secular world'.[44] This, according to Gilbert, was precisely Cardinal Heenan's view of the matter. As he put it:

'He (Cardinal Heenan) had rejected totally the idea of a Church re-united on the basis of compromise with the beliefs and values of the post-Christian age, and he feared a softening or abandonment of traditional doctrines designed to make the historic gospel more acceptable to secular men.'[45]

By and large, however, this does not seem to be the view of the majority within the Church of England, although no doubt there are those who would support this position. Most, in fact, again including the bulk of the Church's leadership, wish to see some degree of dialogue or even 'accommodation' with society in order to make the Church's message more relevant and plausible to that society. On the theological front, perhaps the most spectacular example of this in recent times within the Church of England was the publication by John Robinson, then Bishop of Woolwich, of *Honest to God*.[46] Accommodation can also be found on other fronts within the Church of England – in

[43]See H.R. Niebuhr, *op. cit.*, Ch. 2.
[44]A.D. Gilbert, *op. cit.*, p. 130.
[45]*Ibid.*.
[46]J. Robinson, *Honest to God* (London: SCM Press, 1963). See also the debate engendered by David Jenkins' (Bishop of Durham) review of the Church's credal formulae in C. Longley, "Mysteries that Science Cannot Solve", *The Times*, May 14 1984; "Seeking a Solution to the 'Durham Quarrel'", *The Times*, June 18 1984, and the letters on June 9, 1984 headed 'Historicity and Christian Orthodoxy'.

recent liturgical reform, the development of specialized, non-parochial forms of ministry, democratization of the Church's internal mode of decision-making by the introduction of synodical government, attempts to soften the Church's position on the marriage of divorcees and on homosexuals and its ecclesiastical treatment of women. Not least, the changed basis of recruitment of bishops towards those with more pastoral experience in society can be taken as an indicator of the new seriousness with which the Church is seeking to come to terms with a much-changed and still rapidly changing society.

Politically, this does not necessarily imply a 'sell-out' to secular ways of thinking, although this is, of course, the charge made by Edward Norman. But it does entail a sustained and open debate with proponents of secular political ideologies, a questioning of inherited patterns of religio-political relationships and a prophetic critique both of society and of the Church's own performance. Those who find this happening within the Church of England, and do not like its implications, argue that it represents the final triumph of secularization and the demise of authentic Christianity. To others, however, who see the need for the Church to strike a historically different balance in its relationship with English society and politics, it represents the possibility of a new era of Christian witness, a witness thankfully devoid of the historical incubus of the Christendom model.

1.5: Looking Forward

The consequences of all these trends and currents are, to some degree, difficult to discuss in that the situation is far from stabilizing around any new pattern or consensus. The Church of England as a whole, and its corporate leadership in particular, has indisputably shifted its centre of political gravity to the left (in conventional secular terms), and to some degree raised the priority accorded to its social and political engagement. Nevertheless, and as with other churches moving under similar imperatives, there would seem to be factors operating distinctly to limit any long-term continuation of such movements.[47] One is the sheer 'weight' of those historical arrangements now under question. Though calls have been made for disestablishment, few amongst the episcopal leadership of the Church of England, or in the other Houses of its General Synod, would welcome an outright break.[48] They see the state connection as a symbol of a continuing Christian presence in public affairs, a recognition of the Church's role in England's historical development and, not least, a channel through which the Church can continue to exercise political influence. However, establishment, as the Archbishop of Canterbury is very aware, imposes obligations and circumscriptions. By accepting a privileged status in affairs of state, the Church must to some degree in word and action support that state and the socio-political arrangements associated with it. The end product, therefore, is a careful and restrained balance between supporting and challenging the *status quo* that is the hallmark of current Anglican practice.

One other limit also comes from within the Church - the constraint imposed by the potential divisiveness of a too-radical and too-politicized Church. The Church of England's social roots are substantially within the middle-class, suburban and rural sectors of society. Arguably, it has never penetrated or mobilized significant portions of the urban working class, and certainly has achieved very little influence amongst England's recent immigrant groups from the West Indies and the Indian sub-continent. Though no longer quite the religious manifestation and sanctifier of England's 'ruling class', as once it possibly

---

[47]On the limited shift to the left, see K. Leech, "Is the Church of England Really Moving to the Left?", *Marxism Today* (October 1982), pp. 16-19.

[48]In two surveys conducted by the author in 1975 and again in 1981 amongst elected members of the General Synod, only 14.4% in the former year (House of Laity 17.4%, Clergy 10.2%) and 16.3% in the latter year (Laity 14.3%, Clergy 15.5%) unreservedly agreed that 'the Church of England should be disestablished as soon as possible'. Similarly in the Credo Poll of Anglican clergymen, only 34% thought that 'the Church of England should be disestablished altogether so as to be free from any constraints imposed or implied by Establishment even if it meant losing any privileges which flow from Establishment', whereas 59% disagreed.

was, its social base is certainly to be found disproportionately amongst England's relatively privileged and, therefore, politically conservative groups.[49]

For the episcopate in particular, who provide direction and leadership to the Church, their boldness must be tempered by the need to maintain internal unity and cohesion. There is no point, in other words, in staking out a political path down which few of the rank-and-file will go. Of course, this itself becomes a challenge for the Church's leadership – to enable the laity and clergy in the grass-roots to transcend the particularity of their own situation and perceive the broader issues through some compelling political theology. But it is easier to say than do. The Church's resources are already strained and largely committed in other ways. Furthermore, not all Church leaders feel that they are able to, or even should, undertake the task. Thus, if the Church is going to continue changing the corporate and individual pattern of its political engagement as it has in the recent past, it will do so only very slowly and very diffidently. This may serve to dampen controversy but it will certainly not eliminate it. Thoughtful leadership and sustained theological reflection will still be needed in order to identify the right path to follow. In this way the latent tensions between distinctiveness and worldly relevance, consensus and division, social challenge and social cohesion may then be fruitfully tackled. What will finally emerge out of all this, one hopes, is a relationship between Church, politics and society which is appropriate to these post-industrial times and which achieves a resonance similar to that of the Early Church in its own day.

[49]The 'establishment' argument is put by, amongst others, Gilbert, *op. cit.*, p. 71 and F. Parkin, *Middle Class Radicalism* (Manchester: Manchester University Press, 1968). For some empirical questioning of the view, see G. Moyser and K. Medhurst, "Political Participation and Attitudes in the Church of England", *Government and Opposition*, Vol. 13, No. 1 (Winter 1978), pp. 81-95.

Part One

INSTITUTIONAL LINKAGES

INTRODUCTION

The six papers in this section of the volume are concerned with different aspects of the institutional ties or linkages between the Church of England and the world of politics. In the first of these Peter Cornwell considers how present arrangements evolved historically, pointing out that the mutual involvement of Church and State in each other's affairs is certainly not something new, but stretches back to pre-Reformation times. The single most important event that laid down the basis on which the two subsequently coexisted was the 'nationalisation' of the Church of England by Henry VIII, giving it the privileges of establishment, but also bringing it substantially under state control.

Since then, this framework of close identity between Church, State and society has been gradually broken down as Cornwell documents – the growth of a limited pluralism in religious practice, the 'limited and grudging' development of toleration and a de jure recognition of diversity not fully implemented until well into the Nineteenth Century. At the same time, as Parliament came to be the effective centre of political power, and in turn became itself both more religiously pluralistic and more indifferent to religious issues, so its claims to direct the affairs of the Church were rendered more tenuous and unsatisfactory. The reaction of the Church to this situation in calling for its own internal decision-making powers, Cornwell calls a process of 'autonomization' – a still incomplete trend that he sees as posing important and continuing dilemmas for the Church. For example, is a continuation of the traditional link between Church and State worth preserving as an essential balancing factor to set against the growth of an unbridled and possibly unacceptable degree of pluralism? Even today, therefore, constitutional arrangements, though very 'abstract' to ordinary Church members, clearly involve important issues both for them and for society.

Whatever the benefits to Church and nation of continued establishment, the costs and difficulties are very clearly outlined in Frank Field's contribution. In an essay that looks mainly at the politics of liturgical reform at Westminster, he reveals the complexities and conflicts that the present only semi-devolved legislative arrangements throw up. Over a considerable period of time the Church has tried to make its liturgy more accessible to outsiders and to bring it more in line with contemporary language usage and social norms. But this in turn has led to serious misgivings amongst those Parliamentarians who were hostile to such 'reforms' and, furthermore, felt the General Synod of the Church to be taking too lightly their responsiblility to remain sensitive to the views of Parliament, a body to whom they remain legally accountable. Certainly this seems to be the clear message coming out of the latest 'crisis' over episcopal appointment procedures in 1984. All of this underscores the need to consider anew the constitutional relationship between Synod and Parliament which is now the effective core of the formal ties between Church and State.

Many of those involved very directly in trying to 'manage' the Parliamentary crisis over Prayer Book Reform were diocesan bishops, the majority of whom sit in the House of Lords. This episcopal leadership, and most especially the Archbishop of Canterbury, is the subject of the fourth Chapter by Kenneth Medhurst and George Moyser. They argue that it is these leaders above all, who must wrestle with the dilemmas of pluralism and cohesion, of national comprehensiveness or sectarian exclusivity, of buttressing social integration or emphasizing political criticism and prophecy. The bishops are not, of course, equally responsible for grappling with such issues even though an ethos of collegiality now pervades their deliberations. Those in the House of Lords, for example, necessarily constitute something of an inner core, although their actual contribution to the Church's political role depends 'on the personalities, expertise or pre-occupations of those concerned'. Generally speaking, however, the bishops are not highly politicized, at least not in the traditional sense of occupying positions of national influence to the possible neglect of their pastoral and administrative duties in their local dioceses. Rather, the new breed of bishop is now 'less integrated into traditional local (and national) elite groups' which leaves them somewhat freer to adopt new and more critical political and social positions. But, at the same time, the paper emphasizes that this shift does not amount to the vision of politicized and radicalized clergymen painted by some commentators.

As already mentioned, at the centre of the Church's political and national role, is the Archbishop of Canterbury and he receives special attention in the chapter. He it is who must wrestle in a particularly demanding and personal way with the varied and conflicting pressures currently bearing on the Church. His emphasis on and choice of isssues to address, his handling of the mass media, the way he defines his office, all these, as the paper discusses, give him a unique capacity to 'influence the nature of public opinion or to create a public mood' thereby making a 'significant contribution ... to the nation's public life'. In exercising these heavy responsibilities, the Archbishop now has a staff of aides at Lambeth Palace. These form an important body of individuals who support the Archbishop not only in his national responsibilities but also in his obligations as a religious leader having considerable influence in the shaping of agendas and priorities on the world stage. How he seems to resolve these various tensions and claims is the focus of the chapter's concluding pages.

Alongside Lambeth Palace, the other major bureaucracy of special relevance to the Church's national contribution to social and political affairs is Church House, the home of the General Synod. This body, the Church's 'Parliament', together with its associated Boards, is the subject of Chapter 5 by Giles Ecclestone. Setting aside those forays into public life occasioned by its own internal needs (such as Parliamentary approval of its new liturgy as discused in Chapter 3) and those issues that arise out of its existence as a social institution (such as its tax status), the chapter focusses principally upon the Church's role in national debates, lobbying and representations to government over broad matters of general concern.

The main responsibility for this work falls to the Board for Social Responsibility (BSR). Its problem is that it must (as with the Archbishop of Canterbury) temper prophecy with discretion.

The need for the latter arises through the Church's 'claim to speak for an undifferentiated public good over and against more partial interests'. This singular position has the effect of making politicians pay particular heed to the Church's message. But, as it may also lend credibility and legitimacy to causes that otherwise might lack both, this influence must be used judiciously and cautiously. All of this, he concludes, especially 'on major issues where the choices are complex and there is no obvious moral imperative', tends to induce the Synod as a whole to move with great caution and sometimes to miss important opportunities altogether. In foreign policy, for example, the International Affairs Committee of the BSR has links both with Parliament and the Foreign Office. This provides a channel through which considerable political influence might be brought to bear. In fact, however, the consequence of such a link is to induce 'a cautious incremental approach . . . and to eschew grand gestures'. More generally, the Synod's contributions, he feels, tend to be occasional, to be confined to expressions of opinion and to reflect the fact that the Church of England is itself considerably constrained in what it can say or do by its own internal social, religious and political diversity. Above all, it has yet to decide, when it does speak out, to whom it is speaking and the terms in which the message should be expressed.

The last two contributions to this part of the volume are more concerned with the Church's public and political role at local level. The two principal ecclesiastical institutions here are the diocese and the parish, and it is the former that is the topic of Ronald Bowlby's Chapter 6. In his view, the traditional independence of the parishes effectively prevented the diocese from developing a corporate strategy apart from occasional efforts 'to rally support for a particular cause'. More recently, however, changes of economic circumstance, together with local pastoral reorganization schemes, have presented dioceses with the opportunity for a more direct role and involvement in the expression of the Church's social and political concerns at grass-roots level. In taking up these possibilities, there is still 'little evidence of any consistent policy which might be labelled 'diocesan', but considerable evidence of religious and moral concern'. As with the Church's national style, its aim is not to bind local governments and parties to a particular vision of an alternative Christian order but to nudge it in a non-authoritarian way by (as he quotes Ecclestone) 'an appeal to a shared perception of what is desireable'.

His review of one specific diocese's response to a major social issue (the Brixton disorders of 1981) shows that the Church can and does get involved in local political matters though (as in that case) not necessarily with 'an obvious impact on events'. The discussion then moves on to examine the particular role of the bishop in local politics, the principal issues that arise (education above all, but with a recent emphasis on unemployment, housing and race) and the theological shifts that have underpin-ned the greater prominence now given to social responsibility as a proper dimension of the mission of the local church. Even so, he concludes that, despite the multiplicity of channels through which the Church can exercise local influence, 'there is still a long way to go, and meanwhile many pressing internal problems capture the energies and attention of diocesan leaders and members alike'.

The final paper, Chapter 7 by Gerald Wheale, takes as its remit the assessment of the Church's political accomplishments in one inner city parish – Moss Side in Manchester. For himself as parish priest (and Area Dean), the challenge is 'the moral imperative to identify with and to struggle alongside my parishioners in their search for true humanity'. Such a parish is a 'testing ground' for the development of practical theology relevant to all the Church although 'worked out . . . in the realities of a disadvantaged and poor community'. Unfortunate-ly, in his view, too few in the Church share this vision. Many others find this 'too radical', including some within the 'diocesan establishment'.

Outside the Church, on the other hand, the response can and has been more encouraging, giving it a real 'entre' into the community, allowing it to build bridges where none might have existed before and giving it a role in bringing very concrete benefits to the community it serves. In getting involved himself, however, Wheale eschews party activity, even though political engagement in the broader sense cannot, he feels, be avoided by any priest or Christian. The particular problem of a partisan commitment is that it is essentially divisive, it entails taking sides and the use of a language of social conflict. For his part, he rejects the immagery of 'enemies', and of 'us' and 'them'. But, in a polarized situation, being in the middle may entail being rejected by both sides, a situation which poses important issues about the meaning of loyalty and solidarity and about the relevance of 'reconciliation' in a situation of intolerable repression. Not least in all this are the obstacles to true undestanding by those possibly well-intentioned Christians 'making a facile moral judgement from the comfort of a middle-class armchair'.

So, all in all, he 'remains critical of the Church . . . because of its failure to recognise and significantly engage the political dimension of life'. In consequence, he concludes by calling for more strategic thinking and for changes in training and the allocation of resources so that the Church might at last convincingly take on a role that would 'enable and sustain the ministry of love with the poor and disadvantaged who are at the margins of society'.

Chapter 2

THE CHURCH OF ENGLAND
AND THE STATE:
CHANGING CONSTITUTIONAL LINKS
IN HISTORICAL PERSPECTIVE

Peter Cornwell

2.1: Introduction

'For us "establishment" means the laws which apply to the
Church of England and not to other churches'.[1] This definition,
chosen by the 1970 Chadwick Commission, has the merit both
of steering clear of more vague and emotive uses of the term and of
taking us briskly to the heart of our subject. These laws, at first
sight, seem to constitute a rag-bag of disabilities imposed on,
and privileges granted to, the Church of England. Parish priests
cannot pick and choose those to whom they will minister, for
parishioners, whatever their personal beliefs, have common law
rights of access to the parish church and the ministrations of
their vicar. The bishops are not elected by ecclesiastical
enthusiasts but nominated by the Sovereign on the advice of the
Prime Minister who may be a Baptist, Methodist or unbeliever.
The 1662 Prayer Book, a repository of the Church's doctrine as
well as its official liturgy, is under the ultimate control not of a
Church synod but of Parliament. Final appeal from Church
courts is, in faculty questions affecting property, to the Privy
Council and, in matters involving doctrine, ritual and ceremonial, to a Commission appointed by the Crown. In return for
these restraints, the Archbishop of Canterbury has the right to
anoint and crown the monarch who 'cannot be reconciled with
the see or Church of Rome or profess the popish religion, or
marry a papist', but must swear to maintain 'the protestant

[1] Report of the Archbishops' Commission, *Church and State* (London:
Church Information Office, 1970), p. 2.

33

reformed religion'. In addition, the two archbishops and twenty four senior bishops sit by right in the House of Lords.

What is it that links together these disabilities and privileges? It is the unity of Church and Nation under the Crown. As Canon Gordon Dunstan has written, the statutes of Henry VIII 'restored a unified jurisdiction to the realm. The sovereign became the fount of justice in causes spiritual as well as temporal'.[2] Canon A 7 states: 'We acknowledge that the Queen's most excellent majesty, acting according to the laws of the realm, is the highest power under God in this kingdom, and has supreme authority over all persons in all causes, as well ecclesiastical as civil.' The restrictions and privileges of the Church of England illustrate that Church and Crown are locked together in a more than formal embrace.

Although the constitutional picture suggests the submission of the Church to centralised authority, the realities are otherwise, for power is somewhat more dispersed than the formal arrangement suggests. To begin with, we are not dealing with the exercise of personal regal power but with a constitutional monarchy, the Queen in Parliament. In recent years, Parliament itself has gone further to devolve its own powers to representative Church bodies. The Worship and Doctrine Measure of 1974 gave to the General Synod authority to produce services alternative to those of the Book of Common Prayer and to local congregations and pastors, through their parochial church councils, freedom to choose which services they will have. By agreement with party political leaders, the Prime Minister, who advises the Sovereign in the appointment of bishops, is now herself advised by the Crown Appointments Commission. This body represents both the diocese in which the episcopal vacancy has occurred and the wider Church of England, and submits a list of three names from which the Prime Minister must then choose one or alternatively request further names.

There is nothing very odd about this constitutional development. It is what we would expect from the proven ability of the British constitution to adapt itself to political realities. While

---

[2]G.R. Dunstan, "Corporate Union and the Body Politic", in *Their Lord and Ours*, ed., M. Santer (London: S.P.C.K., 1982), p. 136.

appearances have changed little, modifications of national sovereignty have taken place. Despite Enoch Powell's protests, the Commonwealth, the European Community and N.A.T.O. are realities with which we have, by and large, come to terms. Although politicians, at the time of elections, give us the impression that we are poised to choose the sole masters of our national destiny, we know and they know that the truth is otherwise. In such a small world, not even England is an island. Indeed, there is legitimate concern over the control of the awesome powers of American airforce bases and the democratic accountability of the E.E.C., but we are apt to seek solutions not in constitutional fundamentalism but in a further development of democratic control. The expectation is that our constitution is pliable enough to accommodate such a development as it did the Glorious Revolution of 1688 and the transformation of Empire into Commonwealth.

The constitutional framework of the Church of England gives the illusion of unchangeableness but, once set it in historical perspective, we shall be struck as much by change as continuity. This may help us to see both the opportunities for further change within that framework and the points where change might burst it at the seams.

2.2: The English Reformation and its Aftermath

By the Supremacy Act of 1534, it was enacted that 'the King our Sovereign Lord, his heirs and successors, kings of this realm, shall be taken, accepted and reputed the only supreme head in earth of the Church of England called Anglicana Ecclesia'. The question continues to be asked whether this 'nationalisation' of the Church of England with its rejection of the Papacy was really a revolution or merely one step forward along a path already clearly mapped out. It is, in fact, very difficult to assess the degree of change in any particular event. Those who know little of the background are apt to overdramatise change while those who have immersed themselves in the detail tend to believe that 'there is no new thing under the sun'. Of course, ecclesiastical vested interests come into this. Because the Church of England wants to claim continuity with the pre-Reformation past, its apologists turn to those events which seem to be precursors of the Henrician Reformation.[3] Thus, the mingling of sacred and secular can be seen in the bishop and ealdorman sitting side by side hearing both ecclesiastical and secular cases in the same court.

Kings did not stand aloof from ecclesiastical matters or remain indifferent to episcopal appointments. Even William the Conqueror, who forged stronger links between the English Church and Rome, exercised the old right of 'investiture' of the bishops by giving them both ring and staff. He enjoined the bishops 'not to enact or prohibit anything but what had been first ordained by the king'. The Statutes of Praemunire, imposing the heaviest penalties on any who should seek to draw people 'out of the realm to answer for things whereof the cognisance pertains to the King's court', were statutes not of the Reformation but of the 14th Century.

Certainly, the seeds of ecclesiastical nationalism were sown and mightily assisted in their growth in the 16th Century by the state of the papacy. The latter, so far as England was concerned, could not have been at a lower ebb. It challenged the law and order of a nation struggling for unity. It constituted a drain on national resources. And what did Englishmen get in return for their money? An institution apparently incapable of effecting those reforms which so many saw were necessary; an institution, being in the pocket of rival national leaders, which appeared more secular than sacred. Add to this that there were Popes of less than edifying character and, indeed, a time when no one knew for sure who was the Pope, and it is plausible to represent the Henrician Reformation as a step in a direction established of old.

And yet that is not quite the whole picture. Tension there might be between King and Pope but never any indication that the Ecclesia Anglicana seriously considered itself to be a separate national church cut free from papal bonds. The theological justification for the papacy was still hotly debated. There were

[3]See Appendix I. Report of the Archbishops' Commission on the Relations between Church and State, *Church and State* (London: Press and Publication Board of the Church Assembly, 2nd edition, 1936).

those with a high doctrine and those with a low one. Yet, however tiresome it might on occasions prove to be, the papacy was an accepted part of the Christian 'kit', something you had to learn to live with. So Z.N. Brooke showed that, in the 11th. Century, 'there was nobody in England or elsewhere who questioned the essential unity of the Church or who denied that it was under papal headship'.[4] Although the Roman centralising policy of the 11th. and 12th. Centuries was resented both by local monarchs and the episcopate, yet 'everywhere they were forced to accept it, the bishops first, because conviction gradually came to them from the study of the law and authorities they all revered, the king later, as circumstances forced them, most reluctantly, to yield'.[5]

The attitude of an enlightened English Churchman to the papacy at the time of the Reformation is probably to be seen in Thomas Moore. As Brian Gogan has shown, Moore did not have a particularly high doctrine. He accepted that its dominical institution was an open question and never believed the Pope to be above a General Council. He is sternly realistic about the papacy's political entanglements and had no hesitation in advising Henry, then in a militant anti-Lutheran and pro-papal mood, that the Pope's authority be 'more slenderly touched':

'I must put your Highness in remembrance of one thing, and that is this. The Pope, as Your Grace knoweth, is a Prince as you are, and in league with all other Christian Princes. It may hereafter so fall out that Your Grace and he may vary upon some points of the league, whereupon may grow breach of amity and war between you both.'[6]

The development of the reforming movement was to drive Moore to a more theological understanding of the papacy, but all the way through he saw it 'as an ecclesiastical institution established and approved by the Christian community and therefore as part of the common law of Christendom'.[7] In a

[4]Z.N. Brooke, *The English Church and the Papacy* (Cambridge: Cambridge University Press, 1952), p. 23.

[5]Brooke, *The English Church and the Papacy*, p. 227.

[6]Anthony Kenny, *Thomas Moore* (London: Oxford University Press, 1983), p. 51.

[7]B. Gogan, *The Common Corps of Christendom* (Leiden: E.J. Brill, 1982), p. 266.

letter to Cromwell he writes: 'The papacy is at the least wise instituted by the corps of Christendom and for a great urgent cause in avoiding of schisms.'[8]

If the seeds of conflict had lain deep in the past, at the end of the day something happened which few thought would happen, the Papacy was rejected and its powers not abolished, but transferred to the Crown. The papal enthusiast Henry broke with it, while the papal critic Moore died for it. The comparative ease with which the revolution was carried through continues to mystify us and yet it is certain that this act of nationalisation rang bells with a longing for independence from foreign interference and for internal law and order under one strong head. In the historical plays of Shakespeare, we may not always meet good history but we do taste something of this Tudor passion; horror of the 'civil broil' of the Wars of the Roses and the high hopes which were set on a strong monarchy. While 'England hath long been mad and scarr'd herself', Henry Tudor now comes to 'enrich the time to come with smooth-faced peace, with smiling plenty and fair prosperous days'.[9] In such a mood, the failure of Katherine of Aragon to produce a male heir and so secure the succession was something more than a minor domestic misfortune or even a cause of unease to the King's conscience. The longed-for national stability was once more threatened.

The actions of Henry, by breaking with outside interference and establishing one fountain of law in the land, responded to this national sentiment. Although the clergy might try to qualify their acceptance of the Royal Supremacy with the saving clause '*quantum per Christi legem licet*', Elizabeth might tone down the title to 'Supreme Governor', and Richard Hooker might insist that even kings are subject to the rule of law and to the Law of God, yet the sovereigns were not over sensitive in their exercise of these powers. After all, the Supremacy Act had passed with no saving clause for tender clerical consciences, it had insisted that the King had 'full power and authority from time to time to visit, repress, redress, reform, order, correct, restrain and amend all such errors, heresies, abuses, offences, contempt and

[8]Gogan, *The Common Corps of Christendom*, p. 256.
[9]William Shakespeare, *Richard III*, Act 5, Scene 5.

enmities, whatsoever they be which by any manner spiritual authority or jurisdiction ought to be so treated'. Similar powers were 'united and annexed to the imperial crown of this realm' by the 1559 Act of Supremacy under Elizabeth. These powers did not languish, they were firmly exercised under both Henry and Elizabeth. The Queen had her own views about ornaments in the church, clerical garb and about those gatherings for clerical education commonly called 'prophesyings', which she energetically promoted. Indeed, such initiative in ecclesiastical reform had long been expected of the 'Godly Prince'. The English Reformation underwrote this mingling of sacred and secular and gave it firmer theological support.[10] Bishop Gardiner is thus opposed to 'the old accustomed distinction which doth put a handsome difference between the government of a Prince and of the Church'.[11] Must, he asks, 'every man in his own private care seek the kingdom of God and must a Prince in his administration neglect it or at least not care for it?'.[12] The Prince as prince of all the people is one 'whose office is to take charge not only of human matters, but much more of divine matters'.[13] Bishop Jewel is equally insistent that a Christian prince 'hath the charge of both tables committed to him by God, to the end he may understand that not temporal matters only but also religious and ecclesiastical causes pertain to his office'.[14] Richard Hooker, unwilling to restrain 'the name of the church to the clergy excluding all to the residue of believers, both prince and people',[15] claims that the concern of the state is not simply to 'provide for life but also for means of living well' to 'care for that which tendeth properly unto the soul's estate'.[16] 'It is a gross error to think that regal power ought to serve for the good of the body and not of the soul, for men's temporal peace and not for

[10]See P.D.L. Avis, *The Church in the Theology of the Reformers* (London: Marshall Morgan and Scott, 1981), Chapter 9.

[11]Ed., Pierre Janelle, *Obedience in Church and State, Three Political Tracts by Stephen Gardiner* (New York: Greenswood Press,1968), p. 103.

[12]P. Janelle, *Obedience in Church and State*, p. 105.

[13]P. Janelle, *Obedience in Church and State*, p. 117.

[14]Ed., J.E. Booty, *An Apology of the Church of England by John Jewel* (Charlottesville: The University Press of Virginia, 1974), p. 115.

[15]Richard Hooker, *Of the Laws of Ecclesiastical Polity*, Book 8, Ch. 1.4.

[16]Hooker, *Of the Laws of Ecclesiastical Polity*, Book 8, Ch. 1.4.

their eternal safety as if God had ordained kings for no other end and purposes but only to fat men up like hogs and to see that they have their mast.'[17]

The Royal Supremacy was given by the reformers the backing of a high doctrine of the Laity and of civil government. Yet the personal exercise of this supremacy was from the beginning limited. Even Henry VIII did not achieve exactly what he had wanted. Religiously conservative, he yet opened the doors to more radical doctrine notably in his appointment of Cromwell as his Vicar General and Cranmer as Archbishop of Canterbury. How he got more than he had bargained for became clear in the reign of Edward VI as doctrine and liturgy moved far to the left of what he would have tolerated. With Mary Tudor comes that strange reversal in which the sovereign who has set out to reject the Royal Supremacy, has to employ its very powers to do so. Although Elizabeth was the chief architect of the religious settlement, she was most successful when she was able to work through her leading moderately reforming bishops. [18] Even Elizabeth did not have things all her own way. Men driven into exile on the continent under Mary returned zealous for a more complete reformation. They were sharp in their dislike of church ornaments and ecclesiastical garments. In these matters the Queen had to compromise. If she retained the hated crucifix in her own chapel, she had to acquiesce in the further denuding of parish churches. If she was able to make the surplice a sticking point, she had less success over the traditional eucharistic vestments. Although she might press her bishops to restrain those troublesome 'prophesyings' through which the continental theology was spread, yet relentlessly, through an alliance of reformed pastors and leading laity, parish life was more conformed to the model of Geneva than she would have liked. The high doctrine of the laity was beginning to spread downwards from the Godly Prince to the squirearchy. The contagion spread from Parliament to the parishes where it was proving unstoppable.

Moreover, those who had returned from exile, were less

[17]Hooker, *Of the Laws of Ecclesiastical Polity*, Book 8, Ch. 3.2.
[18]See W.P. Haugaard, *Elizabeth and the English Reformation* (Cambridge: Cambridge University Press, 1970).

willing to go along with that reverential doctrine of the Royal Supremacy expounded by Gardiner and Cranmer. One could not help noticing that both these enthusiasts for regal powers had been hoisted with their own petard. Gardiner found that the 'true obedience' cost him his see under Edward VI, and Cranmer, under Mary, was piteously torn between adherence to Reformation doctrine and an exaggerated deference to the sovereign. The returning exiles had learned a less complaisant doctrine. In December 1576, Grindal, the Archbishop of Canterbury, is to be found writing to her Majesty pleading that she would 'refer all these ecclesiastical matters which touch religion, or the doctrine and discipline of the church, unto the bishops and divines of your realm, according to the example of all godly Christian emperors and princes of all ages'. She was asked, in matters of faith and religion, 'not to. . . .pronounce so resolutely and peremptorily as ye may do in civil and extern matters'. Dangerously invoking the ghost of Ambrose in his conflict with the Emperor Theodosius, he quotes the defiant prelate: 'Look not only upon the purple and princely array wherewith ye be apparelled, but consider withal, what is that that is covered withal. Is it not flesh and blood? Is it not dust and ashes? Is it not a corruptible body, which must return to his earth again, God knoweth how soon?'[19] It is not surprising that Grindal was suspended from his Archepiscopal functions. Yet only a few years later the protest of this essentially moderate man was to seem tame compared with the hostility which Charles I encountered. Charles made the tactical error of hitching the royal wagon to the small 'high church' party which proved to be a less effective force than that of the godly squires. The Civil War was to show once and for all that a personal exercise of the Royal Supremacy would not work.

Despite tense relations with the Papacy and early seeds of restless nationalism, despite Bishop Jewel's attempt to represent it as a conserving of a more primitive past, the English Reformation involved radical change. It broke with centralism and stood for the traditions of an independent national church.

[19]C. Cross, *The Royal Supremacy in the Elizabethan Church* (London: George Allen and Unwin, 1969), p. 173. See also P. Collinson, *Archbishop Grindal* (London: Jonathan Cape, 1979).

'The Bishop of Rome hath no jurisdiction in the realm of England.' (Article 37) 'Every particular or national church hath authority to ordain change and abolish ceremonies and rites of the Church ordained only by man's authority.' (Article 34). It was against such national independence that, in the end, Thomas Moore was to stand, in the belief that 'this realm, being but one member and small part of the Church, might not make a particular law disagreeable with the general law of Christ's universal Catholic Church, no more than the City of London, being but one poor member in respect of the whole realm, might make a law against an Act of Parliament to bind the whole nation'.[20]

Yet if, in its insistence on unqualified national autonomy, the English Reformation was radical, it was profoundly conservative in its identification of Church and nation. The common law rights of parishioners to access to their parish church and to the ministry of their parish priest lie well back beyond the Reformation. For all their differences in doctrine, both roman-ists and reformers would agree with Edwin Sandys when he wrote: 'One God, one king, one faith, one profession is fit for one monarchy and commonwealth. . . .Let conformity and unity in religion be provided for; and it shall be a wall of defence unto this realm'.[21] A society in which a variety of beliefs and unbelief could be accepted was simply not seen to be a possibility. It is this rejection of a pluralist society which gives cohesion to the view of the Royal Supremacy and the National Church. When Hooker wrote: 'there is not any man of the Church of England but the same is also a member of the commonwealth, nor any man a member of the commonwealth, which is not also of the Church of England',[22] he was both echoing an old and accepted doctrine and laying the essential foundation of the Church as by Law Established.

Elizabeth strove to make Hooker's dream a reality; she fashioned a National Church as capacious as she could make it, one which could include all but the most perverse. Sorely would

[20]Gogan, *The Common Corps of Christendom*, p. 288.

[21]P. McGrath, *Papists and Puritans under Elizabeth I* (Poole: Blandford Press, 1967), p. l.

[22]Hooker, *Of the Laws of Ecclesiastical Polity*, Book 8, Ch. 1.2.

she have liked to have seen the Marian bishops providing the continuity with the past. Her liturgical tastes were probably more than personal conservatism in religious matters, they showed her desire to soften the appearance of change. But there were more practitioners of the Old Faith than traditional English history has allowed. Behind the thin red line of the Mission Priests with their colourful exploits and heroic sufferings were many more who, loving their country and wishing to be recognised as patriots, sailed as close to compromise as they dared and yet longed for the Old Faith always and practised it when they were able.[23] The Papal Bull of 1570 excommunicating the Queen made life not only impossible for the recusants but also for any further attempt to woo them to the settlement. And, of course, always at Elizabeth's heels there snapped the 'precisionists' (Puritans). Bend though she might to the reforming winds, they were never satisfied and, at the end of the day, the Queen had to accept that comprehension in this direction too had its limits. No sooner was the ink dry on Book 8 of Hooker's Ecclesiastical Polity than the settlement was bursting at the seams. It took only a monarch whose principles were firmly set against the prevailing trend, and who lacked Elizabeth's pragmatism, to finish the settlement off.

2.3: The Post-Restoration Period

After the Restoration of the monarchy, it became clear that the pluralist society had come to stay. For a while, 'plain and moderate episcopal men' sought a new settlement which, while excluding independents, baptists and other sects, would comprehend main-stream presbyterians. This was not a particularly high-minded attempt. Charles II and James II hankered after toleration which would include Roman Catholics. Churchmen thought that an alliance with presbyterians was preferable to that, and could constitute 'a necessary defence against recusants and sectaries'. As it proved, the restored Church of England was

[23]See J. Bossy, *The English Catholic Community 1570-1850* (London: Darton, Longman and Todd, 1975).

not willing to bend to allow comprehension on terms other than humiliating to the dissenters. With James II out of the way and the popish threat thereby removed, hesitating steps could be taken in the direction of toleration. The Toleration Act of 1689, though of a limited and grudging nature, opened the doors to the building of dissenting chapels. These doors were never to be closed.

This movement towards toleration was nothing like so smooth as those who see Establishment as the very bastion of liberality would imagine. For every two paces forward, one was taken back. There were the Reactionary Schism Act of 1714 and the Occasional Conformity Act of 1711. Yet these proved ineffective and survived only until 1718. The battle for toleration was, in principle, won, attempts to revive a comprehensive national church were abandoned; the pluralist society, it was recognised, had come to stay.[24] No longer could it be said that 'there is not any man of the commonwealth which is not also of the Church of England'. That is not to say that there were not those who still hankered after Hooker's dream. Even in 1833, Thomas Arnold could revive the hopes of a new settlement. Broaden the establishment just a little, smooth down some of its rougher dogmatic edges, and nonconformists could be induced to be conformists. Yes, it would be a return to comprehension, a reversal of the drift towards toleration and the pluralist society. Only those who would conform to such a broader establishment, Arnold believed, should be afforded the rights of citizenship. Those who resisted, and he knew that Jews and Roman Catholics would, must either keep quiet and endure the loss of civil rights, or emigrate. 'I should earnestly deprecate the admission of Jews to a share in the national legislature', he wrote, 'It is a principle little warranted by reason that the sole qualification for enjoying the rights of citizenship should consist in being locally an inhabitant of any country.'[25]

The nation chose not Arnold's dreams but a coming to terms with reality. The whole movement towards toleration and the

[24]N. Sykes, *From Sheldon to Secker* (Cambridge: Cambridge University Press, 1959), Chapter 3.

[25]Thomas Arnold, *Principles of Church Reform*, eds., M.J. Jackson and J. Rogan (London: S.P.C.K., 1962), p. 167.

pluralist society created problems for the Church of England; not only did it lose its status in the nation but found its ability to shape and direct its life reduced. In 1717, the Convocations were suspended and for a century and a half it was considered inexpedient that they should meet for any but formal business. But who then could provide for the developing life of the Church, enrich the Prayer Book by making provision for preparing of the condemned for death or for consecrating new churches, or speak the mind of the Church against the deviant views of a Whiston or Toland? None could act or speak for the Church save Parliament. In the theory of Hooker, that might be just and reasonable for the House of Commons contained none but laity of the Church of England and the House of Lords held a place for the Lords Spiritual. Yet pluralism and, indeed, indifference had worked their way into Parliament, so that such a warm defender of establishment as Warburton could claim that 'to have laws framed and modelled solely by the state and imposed upon the Church is making it the meanest and most abject of all the state's creatures'.[26] If we are to speak of Erastianism in the sense of the unqualified control of the Church by the State, then it is of the 18th. Century Church of England of which we must speak. The demise of the Convocations came at the very moment when the personal powers of the monarch had been most reduced and the authority of Parliament notably enhanced. Ecclesiastical action, whether liturgical reform or pastoral re-organisation, had to be carried out by a Parliament whiggish in political tone and latitudinarian in religious temper. Only by recognising this can we understand John Keble's Assize Sermon of July 1833 as other than a lot of fuss about nothing. Parliament's action in the suppression of the Irish bishoprics was but a reasonable husbanding of resources, yet it pitifully revealed the Church as a mere department of the State.

The Oxford Movement, with its apostolical principles and high doctrine of the Church's identity, rose to challenge the establishment's subservience. 'The Tracts for the Times', Newman later wrote, 'were founded on a deadly antagonism to what in these last centuries has been called Erastianism or

[26]Sykes, *From Sheldon to Secker*, p. 66.

Caesarism. Their writers considered the Church to be a divine creation, "not of men, neither by men, but by Jesus Christ".[27] Keble and his friends powerfully reinforced the self-consciousness of the Church at a time when secular trends were forcing Church and State apart. The corollary of the pluralist society, with dissenters and eventually Roman Catholics free to go their own way and enjoy full civil rights, must be that the Church of England should be free to go its own way. Theological conviction and secular trend pushed the Church towards self-government.

2.4: The Modern Era

From the middle of the 19th. Century, the Church of England became more and more autonomous. In 1852, the Convocation of Canterbury resumed debate followed by the Convocation of York nine years later. At the end of the century, it was recognised that the laymen in Parliament were not so 'godly' as Hooker had wanted them to be, and that to fulfil the aspirations of the Reformation, a place for the laity had to be found in the Church's own organs of government. A cautious start was made with Houses of Laity attached to the convocations and, at the local level, the development of parochial church councils. In 1919, the Representative Church Council was turned into the Church Assembly with the right to pass measures which, with the assent of Parliament, would have statutory force. The Synodical Government Measure of 1969 reconstituted a representative system which spread from the parish, through deanery and diocese, to the national General Synod in which bishops, priests and laity were to meet together to make decisions on all matters, doctrinal and liturgical as well as administrative. It was this new General Synod which received the 1970 Chadwick Commission Report, a document arguing that Church and State should stand further apart. It was also this Synod which forwarded two of that Commission's most important recom-

[27] J.H. Newman, Letter to His Grace the Duke of Norfolk, in *Newman and Gladstone. The Vatican Decrees*, ed., A.S. Ryan (Notre Dame: University of Notre Dame Press, 1962), p. 92.

mendations. The Worship and Doctrine Measure of 1974, while leaving the 1662 Book of Common Prayer under the ultimate control of Parliament, gave to the Church the freedom to produce services which would be lawful alternatives to those of the Prayer Book. The Synod, having decided that the Church should have 'the decisive say' in the appointment of bishops, declared itself satisfied with the arrangements made by Lord Coggan and Sir Norman Anderson with the party political leaders and which led to the setting up of the Crown Appointments' Commission to advise the Prime Minister.

The middle of the 19th. Century until the present day has seen 'a steady movement towards autonomy' for the Church. Although the process was essentially a coming to terms with a reality which the State had already recognised, it was not smooth nor without the need for pressure and protest. The prosecution and imprisonment of some ritualistic priests in the late 19th. Century by secular courts was felt to be unacceptable by all but protestant fanatics. The rejection of the 1928 Prayer Book by Parliament came as a deep shock and drove even such a staunch upholder of the National Church as Hensley Henson into the camp of disestablishment. Nor was the unease felt only by ecclesiastics. Members of Parliament, finding themselves in 1964 having to debate what clothes a clergyman should wear when officiating in church, found it distasteful and pleaded that the Church of England should be free to decide such matters for itself. The ebb and flow of dissatisfaction, at various intervals during this period, was reflected by commissions which, though far from radical in tone, helped to nudge the Church towards self-government.

So far the movement towards autonomy has been contained within the constitutional framework. The Royal Supremacy remains. The Sovereign still appoints bishops on the advice of her responsible minister. Parliament still retains ultimate control over the Book of Common Prayer. The final court of appeal from the Church Courts is, in faculty cases, the Privy Council and, in matters of doctrine, ritual or ceremonial, a Commission of Revision appointed by the Crown. The 1970 Chadwick Commission was confident that this development could be continued within the existing constitutional framework. 'It is not a wild prediction that (unless the constitution of Britain were shattered out of its steady development by some cataclysm) the trend will continue, until the Church of England is autonomous and the intervention of the State will vanish, except so far as States must always be prepared to ensure that every Church is faithful to the trusts by which it is a corporate entity.'[28]

2.5: The International Dimension

This picture of development would not be complete without some attention to the effect which the spread of the Anglican Communion has had on the Church of England's understanding of itself. The Reformation emphasis on autonomous national churches was challenged by the fact that where the flag of empire went there the ministrations of the established church followed. Some of the difficulties were foreshadowed in the relations of the Church of England with the Episcopal Church in Scotland. The latter church was not established and it was tainted with the suspicion of Jacobite rebellion. Despite the closeness of the two churches in worship, order and doctrine, an act was passed in 1748 prohibiting Scottish priests from officiating in the Church of England. Although, as anti-Hanoverian sentiment decreased, relationships improved, the 1840 Act of Parliament gave only grudging permission for English bishops to license a Scottish priest to officiate and preach 'for any one or two days and no more'. The American War of Independence highlighted the problem. To whom could the faithful children of the Church of England turn to have their bishop consecrated?

Archbishop Moore of Canterbury, in declining the invitation, perceived as an insuperable difficulty the necessity, according to the English rite, of swearing allegiance to the English Sovereign. It was to the Episcopal Church in Scotland that Seabury had to turn for his consecration. Even when in 1787 it was made possible for the archbishop to consecrate bishops who were subjects of foreign states without requiring the oath of allegiance, there were still strings attached. The archbishop had to obtain the King's license to consecrate and the bishops so

---

[28]Report of Archbishops' Commission, *Church and State,* 1970, p. 15.

consecrated were forbidden to exercise their ministry in the King's domains. In the early days of the Anglican Communion, the arms of establishment reached out far and wide. The clergy sent out to the colonies were paid by the State and were firmly subject to state officials.

Even as the churches of the Anglican Communion established themselves as autonomous national churches, their relationship to the English establishment remained troublesome. In 1866, Bishop Tait of London was still asking as a real question: 'How far the Royal Supremacy, as acknowledged by the united Church of England and Ireland, can be maintained in our Colonial Churches?' [29] Bishop Colenso of Natal wrote a book on the Pentateuch which many considered heretical and many more simply foolish. Bishop Gray of Capetown moved against his suffragan and set up a court in which Colenso was denounced and excommunicated. His see was declared to be vacant. To whom could the aggrieved Colenso appeal but the Queen in Council? In 1865, the Lord Chancellor judged in Colenso's favour holding Gray's sentence to be null and void in law. The incident revealed both deficient justice in Gray's proceedings and the impossibility of maintaining the Royal Supremacy throughout the Anglican Communion. This communion of autonomous national churches needed some new link or links. Both the narrow issue of how to deal with Colenso's views, and the wider issue of whether these churches could act together independently of the English establishment, haunted the preparations for the first Lambeth Conference of 1867. The overseas bishops wanted a proper synod of the Church. Archbishop Longley of Canterbury, while welcoming an opportunity for 'brotherly communion and conference', insisted that such a meeting 'would not be competent to make declarations or lay down definitions on points of doctrine'.[30] It was with considerable skill that Longley, in the teeth of some English hostility, made the conference possible while defusing any attempt to turn it into a synod.

[29]R.T. Davidson and W. Benham, *Life of Archibald Campbell Tait* (London: Macmillan and Co., 1891), Vol. 1, p. 370.
[30]A.M.G. Stephenson, *The First Lambeth Conference* (London: S.P.C.K., 1967), pp. 187-188.

The very fact that the Lambeth Conference met and, at intervals, has continued to meet, has moderated the isolation of the English national church. The autonomy of national or particular churches has always been jealously preserved; the bishops can give advice but they cannot legislate. However, in recent years, this has seemed inadequate. What does the Anglican Communion do when faced by the fact that some of its member churches ordain women and some do not? The 1978 Lambeth Conference seemed torn between a reassertion of local autonomy and an uneasy awareness that this was not quite enough. Thus, its Report refers to 'the autonomy of each of its member churches. . . .to make its own decision about the appropriateness of admitting women to Holy Orders' but has to admit 'that such provincial action has consequences for the Anglican Communion as a whole' and recommends that no decision to consecrate women as bishops 'be taken without consultation with the episcopate through the primates'.[31] Local action over the ordination of women has indeed proved to have consequences for the whole communion. Provincial decisions to ordain women have been countered by other provincial decisions not to accept their ministrations. The Anglican Communion has been weakened in that we can now only speak of mutual acceptance of ministers, one of the marks of such communion, with some qualification. Painfully the lesson is being learned that there are limits to local autonomy. The Anglican Consultative Council has been set up, the Primates of the Anglican Communion meet regularly and the Archbishop of Canterbury is called upon to exercise a more international ministry.

The issue is further sharpened by those negotiations for church unity which are conducted not at the national level but between the Anglican Communion and other world wide Christian churches. At the stage of study and discussion no great problems arise but, if and when the point of decision is reached, it has to be asked how the Anglican Communion as a body can do it. In the case of the consideration of the Anglican Roman Catholic International Commission report, there will be a process of decision-making by separate national churches but

[31]Lambeth Conference, 1978, Resolutions 21 and 22.

this, in the end, will have to culminate in a Lambeth Conference. The very thing which Bishop Tait so feared and Archbishop Langley so carefully avoided may yet come to pass. It looks as if the mind of Anglicanism has somewhat altered since the nationalist days of the English Reformation. Beneath the unchanging appearance of its constitutional face, the Church of England has greatly changed.

Is this authentic development or a silent revolution in which we have turned our backs upon the past? With its system of self-government within, and the international bonds it forges without, it looks very unlike the church of Henry VIII or Elizabeth I. Yet there are bonds of continuity more substantial than the continued life of old parish churches and the ceremonies of the establishment. The Church of England goes on believing that local particular churches ought not to be dominated by a centralised authority but have a life and vigour of their own. It goes on believing, despite the erosion of religion, that secular government ought to be concerned with the 'good life' and values, difficult though this is in a pluralist society. It goes on believing that the governing body of the Church should involve laity as well as bishops and priests. While other Reformation beliefs, like the Royal Supremacy, have proved mistaken, or one-sided, or simply incapable of export beyond this country, these have in fact spread throughout the world and can be called identifiably Anglican beliefs.

2.5: Present and Future

But is the life of the Church of England within such a pliant constitutional framework capable, as the Chadwick Commission believed, of much more development both towards self-government at home and internationalism abroad? In recent years, hints have been dropped that there may be limitations on this development. When the Worship and Doctrine Measure was debated in 1974, more opposition was encountered than some had expected. Nicholas Winterton was not the only M.P. who saw it as 'a very radical spiritual and constitutional change'.[32] Enoch Powell believed that the issue was 'whether the worship and faith of the Church of England should continue in future, as heretofore, to be regulated by the law of Parliament', and that he saw to involve 'no less a question than the establishment of the Church of England itself – to be or not to be'.[33] Although the Measure passed through Parliament, it did not do so without a warning shot fired across the bows of those zealous for further development.

A similar message was received by the General Synod after it had voted for the Church's 'decisive say' in the appointment of bishops and dispatched its delegates to negotiate with the party political leaders. The answer was that, within the present constitutional framework, the Church could be a partner in the process of selection but could only have 'the decisive say' outside of establishment. In 1981 both Houses of Parliament gave a second reading to the Prayer Book Protection Bill. Because the Bill was dropped, the event was less notable for its attempts to impose upon parishes the monthly use of the 1662 Prayer Book at the main morning service if requested by any twenty parishioners, than the opportunity the debate provided for a vigorous reassertion of Parliament's ultimate control over the Church's worship. Members of both houses believed themselves to be fighting for those rights of English people to participate in the liturgy of Cranmer which seemed threatened by an unrepresentative General Synod and by clerically dominated parochial church councils. Again, the limitations on development were revealed. As long as the Church enjoyed the privileges of establishment, the constitutional framework could be no fiction. 'Either the Church of England retains the privileges of establishment and if so Parliament retains the right to intervene, or Parliament surrenders that right and the Church of England surrenders its privileges.'[34]

This could confront the Church of England with something of a dilemma. The forces which have led to its increasing self-government and its decreasing national isolation have not abated. English society continues to be pluralist with a Parlia-

[32]*Hansard*, Vol. 882, No. 31, p. 1663.
[33]*Hansard*, Vol. 882, No. 31, pp. 1669 and 1667.
[34]*Hansard*, Vol. 419, No. 67, p. 634.

ment which rightly legislates for such a society. In no area can this be seen more clearly than in the question of the reform of matrimonial laws. The State, reflecting the current secular view that marriage can be a temporary relationship, makes ever easier divorce laws, leaving the Church to decide whether to limp in its train or to assert its own distinctive understanding of marriage as a life-long commitment. But, if the Church were to part company with the State and decline to be the nation's registrar, what would this do to the common law rights of English citizens to be married in their parish church? Neither have the forces, which would diminish the isolation of national churches, declined. Both the problems of the Anglican Communion and the hopes for Christian unity remain.

But trends do not go in one direction only. In Enoch Powell's complaint about the Queen's 1983 Christmas message, there is a nationalist spirit moving against what is believed to be a bogus internationalism and which is often hostile towards both the Commonwealth and the United Nations Organisation. This spirit also resists the trend towards a more pluralist society, reaffirming what it calls distinctively 'English' and 'Christian' values. If there are extremist voices calling for a return to a white Anglo-Saxon culture, there are other gentler souls who look for more than unbridled pluralism and the reduction of common values to mere matters of taste. When Members of Parliament come reeling out of a showing of 'video nasties', they have seen that tolerance is not enough. When the House of Lords debates violence, they have seen crime as a symptom of a wider moral sickness and call for the reassertion of Christian values. This anxiety about the shape and coherence of our society is not merely foolish and reactionary. The Archbishop of York in his recent book has claimed that 'the growth of tolerance has always depended on a residual sense that there are some things which still hold us together as a nation. The greater the diversity the stronger these residual unifying factors need to be, if the nation is not to be dangerously fragmented'.[35] While in the 1960s Christians celebrated the pluralist society, we have now all become more aware of its dangers. The Archbishop perceives, beneath

---

[35]J. Habgood, *Church and Nation in a Secular Age* (London: Darton, Longman and Todd, 1983), p. 30.

undoubted pluralism, sufficient religious foundations for the Established Church to remain, in alliance with the Crown, an effective unifying force. Thus, the National Church could become both the articulator and supporter of those common values which are present but submerged beneath the free-for-all of the pluralist society.

In this mood of anxiety about the fragmentation of the nation, might we not be about to see another point in our history, when a combination of Christian ideology and national sentiment leads to a reversal of trends? Whether in that situation the Church would be able to retain its own integrity and keep itself free from capture by forces darker than the Archbishop imagines, is a sombre but real question which lies outside the scope of this essay.

One thing is clear. There are forces which could further erode the Church of England's constitutional position and forces which could strengthen it. Soon we shall discover that it is not enough to be carried by tides. A decision will have to be made concerning the direction in which Christian conviction should move us. That decision will involve something more than questions of constitution and history. Although the English people do not like to wind themselves up to abstract arguments, there are times when this uncongenial task is thrust upon them.

Chapter 3

THE CHURCH OF ENGLAND
AND PARLIAMENT:
A TENSE PARTNERSHIP
Frank Field

3.1: Introduction

To write about 'a tense partnership' between the Church of England and Parliament is to seek an understanding as to why the Prayer Book has emerged once again as a bone of contention between some members of the Lords and Commons on the one side, and leading figures of the General Synod on the other. The forces which have been at work are considered in this chapter. Some Members of Parliament now believe themselves to have been tricked into losing Parliament's right to approve the form of non-experimental Church of England services. What began as experimental liturgical reforms have resulted in the Church gaining a new Prayer Book without parliamentary approval. And while senior Church leaders have endlessly claimed that the new services are only alternatives, it is now clear that it is the Prayer Book which has taken second place to the Alternative Services Book. To help understand why the Church proceeded by a rather circuitous route to achieve a new Prayer Book it is necessary to go back to the beginning of the century and, in outline, trace what happened at the last attempts to make a major revision of the Book of Common Prayer.

3.2: Background

As Bishop Bell makes plain in his monumental life of Archbishop Davidson, the attempt to introduce a revised Prayer Book spans the quarter of a century of Davidson's episcopacy.

The first official act after his enthronement in 1903 was for the Archbishop to receive a deputation of over 100 Unionist MPs concerned that ritualism in the Church of England had led to an intolerable degree of ecclesiastical disorder. The result of this deputation, together with parliamentary lobbying, was the establishment in 1904 of the Royal Commission on Ecclesiastical Discipline. The Commission, reporting in 1906, recommended actions which would lead to a proposed new Prayer Book.

While the move for reform was initiated by a pre-War Royal Commission, it was the changes in services brought about during the War which made reform of the Prayer Book much more urgent. Bell maintains that pre-War ritual disputes had largely subsided by the turn of this century into questions concerning the use of eucharistic vestments. What had changed, however, was the frequency with which the Eucharist was celebrated:

'With the War. . . .there came a considerable change. The Eucharist became more and more prominent in the worship of Churchmen, and so more and more prominent in public discussions on the Prayer Book. The debate on Reservation in the Upper House of Canterbury Convocation in 1917. . . .marked a significant stage. The debate in the same place in February 1918, accepting the proposals of the Lower House for an alteration of the central part of the Communion Service (refused in April 1915), was also significant. It was then that the question of an Alternative Order of Holy Communion first took a definite place in the Bishops' proposal for Prayer Book revision.'[1]

The details of the procedure by which the Church itself considered these proposed changes to the Prayer Book do not concern us. What is of importance, however, is that after lengthy deliberations the proposed reforms were considered by the Ecclesiastical Committee (a joint select committee of both Houses of Parliament) who raised no objection to the reform. Consequently, the Archbishop of Canterbury presented what

[1] G.K.A. Bell, *Randall Davidson* (London: Oxford University Press, 1938), p. 1326.

became known as the Deposited Book ('deposited' because the Revised Prayer Book had been lodged with the Clerk of the Parliaments for purposes of identification) for approval of the Lords on 12th December, 1927. After three days of debate, approval was given by 241 votes to 81. The Measure then passed to the Commons where it was lost by 238 to 205. After making revisions to the text, the House of Commons also rejected the revised Measure by 266 to 220.

Why did the Measure fail to gain a majority in the Commons? First, the old 'no popery' fear flared up as it often does 'in an astonishing way at intervals in our history'.[2] It aroused opposition from a variety of Churchmen, both Evangelicals and Anglo-Catholics attacking the proposed reform. In addition, there were the tactical mistakes make by Davidson himself. To this list Bell adds:

'....when all this is said, something more fundamental remains. The deepest reason for the failure was that the whole method was from the very beginning wrong. The revision of Church services and the enforcement of ecclesiastical discipline are different things. A revision of worship, of common prayer, which is intended from the start to be used as an instrument for stopping disobedience is at any rate not likely to produce the happiest results in the realm of worship!'[3]

One of the major reasons put forward during the reform of the liturgy in the 1960s and 1970s was the need to bring greater order and standardisation to Anglican services. And while this time the end result has been for the Church to gain approval of its new services, once again this attempt to deal with unlawful variations in services by way of a major revision of the form of worship has not given rise to 'the happiest of results'.

3.3: The 1965 Reforms

In introducing the 1965 Prayer Book (Alternative Services) Measure, the then Archbishop of Canterbury, Michael Ramsey,

[2] Bell, *Randall Davidson*, p. 1354.
[3] Bell, *Randall Davidson*, p. 1357.

recalled what had happened when the Church last presented an alternative prayer book to Parliament, and went on to remark:

'There is no wish for a repetition of that procedure. Indeed, within our Church we have come to think that the right way of reform in worship is not by the construction *all at once* of a new Prayer Book, but the method of piece-meal change and experiment.'[4] (italics added)

The significance of these words was not fully grasped at the time. Indeed, there was little reason why it should have been for the Archbishop was at pains to stress that the Measure

'. . . .enables a limited – indeed, a very modest – degree of autonomy to the Convocations and the House of Laity to sanction new forms of worship. . . . for limited experimental periods.'[5]

The total debate in the Lords lasted for less than one and a half hours and at the end of the proceedings, the Archbishop remarked how 'the passing of this Measure will be (seen as) an act of mutual trust between Parliament and the Church'.

That may have been the Archbishop's hope, but, far from ushering in a new period of mutual trust, Parliament woke up late in the day to the fact that the Church had set in motion changes which might well result in a new Prayer Book but which would not come to Parliament for approval. Indeed, when Parliament next had a chance to debate this move, the reform was presented in terms of a mere logical outcome of an action which Parliament itself had set in motion.

There was no hint that this was the likely outcome, however, when the 1965 Measure was debated in the Commons. Indeed, efforts were made – no doubt in good faith – to assure MPs that they were doing no more than delegating, for a very limited period of time only, their power over the form of Church of England worship. The Church's spokesman in the Commons gave the understanding that at the end of the experimental period:

[4] House of Lords, *Hansard*, 18th February 1965, Col. 657.
[5] House of Lords, *Hansard*, 18th February 1965, Col. 652.

'. . . .one of two things will happen. Either the Church will revert to the 1662 position, or the Church will ask Parliament for approval of what has taken place during the experiment.'[6]

That is precisely what did not happen when the Church came back to Parliament with the 1974 Church of England (Worship and Doctrine) Measure.

3.4: 1974 Worship and Doctrine Reforms

The assurances given that Parliament had been asked to license liturgical experiments for a limited period only were cast aside when the 1974 Measure was presented to the Lords. Michael Ramsey, still Archbishop, when introducing the Measure recalled how 'the powers given under the 1965 Measure will be expiring round about the year 1980'. And he went on to ask,

'What then? If there is no further legislation, then the only services possessing lawful authority will be those of the 1662 Prayer Book. Is it really possible or desirable to revert to that position? Is it likely that the Church will be able or willing to present to Parliament one Prayer Book – all at once designed to last a long time? No. . . .I think it is most unlikely.'[7]

Because the Archbishop's speech was largely taken up with a review of events since the Royal Commission on Ecclestiastical Discipline, and developments since 1965, only a brief mention was made of what the 1974 Measure entailed. In essence, it proposed that Parliament should cease to have the right to approve the forms of Church of England worship.

The Church had neatly outfooted Parliament. From now on it played two cards with considerable skill. One was that the Church was only in its present position because of the liturgical experiments which had been initiated with State approval. The other was the threat of disestablishment.

[6] House of Commons, *Hansard*, 23rd February 1965, Col. 299.
[7] House of Lords, *Hansard*, 14th November 1974, Col. 871.

This last point weighed heavily with those speakers most critical of the Measure. After reviewing why he was unhappy with the proposal, Lord Waldegrave recalled,

'The Rt. Revd. Prelate, The Bishop of Southwark. . . . has said that if we do not pass this Motion we shall take one step closer towards disestablisment, and I am inclined to agree with him.'[8]

Lord Waldegrave went on to record that, despite his misgivings with the Measure, he would not vote against it because

'I do not think disestablishment is what most of us want. . . . Disestablishment would be dangerous because it would remove the safeguard against a too radical alteration in what kind of church we are to have in England.'[9]

The Worship and Doctrine Measure met with more opposition in the Commons, but there, too, Members had to consider the possibility of sparking off a disestablishment controversy should the Measure be rejected. This did not prevent some plain speaking as MPs realised what the Church had achieved by a less than straightforward approach. The Church was claiming disestablishment, while retaining all the advantages of establishment as was pointed out by one Member:

'I return to the central point which is surely the question of the relationship of this House to the Established Church. . . . (This Measure) is asking the House to retain the status of the Established Church while taking away from this House the power and the responsibility for its existence.'[10]

In 1965, it had been the then Member for Down South, Captain Orr, who had made the most powerful speech against the experimental reforms, warning of the Measure being 'the beginning of the end of parliamentary control over public worship in the Church of England' as well as 'the beginning of

[8] House of Lords, *Hansard*, 14th November 1974, Col. 882.
[9] House of Lords, *Hansard*, 14th November 1974, Col. 882.
[10] House of Commons, *Hansard*, 4th December 1974, Col. 1612.

the end of common prayer'.[11] So, in 1974, it fell to the Member for Down South, J. Enoch Powell, to deliver a magisterial onslaught on what the Church was attempting to achieve. He developed the following argument.

The view that the Church should have the right to order its own worship – a major plank in the Archbishop's case for the reform – was disputed. While such a statement 'seems to be treated as though it were a self-evident verity (it) is clearly not so, historically'. More importantly,

'. . . . for a church to be established by law it must be a specific church, with a specific belief, and specific forms of worship which correspond to that belief. . . . It is the character of the Church of England. . . . that it is such a church. We are. . . . deliberating whether on balance it is wise that it should continue. . . .to remain so.'[12]

Linked to this was the success of those who formed the Prayer Books of 1549, 1552 and 1662 to be comprehensive:

'It could accommodate deism and the philosophy of the 18th. Century. It could accommodate the piety of a Samuel Johnson. . . . it. . . . could accommodate both Simeon and Pusey, that with its aid the Church of England could discover that it had not lost the best heritage of the Catholic Church, and that it could at the same time be a church of evangelism.'

To the argument that the 1965 reform prevented Parliament from doing anything but approve the Doctrine and Worship Measure, the Member for Down South commented,

'It is quite unacceptable that this House, because it has permitted a deliberately delimited experiment to be conducted, should be told that thereby its judgement is pre-empted as to what is to happen thereafter.'

Enoch Powell also dealt with the question that, should the Measure be rejected, the Church would be forced back to a

[11] House of Commons, *Hansard*, 23rd February 1965, Col. 317.
[12] For all references to Powell's speech, see House of Commons, *Hansard*, 4th December 1974, Cols. 1666-1677.

pre-1965 situation. He went on to recall that the Bishop of Durham had insisted that the Church of England had moved into a period of liturgical stability:

'If the experiment has been a success, if it has resulted in forms of worship and formularies being evolved which, as a result of experiment, have shown themselves acceptable to the Church of England, the case is simple. All that is necessary is to present a measure to the House, and to say to this House, "With the powers which you gave the Church, the experiment has been carried out, and now we wish you to authorise the result of that experiment permanently by a measure which will give the force of law to the innovations".'

These argument did not prevail and the stage was set for the friction which has characterised the relationship between the Church, in the form of the Bishops and senior members of Synod, and a number of those MPs who take an interest in Church matters. This tension has surfaced in three main ways: it has been voiced at the regular meetings MPs have with senior Church officials; it was given specific prominence when both Lords and Commons gave initial approval to the Prayer Book Amendment Measure; it erupted throughout much of the time Parliament was considering the Pastoral (Amendment) Measure and, most recently, in the rejection in the Commons of the Appointment of Bishops Measure in July, 1984.

3.5:   Channels of Opposition

Twice a year one of the senior bishops – now the Bishop of Southwark – invites interested MPs to a lunchtime meeting. An agenda is set listing those measures for which the Church will soon be asking parliamentary approval, together with other business on which the Church thinks it may be useful to brief parliamentarians. At these meetings, a number of bishops attend who have special responsibility for, or interest in, matters which are to be discussed at the meeting.

The majority of MPs who attend are Conservative, but a

sizeable minority are Opposition Members. Among the gathering is the Second Estates Commissioner who is, by convention, a Government backbencher. Since 1979, the position has been held by Mr. (now Sir) William van Straubenzee who is known affectionately in the House as 'The Bishop'. Among the duties of the Second Estates Commissioner is to present Church matters to Parliament, to answer Questions on Church policy every six weeks in Parliament, and to act as a channel of communication between Synod and Church officials on the one side, and Parliament on the other. Sir William is an elected member of Synod. Since 1979 it has been the practice of Synod to co-opt the Shadow Estates Commissioner, i.e. the person on the Opposition front bench who 'shadows' his opposite number on the other side of the Commons. From 1979 to 1983, this post was filled by Frank White.

Of the 20-25 Members who attend these regular meetings, only a minority are in support of the direction in which the Church of England is moving. At these meetings, any criticism made of the Church's conduct has been deflected in one of two ways. First, the meetings have been reminded that Parliament agreed to delegate its authority to Synod on matters relating to worship. Second, one or other of the minority of MPs who are largely uncritical of Church policies and attitudes have been quick to run up an anti-Erastian flag whenever criticism has been directed at the Bishops. Both arguments are unsatisfactory. A number of Parliamentarians now feel that the Church has trapped it into delegating parliamentary authority to Synod. Further, to argue on Erastian grounds against the right of the State to regulate the Church is a little strange given that the Church of England 'is by law established'.

Underlying much of the parliamentary criticism in the earlier part of the 1979 Parliament was the feeling that, while going through the motions of seeking State advice and approval, listening to what Parliament had to say was the last thing which Synod believed it important to do. Indeed, little if any notice was taken of the criticisms made at these regular meetings until the Church was pulled up sharply by the difficulties the Synod faced both in gaining parliamentary approval for its Pastoral

Reorganization (Amendment) Measure and by the introduction of the Prayer Book Protection Measure.

3.6:   Prayer Book Protection Measure

The aim of the Prayer Book Protection Measure, 1981, was to ensure that twenty people of a parish could compel their incumbent to hold once a month the principal morning service according to the 1662 Rite. In introducing this measure, Viscount Cranborne remarked that it was 'a sad occasion when any. . . Member should feel compelled to. . . introduce a bill such as this'.[13]

Viscount Cranborne accepted that the 1974 Worship and Doctrine Measure had created a concordat between Church and State, but that the concordat rested on two clear undertakings. The first was given by the then Archbishop of Canterbury during the Lords debate on the 1974 Measure. Michael Ramsey asserted that

'....it is not a Measure for abolishing the Book of Common Prayer. (Rather) it gives to the Book of Common Prayer a secure place.'[14]

When the Commons debated the 1974 Measure, the Church's spokesman in the Commons stated:

'If the Synod should ever wish to alter (the position of the Prayer Book) so that the 1662 Book, or some services in it, were to be abolished, the Church would have to come to Parliament with another measure and thus the Book of Common Prayer is given a secure place in the future of our worship.'[15]

Viscount Cranborne's contention was 'that it is not Parliament which is in danger of breaking the concordat; the Church has breached it'.[16]

[13] House of Commons, *Hansard*, 8th April 1981, Col. 959.
[14] House of Commons, *Hansard*, 8th April 1981, Col. 960.
[15] House of Commons, *Hansard*, 8th April 1981, Col. 960.
[16] House of Commons, *Hansard*, 8th April 1981, Col. 960.

The nub of the Second Estates Commissioner's case for the House rejecting the Bill was that, while the Prayer Book 'was enshrined in the laws of the land',[17] congregations had opted for the new services. This was not a view shared by the majority of MPs present, and despite the work of the Government whips who had been mobilising opposition to the Bill, Viscount Cranborne was given leave to introduce his Bill by 152 votes to 130. Of this 130, over 50 were either part of what is called the pay-roll vote (i.e. members of the Government who can be more easily marshalled than other members to vote in a particular way) or were opposition whips who regularly 'do deals' with their opposite numbers to help get business through, or defeated, in return for minor concessions on usually totally unrelated issues.

The debate in the Commons was followed, later the same day, by the introduction of a similar Bill in the Lords and a debate which covered almost identical ground. A number of speakers drew attention to the inconsistency in recent pronouncements of Church leaders demanding 'absolute freedom of independence combined with all the advantages of establishment'.[18] And other speakers wondered whether Parliament would have delegated its authority to Synod had it been aware of the results brought about by use of that power.

It was Lord Dacre (better known as Hugh Trevor Roper) who summed up the feelings of many participants to the debate when he drew a distinction between a church and a sect:

'The Church', Lord Dacre observed, 'is the congregation of the faithful, clergy and lay alike, and it includes many who loyally adhere without pedantically subscribing. That is the difference between a church and a sect. An established church has a particular duty towards the laity: a duty of tolerance and comprehension. The laity is not to be dragged unwillingly towards a particular road by a party of activists exploiting their customary loyalty and deference.'[19]

[17] House of Commons, *Hansard*, 8th April 1981, Col. 960.
[18] House of Lords, *Hansard*, 8th April 1981, Col. 637.
[19] House of Lords, *Hansard*, 8th April 1981, Col. 638.

The Lord Chancellor spoke twice in the debate, towards the beginning and almost four hours later as the discussion was drawn to a close. On both occasions he warned the House of the constitutional consequences of passing the Measure:

'In the ordinary course of Private Members' Bills Her Majesty's Government adopts a neutral posture. Unhappily, in matters which raise grave questions of constitutional propriety and usage, this cannot be the case. In this case. . . . such issues arise and it is my duty to tell the House without equivocation that on such grounds Her Majesty's Government cannot recommend to the House the passage of this Bill through Parliament.'[20]

The Bill was, nevertheless, given a second reading but despite these two rebuffs the Church had still to begin taking seriously the criticisms made of its behaviour by committed parliamentarians. The Archbishop did, however, accept an invitation to lunch from Viscount Cranborne where he met a small group of parliamentarians, and a follow-up lunch was arranged at Lambeth Palace for a much larger group. And while he has always shown a sensitivity to the reactions of parliamentarians, the general Church complacency continued, but did not outlive the passage of the Pastoral Reorganisation (Amendment) Measure.

3.7:   Pastoral Reorganisation (Amendment) Measure 1982

Before any Synod measure gains the force of law, it has to be considered by the Ecclesiastical Committee of Parliament and then debated and passed by both Lords and Commons. Measures coming to the Ecclesiastical Committee can be accepted or rejected; they cannot be amended. Up until 1982, when the Committee sent back the Clergy Pensions (Amendment) Measure (see below), no measure had been rejected by the Committee. Synod completed its debates on the amendments to the 1968 Pastoral Measure in February 1981. The Ecclesiastical

[20] House of Lords, *Hansard*, 8th April 1981, Col. 627.

Committee began its deliberations in June 1981 and did not give its final approval until February 1982.

Population movements during and after the War have resulted in some parishes being bereft of all, or practically all, their parishioners, while in other areas would-be parishioners have had no accessible church. The original Pastoral Measure provided a machinery for the creation of new parishes, the setting up of what are called 'team' or 'group' ministries, and the procedure by which churches can be made redundant. In the light of the working of this measure, Synod proposed a number of reforms of which two were considered contentious by the Ecclesiastical Committee. In addition, as meeting followed meeting, a number of Committee members became critical of the performance of Synod officers. It may have been Synod's view that the Measure was largely uncontroversial, hence the somewhat relaxed manner in which officials approached the Committee. But, on a whole series of questions, officials were not able to provide information considered satisfactory by the Committee. In addition, because of their concern, members debated at some length two of the Synod's proposals: the abolition of appeals on church redundancies to the Privy Council, except in a those few cases where there had been an irregularity of procedure, an excess of jurisdiction or on cogent evidence of an erroneous judgement; and secondly the Advisory Board for Redundant Churches' loss of its veto power over demolition proposals.

The abolition of the appeal to the Privy Council, except on matters of law, was debated at length by the Committee. In the end, members were satisfied that the Privy Council had powers to overrule a redundancy decision only if the procedure by which the decision had been made was unlawful. The Privy Council could not enter into a debate on whether a decision was wise or not. Once this change had been agreed, the rest of the Committee's deliberations centred on the proposal to curtail the powers of the Advisory Board for Redundant Churches.

The original Pastoral Measure had established the Advisory Board for Redundant Churches in order that the views of the intelligent conservationists could be considered along with the pastoral orientation of the Church Commissioners in any scheme which involved the partial or total demolition of a church. To secure an effective status, the Advisory Board was given the power to veto any demolition proposal. Within the space of a few years, the Board, under the secretaryship of Margo Eates, had developed an independence, so much so that the Commissioners became anxious to limit its influence.

During early discussions on the Pastoral Reorganisation (Amendment) Measure, the Advisory Board agreed to the loss of its veto power, but later reconsidered its position. This change of heart came about once it was realised that the proposed reform would tip the balance decisively in favour of the pastoral needs of the Church against its national duties of safeguarding buildings of outstanding architectural merit. The Church was, however, placed in a difficult position when the Advisory Board lobbied the Ecclesiastical Committee about its loss of veto power before telling Church authorities of its changed stance. Its submission made two important points.

In the first place, the Board argued to the Ecclesiastical Committee:

'Again cases which have arisen during 1980–81. . . . have convinced the Board that it would be unwise to leave decisions in the hands of the Church Commissioners, if only because it would be extremely difficult for a pastorally orientated body like the Commissioners to resist the diocesan pressure that would be brought to bear on them to reject the Board's advice and to ignore restrictions which the Board might, on valid historic or architectural grounds, strongly recommend.'[21]

The Board also argued that its powers of veto had resulted in the saving of some churches which would otherwise have been pulled down. For example,

'. . . . the Advisory Board's refusal of Certificates, in the face of strong pressure, resulted in saving Holy Trinity, Tunbridge Wells. . . . lately upgraded and converted for use as a theatre; St. Stephen, Rosslyn Hill. . . . which is now under consideration for vesting in the Redundant Churches Fund; Holy Trinity,

[21] House of Commons, *Hansard*, 17th June 1982, Col. 1194.

Sloane Street. . . . which is now being retained in parochial use; St. Hilda, Cross Green. . . . which is again in active parochial use; Christ Church, St. Albans. . . . now converted to use as a recording studio; St. Gregory the Great, Canterbury. . . . now converted for educational purposes.'[22]

Given this evidence, many members of the Committee were unwilling to pass the Measure until there had been a joint meeting of the Committee with Synod's Legislative Committee; members wished to express their opposition to the proposal without voting against it. This idea was resisted and as the meetings dragged on an unofficial proposal was canvassed by John Selwyn Gummer (who happened also to be a Synod member) for such a meeting to take place on the understanding that it would be followed immediately by the Committee giving approval to the Measure. This proposal was accepted by the critics. Their main wish was to meet with their opposite numbers in Synod and register a protest centring as much on the style as on the content of Church politics. As a matter of courtesy, John Selwyn Gummer informed the Second Estates Commissioner what was being planned. At the following Ecclesiastical Committee meeting on February 4, 1982, a number of those who had backed the idea of a joint meeting switched sides, including the Revd. The Lord Sandford. A few days later the Court Page of *The Times* carried the announcement of his appointment as a Church Commissioner.

Considerable anger was expressed at the end of the Ecclesiastical Committee meeting when the compromise suggestion was forced off the agenda. A vote was forced on either an acceptance or rejection of the whole Amendment Measure. This undermining of the compromise proposal was described in *The Times* by one of the Committee members as 'the most squalid little political manoeuvre I have seen this Parliament'.[23] Following the meeting, feelings ran so high that, for example, one of the senior members, Mr. (now Sir) Peter Mills intimated that if this was the way the Church was going to behave, he could see little use

[22] House of Commons, *Hansard*, 17th June 1982, Col. 1194.
[23] *The Times*, 16th April 1982, p. 7.

remaining on the Committee. Sir Peter, it should be remembered, was one of those who, while being a member of the Church Assembly, had argued for parliamentary approval of most of the reforms considered by Parliament during the previous fifteen years or so. His criticism was, therefore, particularly important.

This anger at last registered over at Church House and the Ecclesiastical Committee was offered, not a meeting with the Legislative Committee, but a delegation led by the Archbishop of Canterbury. At this meeting on 22 June 1982, Committee members were able to talk directly to senior Synod leaders, rather than through intermediaries. During the meeting, the Archbishop and his senior colleagues gained some idea about the Committee's unease on matters of Church policy and, more importantly, on what the Committee felt to be the Established Church's unwillingness to enter into a proper dialogue with interested parliamentarians.

At the end of the meeting, the Archbishop suggested that this should be the first of a series of meetings. What effect these two meetings will have it is difficult to judge. None of the promised, follow-up meetings has yet materialised. And, while Synod is much more careful about trying to explain its measures to Parliament, this change in attitude has only come about after the Ecclesiastical Committee forced Synod to withdraw the Clergy Pensions (Amendment) Measure due to its extensive drafting faults. In some important respects, the Measure as submitted to the Committee would have had the opposite effect to that intended by the Synod.

3.8: The 1984 'Revolt' over the Appointment of Bishops Measure.

I turn finally to the latest manifestation of rising tension between Church and Parliament. Once again, the chief protagonists were, on the one hand, a group of back-benchers in (on this occasion) the House of Commons led by Enoch Powell and, on the other hand, the General Synod. The specific subject on which anger was expressed concerned changes recommended to

Parliament by the General Synod in, as the latter saw it, the relatively arcane and anachronistic procedures through which bishops in the Church of England are legally vested with their powers. The aim of the new Measure, had .it been approved, would have been to erase the 'farcical' arrangement whereby Cathedral chapters are required to obey a royal command to vote for, and thus elect, the person duly nominated by the Crown. Instead, the method of archiepiscopal confirmation, also allowed for in the original Appointment of Bishops Act (1533), but not in fact used, was now seen as more seemly.

In proposing this change, however, some Parliamentarians once again saw the General Synod intent upon a process of creeping disestablishment, a process whose effect was 'to keep in place the symbols of establishment. . . . while chipping away at the substance.'[24] It was against such attempts to shift the fundamental character of the Church (as he saw it) that Enoch Powell railed. Setting himself up once more as the guardian of the historic and traditional nature of the Church of England, he attacked the Measure in very sharp terms,

'.... this (Measure) appears to be an act of wanton vandalism – an act which illustrates the gulf between the General Synod and the ordinary feelings of the general public, and the gulf between the bureaucracy of the Church and the nature and historical sense of the Church of England.'[25]

For him, an internally self-governed church, able to appoint its own bishops without reference to Parliament, would no longer be a national church, no longer the Church of England as it had been known since the Reformation. The General Synod was therefore betraying that historic arrangement, that essential national significance of the Church, and trying to turn it into no more than a sect.

Some of Powell's colleagues who also spoke in the debate were equally incensed by the behaviour of the General Synod and other senior leaders within the Church but perhaps for more short-term reasons. they had in mind the recent elevation to the

---

[24] Clifford Longley in *The Times*, 23rd July 1984.
[25] House of Commons, *Hansard*, 16th July 1984, Col. 134.

See of Durham of Bishop David Jenkins, a man whom Patrick Cormack hinted 'professes agnosticism on some of the main tenets of the Christian faith.'[26] This event, he suggested, was but one of 'many. . . trends in the established Church of England' about which 'honourable Members who take an interest in such affairs. . . have been profoundly concerned.'[27] The trends he had in mind, and was obviously disturbed by, were those of a Synodical and episcopal leadership being seemingly bent on a course of action that would carry the Church down historically novel and unwelcome paths. Amongst other consequences this would subvert Parliament's ultimate authority in ecclesiastical matters. He couched his experiences in these terms:

'Those of us who sit on the Ecclesiastical Committee are sometimes a little perturbed about the arrogance – I use the word advisedly–of the Synod of the Church of England when it comes to consider the role of Parliament because in effect it says, "If you question the wisdom of what we are doing in Synod, you are moving us towards disestablishment." That threat is implicit, time and again, in what is said to the Ecclesiastical Committee.'[28]

On this evidence, therefore, Church and at least a part of Parliament seem destined to remain in a tense partnership. For, as the Church continues to press for further de jure self-government, continues to espouse postures that challenge traditional understandings and, not least, recruits into its leadership men who adopt apparently novel positions on doctrinal matters (though not on social matters where Parliament has increasingly accepted the Church's right to be involved), so certain sections of conservative opinion within Parliament will seek vigorously to resist.

[26] House of Commons, *Hansard*, 16th July 1984, Col. 139. For subsequent developments, see also *The Times*, 9th and 11th February, 1985 the Preface of the *Church of England Yearbook*, 1985 (London: CIO Publishing) and the intended debate in the General Synod during the same month on doctrine in the Church of England.
[27] House of Commons, *Hansard*, 16th July 1984, Col. 138.
[28] House of Commons, *Hansard*, 16th July 1984, Col. 139.

3.9: Conclusion

Where does all this leave the relationship between the Church of England and Parliament? It is important to note the change in the nature of the tension between the two bodies now and in 1927. In the 1920s, the concern was that the Church was in danger of losing its protestant ethos. Now the grounds of complaint centre on the manner in which the Church has begun fundamentally to change the link between Church and State.

While some Synod members may congratulate themselves on their successes, there has been a cost which is over and above the worsening of relationships between the two bodies. The introduction of the Prayer Book Protection Measures resulted in breaking the convention whereby ecclesiastical legislation originates only in the Synod. Considerable stress was put on adhering to this convention, particularly in the behind-the-scenes lobbying to prevent the introduction of this measure in the Lords and Commons. As every student of the constitution knows, once a convention is broken it is easier for further breaches to be made.

There are two reforms which are likely candidates for further breaches of this convention. If the Church does nothing to stop the further decline in the use of the Book of Common Prayer, a new Prayer Book protection measure may be introduced. More importantly, and irrespective of action to protect the position of the Prayer Book, lobbying may well begin in earnest for a reform allowing the Ecclesiastical Committee powers to amend Church measures. The events since 1979 have shown the unsatisfactory nature of the current position whereby any part, no matter how small, of a proposal cannot be changed by Parliament or Synod, once the measure has been introduced to the Ecclesiastical Committee.

A reform along these lines may well lead Church officials to raise the cry for disestablishment. Such threats were made at the introduction of the Prayer Book Amendment Measure in 1981 and again in 1984, but Church officials have made no attempt to follow up on their suggestions. The Church's insistence that disestablishment might result from passing the Protection Measure did, however, set some parliamentarians thinking through what such a move would involve. The conclusion was that a measure of this kind would be likely to take a great deal of parliamentary time, so much so that it would disrupt the timetable for the Government's own business. The Church may, therefore, be faced with the position of disestablishment becoming an empty cry, not because Churchmen will cease to demand it, but because Parliament would not conceive of surrendering the amount of parliamentary time such a move would undoubtedly involve. If events were to unfold in this way, the Church will be left in an unenviable position and those who were most pleased with the way they at least engineered a new prayer book, may yet live to have second thoughts. Certainly, judging by the events of 1984, a more cautious and sensitive consideration of Parliamentary opinion by the Synod and its leadership would seem in order.

Chapter 4

LAMBETH PALACE, THE BISHOPS AND POLITICS*

Kenneth Medhurst and George Moyser

4.1: Introduction

In secularized society, it is readily assumed that the churches have, at best, a marginal role to play in national political life. Political divisions in English society do not run along confessional lines and issues of obviously religious provenance have not loomed large on the political agenda. However, some recent developments have suggested that the major churches may be seeking a somewhat redefined and more clearly relevant political role. This is true, not least, of the Church of England whose distinctive history leaves it occupying a position which, even now, is of particular importance for the society.[1]

It is of course the case that both legal and de facto religious toleration have now become the order of the day and that, within the context of a pluralistic society, the Anglican Church has been constrained to abandon its monopolistic pretensions. Nevertheless, it remains established and sees itself occupying a symbolically important position in a still ostensibly Christian society.

For some of the Church's critics, this situation signifies the persistence of unhealthy anachronisms wedding the institution too closely to the *status quo*.[2] For others, the situation constitutes

* We wish gratefully to acknowledge the financial support of the Economic and Social Research Council for the project from which this chapter is drawn.

[1] On the whole subject of 'secularization' as it affects England, see A.D. Gilbert, *The Making of Post-Christian Britain: A History of Modern Society* (London: Longman, 1980).

[2] The case for disestablishment is argued in P.R. Cornwell, *The Church and the Nation: The Case for Disestablishment* (London: Basil Blackwell, 1983). More 'orthodox' perspectives are represented by J. Habgood, *Church and Nation in a Secular Age* (London: Darton, Longman and Todd, 1983).

a challenge or opportunity either to reaffirm traditional under-standings or else to articulate Christian values within the widest possible social and political contexts. Certainly, our evidence suggests that the vast bulk of the Church of England's present episcopal leadership has no desire to sever the State connection though, as we shall see, there may be some pressure to redefine it.[3] Inevitably, the persistence of traditional, if now loosened, bonds involves tension if not ambivalence on the Church's part. There is resistance to the idea of a sectarian position and there is acceptance of a need to be supportive of all sectors or facets of the society. But that necessarily may entail difficulties when it comes to the exercise of a prophetic or politically critical ministry.[4] There is a problem for a Church which sees itself as a national body but which may, on occasion, feel constrained to speak out, at least by implication, against particular tendencies or groups within the fold. There is a difficult balance to be struck between its politically encouraging or integrative role and its politically critical functions.

Close to the heart of these controversies lie the Church's episcopate who constitute the focal point of this essay. It is they, particularly, who must wrestle day to day with the problems that we have identified and who may experience the tensions thus engendered. Within the public and political spheres, they have special significance, for those charged with episcopal oversight are vested with an especially authoritative and symbolically significant form of leadership. The nature of the episcopal office, and of the expectations attached to it, give to bishops a particularly salient if not vulnerable position within the public domain.

4.2:   The Bishops and Politics

In assessing relationships between the episcopate and politics, it is possible to discriminate between three levels of activity,

[3] This is the conclusion we have reached having talked at some length with diocesan bishops from all but one of the English dioceses as well as with other senior Church leaders.

[4] For some questioning of the whole idea of a prophetic ministry on the part of official Church leaders, see R. Gill, *Prophecy and Praxis*, (Basingstoke: Marshall, Morgan and Scott, 1981).

namely the local or diocesan, the national and the international. We also wish to distinguish between different elements within the episcopate – elements characterized by differing priorities and responses to the public arena.

Firstly, we distinguish between those bishops who, by virtue of their sees, or seniority, occupy seats in the House of Lords and those not yet in that position. The former do not necessarily accord a high priority to their parliamentary responsibilities and do not inevitably make substantial and influential contributions to public debate. In reality, those concerned acknowledge that there are differing levels of commitment to this type of activity.[5] Individual contributions depend on the personalities, expertise or pre-occupations of those concerned. Moreover, degrees of involvement vary from time to time, and from issue to issue, depending upon the particular qualifications or experience that bishops bring to bear. A debate on unemployment, for example, is more likely to invite the contribution of a bishop from an industrial area than one from a primarily rural see. Equally, for most contemporary bishops, pastoral activity within the diocese rates higher than national involvement. This applies not only to involvement in the parliamentary and secular arena but also to involvement in the Church's own central organs.

Nevertheless, one should separate out those offered the opportunity to make a mark in national debate. At the least, membership of the House of Lords does entail periodic attendance to lead prayers which, to put it no higher, affords opportunity for two way flows of influence between the bishops concerned and members of the national political elite. It certainly appears as if membership of the Lords, even when it does not involve obviously significant contributions to public discussion, may well involve informal contacts that provide bishops with opportunities, albeit in small ways, to shape the priorities and thinking of some of their secular counterparts. Indeed, for many of the Lords Spiritual, the influence exercised is chiefly of a personal, informal and somewhat diffuse kind. The existence of such contacts, however, puts them in a more 'privileged' position than episcopal colleagues denied such regular or guaranteed access to national figures.

[5] This and subsequent points also stem from our interview evidence.

The tendency noted above for bishops to give priority to local pastoral concerns is one that seems characteristic of the contemporary Anglican episcopate. In case this seems obvious, it must be indicated that, in previous eras, membership of the episcopate might well involve participation in an upper-class life style and a share in national public life that could lead to long absences from the diocese. Possible reasons for the change we have explored elsewhere.[6] On the one hand, the Church has been relegated to a less significant position in English society; on the other, there has been some theological re-evaluation of the episcopal office.[7] Here it seems sufficient to say that the maintenance of autonomous ecclesiastical institutions and, more importantly, the care of local clergy and their congregations, now claim more attention from bishops than once was the case.

Similarly, bishops are now relatively less integrated into traditional local elite groups. They have been recruited less and less from upper class or aristocratic backgrounds and become, therefore, less closely allied with local land-owning groups.[8] Bishops may still interact with such elements but less frequently and more formally than was the case. A bishop, for example, may have routine dealings with the Lord Lieutenant of the county but is now unlikely to be a member of the latter's immediate social group or to share the latter's values and assumptions. If anything, local landed interests, as well as local business leaders, may be more likely than the bishop himself to think of the episcopate as naturally aligning itself with their interests. In such quarters there is still a tendency to see the Anglican Church's episcopate in terms of a traditional hierarchical society. These preconceptions may well give rise to misunderstandings and tension.

In principle, the process of disengagement may leave Church leaders freer than before to exercise localized forms of social or

[6] See K. N. Medhurst and G. Moyser, "From Princes to Pastors: The Changing Position of the Anglican Episcopate in English Society and Politics", *West European Politics*, Vol. 5, No. 2 (April, 1982) pp. 172-191.

[7] For general reflections of a theological kind on the episcopal office, see P. Moore (ed), *Bishops: But What Kind?* (London: SPCK, 1982).

[8] See K. N. Medhurst and G. Moyser, *op. cit.*. See also A. Russell, *The Clerical Profession* (London: SPCK, 1980).

political influence along alternative and more socially critical lines. To some extent this is also true in practice. Thus, bishops are now unlikely to be the co-opted hostages of traditional socially conservative elites. Indeed, episcopal pronouncements from the pulpit and diocesan magazines, or from more secular platforms, may quite frequently lead, in our day, to at least muted criticism from the elite groups in question. This is true of pronouncements on such diverse matters as race relations, national defence, law and order and unemployment.

On the other hand, many bishops are constrained to give second importance to such matters; they devote relatively limited time to fighting public causes or to lobbying for non-ecclesiastical groups. Few bishops can, in this sense, be regarded as highly 'politicized'. Rather there is a tendency for most of the bishops for most of the time, to emphasize pastoral over-sight and 'domestic' ecclesiastical affairs. To this extent, the evidence seems to point away from the picture of the contemporary episcopate presented by some conservative commentators.[9] Indeed, a minority of more radicalized Churchmen might even suggest that their leaders are insufficiently politically aware or outspoken.

Many factors may be adduced to account for these priorities. Firstly, there are revised theological understandings pointing to the bishop as pastor and servant rather than as prince and hierarchical superior. There is a tendency to see the bishop as lying at the centre of a local community rather than at the apex of a diocesan hierarchy; educating or enabling the local Church to play its proper part in society rather than claiming to be the Church's chief or sole authoritative spokesman. In part this involves highlighting important issues, articulating relevant theological insights, educating the Church's own laity and, not least, intermittently reaching out to a wider public in order to nurture the general concept of Christian social concern. But the stress remains upon the mass of Church members as having the prime responsibility for contributing an active Christian presence in politics.

Secondly, there are constraints pointing clerical leaders

[9] See, for example, E. R. Norman, *Christianity and the World Order* (London: Oxford University Press, 1979).

towards a quest for consensus and harmony rather than confrontation and conflict. Theologically, there is the concept of the bishop as an essentially eirenic figure exercising a reconciling or healing mission amongst possibly discrepant groups within the Church, and even the wider society. Culturally, there is the perhaps characteristically English concern for maintaining stability and avoiding radical discontinuity. In principle, this might suggest a certain neutrality towards, or a transcending of, conflict on the part of ecclesiastical leaders. Thus, many English bishops see the idea of a national Church as being incompatible with any notion of ecclesiastical bias towards the interests of any one social group. Within the episcopate itself, however, an arguably more radical voice may be heard suggesting that the otherwise legitimate search for consensus may too readily be confused with an ignoring of latent conflict and an unwillingness to face up to the persistence of social injustices.[10] The same 'radical' critics also suggest that the existence of order and stability can be too readily mistaken for widespread consent to, or support for, existing arrangements. In practice, apparent social or political harmony may cloak sullen acquiescence or even massive alienation perhaps having long term de-stabilizing consequences. From this perspective, true reconciliation or harmony presupposes an initial acceptance of real, if hopefully constructive, conflict. It is at such a point that tensions are engendered within the episcopate, and even within individual bishops, as a result of trying to accommodate inherited understandings of a national Church to a changing theological and political climate.

A third factor bearing on altered episcopal priorities are the constraints experienced by bishops that derive from the new demands of their office. Thus, pressures for extended participation manifested in synodical and related structures make great demands on the episcopate. Such structures represent an attempt to wed traditional hierarchical conceptions of authority to more democratic conceptions, and to work out an as yet ill-defined balance between these diverse understandings. They consequently present bishops with novel difficulties. On the one

[10] See D. Sheppard, *Bias to the Poor* (London: Hodder and Stoughton, 1983).

hand, there are pressures for extended lay participation but, on the other hand, much deference is still extended along with the expectation that bishops should supply leadership to which others may respond. The net result is a situation in which bishops are caught up in a round of 'domestic' meetings, committees and debates.

Of course, such gatherings may in part be concerned with forming the mind of the Church on public issues. To that extent, bishops are engaged, along with others, in the task of educating or mobilizing opinion within the Church and even, to some extent, without. Indeed, bishops may have particularly decisive contributions to make to these activities.[11] Nevertheless, the impact upon the wider society is largely indirect and arises initally from 'in-house' discussion rather than communications aimed primarily at the general public.

Naturally, one cannot always readily discriminate between the impact of episcopal leadership upon a Church audience and upon those beyond. For example, when the Archbishop of Canterbury preaches a sermon on such an occasion as the Service in St Paul's Cathedral, following the Falklands' War, it is apparent that it is part of a national and State occasion having implications felt well beyond the frontiers of the ecclesiastical community as conventionally understood. Indeed, on such an occasion, the Church of England, in rather dramatic form, is seeking creatively to reaffirm its special position as a custodian of what are taken to be the nation's most fundamental values. These occasions, however, are exceptional. In the main, contemporary Church leaders are under some pressure to turn inwards to the ecclesiastical community rather than cutting an obvious dash upon the wider public stage.

The bishop's task may be further complicated by a relative absence, certainly at the local level, of appropriate resources. Thus, with some notable exceptions, bishops lack advisors of the sort which could enable them to discharge their task with suitably high levels of information or expertise. Bishops do, of course, possess specialized advisors, of frequently high calibre,

[11] The example of John Baker, Bishop of Salisbury, in the field of nuclear disarmament, is a recent spectacular example. See Ch. 8 of this volume for further details.

in such realms as education or industrial mission. But a dearth of manpower and economic resources may quite often mean that the important staff jobs have to be delegated to an already hard-pressed handful of lay officials or else to already hard-pressed parochial clergy.

For example, in a media-soaked environment, it might be argued that the bishops should give fairly high priority to developing expertise in the use of the means of mass communications. In practice, however, there has been some reluctance to generate and allocate the appropriate resources. The job of diocesan information officer has, in consequence, either not been established or has passed to a clergyman with other major responsibilities.

Similarly, many of the bishops themselves feel that their own training and background does not always equip them to speak with authority on complex social, economic or political matters. Likewise, with or without appropriate expertise, there is always the danger of becoming over-exposed or of making counter-productive statements. The timing of initiatives and the allocation of relevant priorities is itself a matter of quite fine 'political' judgement which does not always come easily to those whose previous responsibilities may well have lain in far less exposed ecclesiastical structures.

Inhibitions of this kind may be partly associated with the assumption, already mentioned, that ultimate responsibility for Christian political engagement lies elsewhere and that for bishops to obtrude in this sphere would be to undermine the credibility of such a view. In part, however, it may also be a question of traditional theological training and pastoral experience leading to the view that personal one-to-one relationships are the crucial factor in any situation – a view possibly leading to some undervaluing of structural factors.

Some bishops explicitly take the view that the Christian's political responsibility is essentially a matter of moving individual hearts and minds in order that the activities of such individuals may ultimately lead to a moral regeneration of society.[12] There is an alternative view, however, also repre-sented within the episcopate, that a proper concern for indi-viduals must co-exist with a heightened awareness of the constraining effect of impersonal structures and of the need for structural as well as person regeneration.[13] It is, perhaps, fair to say that, should this latter view be accepted as legitimate, then only a minority of bishops have relevant experience or training. Put another way, a bench of bishops rich in other respects, is relatively lacking in members with sociological forms of understanding.[14] This may even be part of a still wider problem, namely continuing difficulties in coming fully to terms with all the implications of 'the Enlightenment' or of scientific ap-proaches to the understanding of the universe.

The issue of sociological understanding may be of particular importance when it comes to the question of seeking conscious-ly to nurture continuing, but fresh and creative, links with the Church's transformed environment. Certainly, it is now appa-rent that, in the political realm, the Church of England is no longer simply 'the Conservative Party at prayer'. Rank and file Anglicans may even yet be disproportionately drawn towards the Conservative Party, and many of those concerned may see membership of the Church as part of a given culture of an arguably backward-looking kind.[15] Nevertheless, a significant proportion of those manning synodical structures, and a clear majority of the English episcopate, have been propelled towards a range of attitudes that is somewhat at odds with traditional expectations. In other words, a measure of disengagement from

[12] See the views of Graham Leonard the present Bishop of London in, for example, G. Ionescu, "Speaking Notes with the Bishop of London on how and why the Church might be losing its nerve and its role in modern society", *Government and Opposition*, Vol. 17, No. 3 (Summer, 1982) pp. 351-361.

[13] See D. Sheppard, *op. cit.*.

[14] This is, perhaps, hinted at in J. Habgood, *op cit.*, which is an unusual attempt, by a senior Churchman, to make use of sociological forms of understanding.

[15] For relevant empirical evidence on voting patterns, see K.D. Wald, *Crosses on the Ballot: Patterns of British Voter Alignment Since 1885*, (Princeton: University Press, 1983). See also W. L. Miller and G. Raab, "The Religious Alignment at English Elections between 1918 and 1970", *Political Studies*, Vol. 25 (No. 2, 1977) pp. 227-251.

traditional alliances has gone hand-in-hand with a certain redefinition of the episcopate's overall position on the conventional political spectrum. Sociological, economic, cultural and generational factors (that we have explored elsewhere)[16] have conspired with shifts of theological perception to produce this situation.

Disengagement and change, however, have not always been accompanied by re-engagement along fresh lines. Large sections of the society remain substantially unaffected by the Church, except perhaps in limited residual senses, and this is particularly true of the working class and of inner city dwellers. Despite some creative thinking and effort, the Church as a whole has not felt willing or able to re-order its priorities so as more effectively to penetrate such strata or the economic and other structures largely governing their lives. To cite a particularly obvious example, though individual Anglicans may have been active in the Trade Union Movement, senior Churchmen seem, as a rule, less likely to receive a welcome from trade union gatherings than they would from gatherings of professionals or businessmen. There is, if you will, a persisting social distance between the Church's leaders and Labour's spokesmen. The gap may be bridged by particular individuals, including particular bishops, and there are even now examples of Church leaders being able privately and unofficially to use their good offices in order to promote a measure of dialogue between different sides of industry. There are others who have more publicly attempted peace-making initiatives as in the 1984-5 Miners' Strike. Such activities, however, perhaps testify to possibilities open on this front rather than to any systematic narrowing of the gap.

To a considerable extent this is a question of the relevant groups having understandably stereotyped, if historically outmoded, images of the Church and, as a consequence, deliberately keeping their distance. To a substantial degree, however, it is also a question of the Church having as yet failed to devise a strategy or the means of communication arguably necessary for getting alongside such groups and dispelling long standing suspicions. We hasten to add that the episcopate as a group cannot possibly be held chiefly, still less solely, responsible for

[16] See K. N. Medhurst and G. Moyser, *op. cit.*

this situation. Their formation and pattern of recruitment is just one part of a much wider and more complex picture having very deep-seated historical origins. But, by that same token, this arguable need for greater structural awareness, to which we have referred, is related to a need for an enhanced understanding of the frequently resistant character of inherited structures and of the need to devise appropriate forms of analysis and action if the resistance is to be overcome.

Having said all this, it may be suggested that, as part of the possibly troubled transitional phase through which the Church of England is currently passing, there are signs of growing attempts creatively to grapple with the issues concerned and, in a sense, to seek after appropriate strategies.[17] Equally, there are signs of a growing acceptance on the episcopate's part that it has a distinctive though certainly not monopolistic role in the redefining of priorities and objectives. It is recognized, in other words, that the nature of the leadership to be supplied by the episcopate may need some re-evaluation. In the rest of this discussion we hope to explore these related questions of leadership and the re-assessment of mission as it affects the Church's presence in the public domain.

In discussing leadership, it is important to note that there exists within the House of Bishops, a relatively small core of figures exercising special influence *vis à vis* Church matters in general, and our field of interest in particular. In part, this is a question of the seniority of those concerned (as measured by their date of appointment or by the see they occupy). Thus, the two Archbishops, by definition, fall into this category, and there still persists the time-honoured tradition of according special precedence to the Sees of Durham, London and Winchester. These five bishops have automatic access to the House of Lords irrespective of their date of appointment and, in practice, it is manifest that appointments to those sees are made from amongst those who, potentially or actually, are regarded as the Church's chief statesmen. In the case of the Archbishops, one might generally say that this is self-evident. In the case of the Bishopric of Durham, it has proved to be a stepping-stone to the Church's

[17] Note, for example, the establishment in 1983 of a Commission of Enquiry into the Inner City by the Archbishop of Canterbury.

very highest offices.[18] London, for obvious geographical and historical reasons, is conventionally regarded as next only to the Archbishop of Canterbury when it comes to personalized links between the Church, the City of London and the State. Similarly, there is reason to suppose that, in appointing to such sees as Southwark and Rochester, which are close to centres of decision-making, at least some consideration is given to the contributions that candidates could make to the influencing of policy in both the ecclesiastical, and the more obviously secular spheres.

The existence of such gradations within the ranks of the episcopate, based on a mixture of see, seniority and reputation, has obviously been a time-honoured fact of life. What seems to be a relatively new departure, however, is for such an 'inner ring' to acquire a semi-institutionalized status. Thus, the practice has apparently developed of periodic informal meetings under the chairmanship of the Archbishop of Canterbury in which minds are explored, positions clarified and issues ventilated. It is also an effort to create a stronger sense of *esprit de corps* and to give a clearer sense of direction, to episcopal deliberations. Not least, it may provide a useful sounding board for initatives being mooted in Lambeth Palace. The bishops concerned may be by no means agreed about the matters concerned, but the clarifying of alternative possibilities could be part of the overall process of giving greater structure to the conduct of episcopal discussions. That stucture is an integral feature of a now more generalized attempt to manage the House of Bishops' affairs on a more planned and coordinated basis. Thus, for example, the House of Bishops' work is now more characterized by delegation to committees than was formerly the case. Equally, more studied attempts are being made to develop a generally more collegiate approach to episcopal dealings with the rest of the Church, and in particular with the General Synod of which the House of Bishops is itself a major component.

The steps are necessarily tentative for the notion of collegial-

---

[18] The present Archbishop of York was previously Bishop of Durham (1973-1983). Another recent example is Michael Ramsay who was at Durham from 1952 to 1956, and was subsequently 'promoted' to York in the latter year and thence to Canterbury in 1961.

ity in the Anglican context seems likely in practice to come up against obstacles, or to experience limitations, that are much less evidently present in the case, for example, of the Roman Catholic Communion. In part, this is a theological matter, for the Anglican Church obviously continues to represent a continuing historic '*modus vivendi*' embracing contrasting theological traditions of a sort not explicitly acknowledged within the Roman Church. Indeed, the diversity inherent within the Anglican tradition is effectively acknowledged and entrenched as a result of the practice of securing representation on the episcopal bench of representatives of different theological formations. Such representatives, by virtue of their experience and responsibilities, are unlikely to adopt extreme or intransigent positions of the sort represented elsewhere in the Church. But they do ensure that there is no false consensus at the top of the Church's official structures.

Those structures have also operated, in their own right, to stand in the way of a single episcopal voice. Thus, from the parochial level upwards, there is a powerful tradition of the benefice holder being very much an autonomous actor tending to be unaccountable on a day-to-day basis to outside agencies. By the same token, potent local identities or institutional interests have been established which stand in the way of any radical territorial reorganization, and also may nurture the idea of the bishop as a unique individual rooted in a specific community rather than as the member of a team offering the Church a measure of collective leadership. In present circumstances, and into the indefinite future, one may expect tension between impulses toward collegiality and much more centrifugal tendencies.

A further measure of the difficulty that may be experienced in seeking after new models of episcopal leadership is the existence of differing approaches to doctrinal and to ethical or political questions, which do not necessarily correlate with traditional evangelical, catholic or liberal divides. As already hinted, there are differences between those who see the Church's prime role as being a stabilizing or integrating force within society and those who see it as having a more challenging and even change-inducing function. Similarly, there are divisions between those tending to repudiate many of the characteristic features of modern secular life as being inimical to inherited Christian understandings and those more likely to see movements of secular opinion as a legitimate source of insight that might lead to some reinterpretation of received wisdom. This would be true, not least, of sexual matters and of attitudes toward relevant legislation of a more 'permissive' character. At a more basic level there are differences that have always existed amongst custodians of the Christian tradition between those who take an essentially pessimistic and hence conservative view of human potentialities and those who see the Christian vision pointing towards more optimistic conclusions.[19] The latter would entail the possibility of Christians positively contributing to the realization of programmes of purposive political change. Put another way, the Church's leaders will reflect the existence of deeper-seated divisions of either secular ideological provenance or theological understanding. Part of the process of seeking something more approaching a common mind might be a clearer recognition of the distinction between ideological differences and theological ones.

4.3: The Archbishop of Canterbury and National Politics[20]

At the very centre of the processes and dilemmas we have sought to outline is the Archbishop of Canterbury (and his team of advisors), who has an arguably unique role to play in wrestling with the issues under review. There is obviously no equivalent of papal authority inside the Anglican Church but, in terms of formal precedence and symbolic significance, the

[19] Some of the relevant issues are debated in R. Niebuhr, *Christ and Culture* (New York: Harper and Row, 1951).

[20] Much of the evidence in this section of our discussion is derived from interviews that we were privileged to have with the present Archbishop, and with members of his staff. We remain deeply grateful for their help. Of course, we accept full responsibility for the use we have made of that evidence and for errors of fact or interpretation that inadvertently remain in our text.

Primate of All England has unique opportunities for influencing the Church's own discussions and for communicating on behalf of the Church with the wider society. Equally, he occupies a position of special symbolic significance within the Anglican Communion at large and so serves as a potent reminder of an added international dimension to all the matters that we are considering. The remainder of this chapter will be primarily concerned to evaluate the role of the Archbishop and of his Lambeth Palace staff against the general background of relationships with other centres of influence inside the Church, with the English polity and with the international community.

It is appropriate, of course, to recall that the Primate is also a diocesan bishop with his own see of Canterbury. To that extent, he remains rooted in a local situation in a way analogous to that of other diocesan bishops. This dimension of the Archbishop's work need not detain us, however, particularly as the present Archbishop seems to have delegated much of the task of over-seeing the diocese to his suffragen bishops in order to free himself for the fulfilling of responsibilities of a national and international character.

The extent to which the Archbishop is caught up in public affairs of a national or international kind gives his office a quality that, diocesan responsibilities notwithstanding, sets it apart from all other episcopal offices in the Church of England. The Archbishop of York can be regarded as sharing the task of national leadership but it seems to be acknowledged by those concerned that the symbolic and substantive responsibilities of the Archbishop of Canterbury are of a different and unique order. The Church of England, the Anglican Communion, and the world-wide Church as well as British and foreign Governments clearly have expectations of the Archbishop of Canterbury that are not attached to even the most senior of his episcopal colleagues. Equally, his responsibilities may well involve, in an uncommonly pronounced way, those opportunities, challenges and dilemmas to which we have already alluded.

In approaching this matter, we would wish, for the purposes of convenience, to distinguish between the Archbishop's national and international responsibilities. We also wish to distinguish between the office of Archbishop and the personality of individual incumbents. In the latter case particularly there is something of an artificial distinction. In any concrete situation, one cannot readily discriminate between the responsibilities attaching to the office and the contribution of the particular office-holder. Perceptions of the office are necessarily mediated through specific persons. On the other hand, specific persons may interpret their role in differing fashions and will inevitably bring differing personal experiences or gifts to bear. Likewise, it is possible for an individual's contribution to lead to some permanently revised understanding of the office.

In saying all this, we are also recognizing that, though the contribution of individuals is obviously in part an expression of their personalities and spiritual or psychological make-ups, they also reflect their responses to, or experiences of, a changing historical or social environment. Individual contributions are obviously likely to vary with changing appreciations of current needs. To take one obvious example, some shift in understanding of an Archbishop's conception of leadership is likely to result from operating within the confines of a synodical system as opposed to the pre-synodical era. Similarly, an Archbishop's understanding of the public side of his office is clearly liable to be conditioned, to some extent, by the advent of the mass media.

The Archbishop's office, irrespective of particular holders, is clearly right at the heart of the Church-State relationship. This is manifested in a number of well-known ways. Firstly, on the symbolic plane, it is the Archbishop who reaffirms the historic Church-State nexus through the Act of Coronation as well as through other public ceremonies involving the Monarch or the Monarch's family. In this regard, it is assumed that the Archbishop of Canterbury will marry senior members of the Royal Family or baptize their children. Equally, and on a more informal yet significant level, access to Royalty may present opportunities for the offering of advice in moments of crisis. Possible examples would be the Abdication Crisis, a projected marriage to a divorcee or non-Anglican. Nowadays, the exercise of such influence has little immediate or manifest political significance, but it does help to create or reinforce a general public image of the office as an integral part of England's traditional governing elite. Indeed, outside the Royal Family itself, the Archbishop of Canterbury ranks second to none – above even the Lord Chancellor and the Prime Minister in terms of established precedence.

Secondly, in terms of the state's formal arrangements, there is the matter of the Archbishop's membership of, and potentially significant role in, the House of Lords. Thus, in major public debates of particular concern to the Church, there is a general presumption that the Archbishop will take the lead in making the Church's contribution. In doing so, an archiepiscopal speech is more likely to receive media coverage than other episcopal interventions and therefore to have some political effect.

Thirdly, the Archbishop's formal position and his membership of the national legislature combine to give him some measure of guaranteed access to national political leaders, up to the level of the Prime Minister, not readily available to less senior churchmen. Opportunities arise, or can be created, for the private and informal raising of public matters of concern to the Church. These may range from the voicing of general disquiet about some implications of official policy to raising very specific questions of institutional or humanitarian concern.

Fourthly, the Archbishop's standing may, in principle, open the door to other and more diversified elite groups within English society. The Office could give its holder access to leaders in such other fields as industry and commerce, education and law. To this extent, unusual opportunities are opened up for generating exchanges of information and for two-way flows of influence. Not least, it may in practice be possible for the Archbishop to bring into private dialogue with himself, and with each other, discrepant groups otherwise lacking opportunities for direct contact. For example, an Archbishop may have the capacity, not equally available to other Churchmen, to initiate informal discussion amongst spokesmen for radically differing approaches to the question of defence and disarmament. Similarly, the Archbishop may be able to bring into discussion groups having some shared interest in race relations. Such exercises not only make possible a better informed Church leadership, and cement relationships between the Church and other bodies, but may also involve the building of bridges between other groups in society. Indeed, it seems instructive that a major Church leader such as the Archbishop of Canterbury may be able to provide the umbrella under cover of which otherwise difficult forms of dialogue may be able to proceed.

It has, however, to be said that there are sections of English society with which communication of the sort alluded to above would not be possible, and within which such a figure as the Archbishop of Canterbury might be perceived with indifference, or even some hostility. This might be true, for example, of some trade unionists, and more especially of spokesmen for radicalized immigrant groups. This is not, of course, a reflection upon the personal qualities of the office-holder, but rather a commentary on the historic development of the Office, its position in the context of established social or political arrangements and the consequent way it may be perceived by groups feeling themselves at a disadvantage in English society, or even wholly alienated from its prevailing assumptions. On the radical left in British politics and amongst some ethnic minorities, the Church of England in general, and its senior leaders in particular, may rightly or wrongly be regarded as an integral and supportive feature of a culture or way of life in which they do not share, or whose benefits tend in practice to be denied to them.

The question of how the office of Archbishop is perceived by differing sections of English society raises the general question of the Archbishop's profile or relationship *vis à vis* the mass public and, especially, in our day, the question of the media. As already implied, the Archbishop of Canterbury more than any other single Churchman has some possibility of using the means of mass communication to command public attention. This partly reflects a tendency on the media's part to personalize issues and so generally to seek out the 'top man' within a given institution.

Such a situation presents the tenant of Lambeth Palace with major opportunities not readily given to other Churchmen. But also it presents him with unusually acute dilemmas. Thus, an Archbishop of Canterbury is perhaps constrained more than any other individual churchman to recognize some sense of responsibility for the total society whilst being particularly aware of specific difficulties standing in the way of an effective or relevant discharge of such responsibilities. There is, in particular, the whole question of maintaining some balance between the Church as supporter or encourager of established institutions, and of their leaders, and the Church as a prophetic or critical voice facilitating change or even representing the powerless. For the individual closest to the heart of the existing Church-State nexus, this raises a number of inter-related problems.

Firstly, at the level of the national governing elite, there is a perceived need to maintain lines of communication through which influence can be exercised, opinions transmitted and counsel given. At the same time, there may be a need to avoid the charge of being co-opted into the service of existing power-holders and an accompanying need to retain a critical independence. In practice, this may involve some sensitive political judgements as to the mode of exercising influence or the issue on which to act. In the first case there is not only a choice between silence and activity or between approval and disapproval, there is also the question of whether reliance should be placed on privileged, private and face-to-face communications, or whether opportunities should be taken to speak out publicly in the House of Lords, on public platforms or in formal ecclesiastical settings. Reliance on private contacts may have the advantage of sustaining relationships of trust with the powerful and, by not embarrassing the latter, may make it easier for them to respond affirmatively. On the other hand, absence of public comment could lay one open to the charge of indifference or even complicity in an unacceptable situation.

In any given case, ethical and pragmatic judgements may be necessary concerning where on balance the advantage lies. On occasion, of course, the decision may effectively be wrested from one's control, for events may occur or pronouncements be made that compel entry into the public arena. When in the public arena, there are other difficulties. In particular, there is always the possibility that the instigator of debate will, in significant measure, lose control over the relevant discussion. Frequently, it is a question of putting oneself in the hands of the media with the attendant risks of selective quotation or even misquotation.

Similar dilemmas are involved in the selection of issues upon which to take some stand. To respond to expectations or pressures in an undiscriminating fashion is to run the risk of rapidly using up one's reserves of credibility with counter-productive consequences for the office one bears and the institution or cause with which the office is associated. This, of course, raises the issue of the criteria governing the choice of appropriate topics warranting archiepiscopal intervention.

Firstly, there is the need to discern those areas or issues to the discussion of which Christian leaders might be expected to bring especially distinctive or valued contributions. There may be a danger of dissipating one's energies by focussing on matters of a relatively detailed, technical variety rather than probing under-lying matters of central theological concern. Equally, there may be the possibility of jumping into some debates too soon and before their real importance or meaning have had time to establish themselves. On the other hand, in the real world of ecclesiastical statesmanship, thes ᐟ dangers have to be weighed against the accompanying danger of speaking in such generali-ties that statements appear platitudinous or even vacuous. Similarly, there is always the danger of entering a debate too late effectively to influence its terms of reference or its course. This latter point is particularly significant given the limited but real opportunities that may be available to prominent Church leaders to influence the content of a given community's corporate or political agenda.

To a great extent, of course, that agenda is determined by international, economic, social or cultural factors of a deep-rooted, long-standing and relatively intractible kind. Britain's economic decline and the perennial East-West conflict would come under this heading. Likewise, the agenda may be dramatically affected by such sudden crises as the Falklands War. In these latter cases, at least, Church leaders along with all other formers of opinion are put into the position of reacting to events as they unfold. On the other hand, there is some scope for the selection of issues to which the Church might wish to give a higher place on the national political agenda or where the Church might, in the light of its own values, seek ultimately to influence the broad thrust of public policy. Such questions as Third World aid, race relations and peace and disarmament could clearly fall under this heading. Indeed, it is in such areas as this that the present Archbishop of Canterbury has most notably gone on public record. In doing so there may on occasion be a question of seeking to influence the specific acts of public policy, or the general tenor of particular Governmental commitments. Attempts to move the present Government away from its negative response to the Brandt Report were a case in point. But this is likely to go hand in hand with the different if related task of seeking, in a broader and more long-term sense, to influence the nature of public opinion or to create a general public mood.

It could be that it is in this latter sphere that Church leaders of the Archbishop's standing have the most significant contribution to make to the nation's public life. It is in the shaping of future opinions, or by effecting shifts in the prevailing public moods, that the Church may ultimately be most likely to influence particular policy outcomes. Of course, there is no need to view the quest for short and longer-term goals as being mutually exclusive, any more than private or public pursuit of objectives may be mutually exclusive. But it is perhaps in taking the longer view that the Church has one of its more valuable contributions to make. It is frequently complained that politicians, by the nature of the constraints to which they are subject, find it difficult to adopt long-term view-points or to raise searching questions about the general long-term evolution of the national or international community. Church leaders are in principle freer to raise the sights of a community above the next set of pressing problems, and to turn the community's attention to underlying moral choices and their longer-term implications.

The whole question of ministering and of agenda-setting at this level must be seen in association with another and possibly unique feature of the Archbishop of Canterbury's office, namely the extent to which he has a special responsibility for conveying to the world a particular image of the Church's underlying nature, priorities and commitments. Not only in word but also in deed, the publicly exposed nature of the office puts its holder in the position of signalling to the wider society, at all levels, potentially potent messages concerning the Church's ultimate purposes and their possible contemporary implications. The present Archbishop's sermon in St Paul's Cathedral following the Falklands War is a prime example of all this. The same sermon is an example of the way in which specific secular events or issues may be the occasion for conveying to an unusually wide audience Gospel teaching – teaching that may well be in conflict with prevailing political assumptions.

This dimension of the task may be related to another possibly distinctive feature of the Archbishop's unique role, namely as an individual 'enabler' or facilitator of the Church's mission deploying the prestige of his office in support of particular causes or innovations which others subsequently take up. Public pronouncements or symbolic gestures on the part of the Archbishop may dramatize and legitimize causes in such a way that those who then become involved can operate against the background of apparently authoritative Church approval. Archbishop Runcie's association with the campaign to over-come housing shortages is a noteworthy example of such an activity. Similarly, at one point he and his staff established contact with senior officials of the World Bank which obviously enabled the Archbishop and his advisors to brief themselves more effectively on relevant economic issues. But also, at least in principle, these contacts opened the door to other and more sustained conversations between representatives of the Church and this important international agency.

The matter of Church contact with such a secular agency as the World Bank raises the further question of the Church's willingness to cooperate with others, outside its own ranks, for the achievement of possibly shared objectives. It is an issue raising dilemmas that come into particularly sharp focus when talking of leaders. Thus, in a society characterized by religious, cultural and ideological pluralism, religious leaders have particu-lar choices to make about the nature and scope of the alliances they deem it appropriate to make with other religious or non-religious bodies.

There is always the question of the extent to which the Church may risk losing its own distinctive identity or 'cutting edge' as a result of incorporation into broader coalitions of interests within the public domain. Equally, there is the question of the extent to which the Church is willing to permit others to legitimize their cause as a consequence of a high level ecclesiastical 'blessing'. Not least, there sometimes are particular difficulties for the Church's most senior leader in seeming to support only one side of a contentious public debate. In such a case, it might be that the Primate would look to episcopal colleagues for the articulation of controversial viewpoints rather than permitting himself to become publicly embroiled. For example, he might prefer the bishop of an economically deprived diocese to be associated with broadly based campaigns on behalf of the unemployed rather than being himself directly engaged. In the same vein, the Archbishop of Canterbury, more than most bishops, could perhaps find it difficult to engage in public debate on terms seeming clearly to indicate across-the-board approval or disapproval for particular political parties. As the chief spokesman for an avowedly national Church, special difficulties seem to attach to the open espousal of partisan postures.[21]

The adoption of very controversial or polarized political positions not only raises problems for Church relationships with the State, but may also entail serious difficulties for the management of the Church's more obviously 'domestic' affairs. In principle, there always exists the possibility of espousing political, or more likely theological, positions that could ultimately tear the Church apart. To some extent he is bound to carry his troops with him and certainly could not be perceived as spokesman for, or defender of, any narrowly conceived ecclesiastical partisan position. Not least, it could be argued, to provoke a truly profound division would be seriously to compromise the credibility and integrity of the Church's mission within the wider society. Expressed somewhat differently, those expecting successfully to fill the Church's most senior positions must remain sensitive to differing theological traditions within their fold as well as to differences of a social or political kind.

The root of this situation can clearly be traced to the very

---

[21] Archbishop William Temple was well known for his general pro-Labour Party sympathies but, significantly enough, he resigned his membership of that Party long before becoming Archbishop. See F. A. Iremonger, *William Temple: Archbishop of Canterbury* (London: Oxford University Press, 1948) esp. pp. 332 and 509.

origins of the Anglican Church with its general thrust towards comprehensiveness. In much more recent times, a new dimension has been added to the situation with the creation of synodical structures that presume extensive lay and clerical participation in the Church's government and the existence, at least in principle, of a sustained debate between bishops, priests and people. On the other hand, as earlier observed, there are still widespread signs of deference to traditional episcopal leaders, and an expectation that they will provide a sense of direction. Implicitly, it is commonly understood that, despite pressures towards conformity or consensus, the episcopate in general, and the Archbishop in particular, have an educative role that must necessarily involve a measure of distance between leaders and led. Part of the task is to lead the Church in new directions and to seek to mobilize its members for the purposes of pursuing fresh or redefined objectives. The difficulty in practice lies in reconciling or balancing the conflicting demands of continuity and continuing consensus on the one hand, and change or prophetic insight on the other.

The complexity of archiepiscopal leadership is rendered all the more apparent by the palpable gap here separating the Church's most senior leaders from the greater part of its local constituents. Empirical evidence strongly suggests that on many of the more political issues that have come to the top of the Church's official agenda, the majority of 'grass-roots Anglicans' cleave to much more traditional or conservative positions than most of their episcopal leaders. This would be true, not least, of their chief official spokesman. To some extent this reflects the already noticed tension between traditional and originally rural-based expressions of Anglicanism and the Anglicanism of those more acutely aware of deep-seated changes in English society and more inclined to seek a redefinition of ecclesiastical links with that society. At the level of the leadership with which we are particularly concerned, it is equally a reflection of corresponding changes in patterns of recruitment into the episcopate, and the formative social as well as theological experience of those concerned.

The present Archbishop, for example, saw service in the armed forces and, perhaps not coincidentally, has been more inclined than immediate predecessors with contrasting experiences to adopt a somewhat more politically conscious and critical position. Equally, changes in his use of personal advisors point to a different and perhaps more collegial mode of leadership. It is to this dimension of the Archbishop's task that we now briefly turn.

4.4: The Role of Lambeth Palace Staff

The Archbishop's demanding office has long required supporting staff work. William Temple, for example, suffered from deficiences on this front[22]. In recent times, however, some potentially significant steps have been taken. For some years now, for example, Archbishops have had the support of a lay assistant. This post's current occupant, Michael Kinchen-Smith, was recruited from a senior BBC position and so brings to bear managerial expertise and knowledge of public affairs. The present Archbishop has further built on such foundations. Thus, a senior bishop, Bishop Hook (formally of Bradford), has been appointed to the Lambeth Palace staff to facilitate communication with senior clergy and to relieve the Archbishop of some of the day-to-day problems that may arise in this quarter[23]. This responsibility could be described as pastoral, involving advice or the smoothing out of difficulties. He also has overlapping responsibilities with the lay assistant for communicating or liaising with such other decision-making centres within the Church as the General Synod and its Boards, or the Church Commissioners. Not least, he shares responsibility for advising the Archbishop on priorities, and the allocation of time in face of conflicting demands. Clearly, the appointment of a bishop to act as 'Chief of Staff' is designed to increase the authority and effectiveness of the Lambeth Palace team and to enable the staff to deal on more equal terms with senior figures in the Church at large.

[22] See F. A. Iremonger, *op. cit.*.

[23] His successor has recently been announced as the present Bishop of Portsmouth, thus maintaining and re-emphasizing the importance and seniority of this still new position in the Church's administration.

The same expanded staff are also responsible for facilitating the role of the Archbishop on other important fronts. Thus, amongst the roles of the lay assistant is a general concern with coordinating the activities of Church spokesmen in the House of Lords. He keeps an eye on the forthcoming agenda and legislative programme of the House in order to ensure that the Church is appropriately represented in important debates. To the same end, he is responsible for seeing that episcopal members are appropriately briefed by the Church's own specialized boards located in Church House, Westminster. Similarly, the lay assistant has responsibility for communication with significant pressure groups and he also assists the Archbishop in the task of communicating with such ecumenical bodies as the British Council of Churches with whom there is much cooperation when it comes to lobbying and allied activities in the social and political spheres.

Awareness of the Archbishop's public role is also reflected in the existence of a personal advisor on his dealings with the media (who additionally acts as the Church's Chief Information Officer). This advisor, currently John Miles, himself having extensive journalistic experience, frequently accompanies the Archbishop on foreign trips as well as handling communications intended for domestic mass consumption. The same consciousness of the Archbishop's actual or potential public role has, for the first time, led to the appointment of a counsellor, Terry Waite, with special responsibility for developing this aspect of the work. It is Terry Waite (on secondment from the Church Army) who nurtures links with strategic governmental and international agencies and who sometimes acts as the Archbishop's roving ambassador. His role in helping to secure the release of missionaries imprisoned in Iran and British 'hostages' in Libya are but two of the most celebrated examples of this type of work and some of the more spectacular fruits of liaising with governmental bodies (in this case the Foreign Office).

In this, as in other matters, there is not always a clear line of division demarcating the responsibilities of Lambeth staff members. There is, to some extent, a deliberate overlapping of responsibilities that goes hand in hand with a certain collegiate spirit amongst those concerned. In part, this reflects the still relatively small-scale and youthful character of the operation. Those concerned sometimes have a wholly new job and so some freedom to define its nature. It is a measure of the transforming capacities of a single Archbishop that future senior staff members may have less freedom to write their own job specifications. They may be constrained by precedents currently being established.

One particular example of converging or overlapping responsibilities is supplied by the existence of two special advisors to the Archbishop on Foreign Relations. They are particularly concerned with facilitating the Archbishop's relationships with other parts of the Anglican Communion and of the worldwide Church. To the extent that this involves foreign travel and, more especially, links with such bodies as the British Foreign Office, there may be a measure of overlap with the responsibilities of the Archbishop's special counsellor. But more importantly from our vantage point, the presence of these advisors serves as a reminder of the existence of a major international dimension to the work of the Church of England and, in particular, to the work of its Primate. It is this dimension that we now examine.

4.5:   The International Political Dimension

In evaluating this sphere of activity, one must indicate that it frequently presents many of the underlying opportunities, challenges and dilemmas that have already been discussed with reference to more purely domestic affairs. In our day, at least two major sets of developments have combined to give the Church of England and its leaders novel international responsibilities. Firstly, Britain's overseas colonial expansion entailed the development of the world-wide Anglican Communion which retains the Archbishop of Canterbury as its symbolic focal point. As part of this, the Archbishop presides over the periodic Lambeth Conferences that have periodically (since 1867) brought together Anglican bishops. Moreover, de-colonization and Britain's declining world role has entailed the emergence of locally-led branches of this Communion with whom 'the

Mother Church' has had to redefine its relationships on a more obviously reciprocal or equal footing. By the same token, de-colonization and declining power ultimately pointed in the direction of closer British relationships with Europe, and hence, for the churches, the potentiality of greater involvement with continental Christians.[24]

This development points to the second of the major developments that have given the Archbishopric of Canterbury a new international importance, namely the modern ecumenical movement. As the Church of England's spiritual leader and the Anglican Communion's senior primate, the Archbishop of Canterbury is clearly in an actually or potentially significant position in terms of ecumenical dialogue and cooperation. It could be argued that the particular historical development of Anglicanism gives it an especially important significance in dealing with, or even mediating between, the Roman Catholic Church and Reformed Churches. Furthermore, the particular interests, experiences and expertise of the present Archbishop highlight the possibilities of dialogue with Christians of the Orthodox tradition.

All this, it needs to be said, has implications going beyond the obviously ecclesiastical. Thus, for example, the existence of the Anglican Communion puts the Church of England at the centre of a worldwide network of contacts and information from which even Governments, on occasion, seek to benefit. The activities of the Church on the ground in Zimbabwe and Namibia, for instance, may make available reserves of information and forms of local insight otherwise not readily available to public policy-makers.

Similarly, the ecumenical movement, not least as it affects the Orthodox Communion, has implications for the situation in the Middle East and, more broadly, for the whole question of East-West relationships. Governments may seek to use Churches in pursuit of their international objectives whilst Churches, in their turn, may seek to influence governments and the general climate of opinion within which the latter operate. Of potential-

---

[24] Some symbolic recognition of this is the relatively recent creation of an Anglican Diocese of Europe with representation in the General Synod.

ly particular significance, Churches are sometimes almost the only non-governmental bodies with regular or institutionalized forms of contact cutting across the East-West divide. To that extent, Churches already play, and have a capacity for still more playing, a bridge-building role, close to grass-roots levels, between communist and non-communist countries. Similarly the Archbishop of Canterbury, as the leader of a significant worldwide Christian Communion, has particular opportunities for building bridges, opening doors and sustaining relationships of interest to governments as well as Churches. Recent archiepiscopal visits to Africa and China are indicators of this. In particular, the World Council of Churches constitutes an important forum not only for the moulding of Christian opinion on a global basis but also for exercises in mutual influence having clear political implications. The Archbishop's role in worship at the WCC Assembly in Vancouver testifies to his perceived symbolic and substantive significance within that forum.[25]

4.6: Conclusion

The Archbishop's position as spiritual head of the Church of England and acknowledged leader of the Anglican Communion raises and brings into sharp focus at least some of the major issues or dilemmas confronting the Church of England's leadership to which, by way of conclusion, we turn. Thus, the Archbishop is at a crucial point of intersection between an international community and a local national Church whose experiences and expectations may frequently be at odds. Archbishops and some other senior Churchmen are to varying degrees stimulated or constrained to adapt to an international perspective and to feed into national Church debates insights, demands and priorities of international provenance. In so doing, they are wrestling with their particular part of the general Christian task of redefining the Church's relationship with a rapidly changing world, and of helping the Church at large to spell out in arguably more compelling terms the Gospel's implications for that world. Equally, and as an integral part of

[25] See *The Church Times* for 19 August, 1983.

the same task, they are seeking to elicit the support of a diminished but still significant local mass membership which, in perhaps the majority of cases, tends to view the Church's task in more obviously particularistic terms.

Such differences of perception, and perhaps gaps in understanding, constitute one major feature of a general problem of leadership on the Church's agenda in the coming decades. They are problems which, as we have indicated at least by implication, arise at all levels of the Church's formal structure but which obviously exhibit themselves in particularly sharp form at the episcopal and archiepiscopal levels. Diocesan bishops at local level, and even sometimes at national level, can still command a degree of attention, even beyond the formal confines of the Church, which puts them in the category of actual or potential opinion-formers. Still more, an Archbishop is in the position of seeking to identify and, in a broad sense, minister to the needs of a national community.

A significant part of this task is to identify, perhaps foster, and certainly supply, a Christian critique of those points of tension or conflict in society that could conceivably herald the emergence of a redefined consensus cohering around restated commitments and values of, at least in part, Christian provenance. In tentatively suggesting this we are, of course, recognizing that this is in no way an inevitable, still less a painless, process. It may require much creative insight and foresight as well as a greater acceptance of the significance and reality of conflict than has hitherto characterized most of English Church life. It may imply, for example, a rather more self-confident Church generally better prepared for going on the 'offensive' and less disposed to adopt a 'defensive' posture *vis à vis* cultural, intellectual, social, economic and political change within the surrounding society. Certainly it seems to imply that a new look at the appropriate balance between the Church's integrative or socially supportive role and its critical or change inducing role. Whilst one need not wholly be sacrificed to the other, it may be that the politically critical function needs to be somewhat upgraded.

There are already some signs of this. Not least is the relatively greater prominence given by the present Archbishop of Canterbury to political judgements of an implicitly or explicitly more critical variety. To some extent, this may naturally reflect Robert Runcie's personal predelictions, priorities and experience. But it may also reflect the extent to which changing theological understandings, on the one hand, and social or political realities on the other, may be tending to force social and political issues somewhat higher up the Church's corporate agenda.

In ensuring that such a trend is fruitful both for the Church and for English society, major responsibility seems to lie with those leaders who have been the main focus of this paper. That, in its turn, raises finally the whole question of the gifts or recruitment of those leaders. On the former point, we of course acknowledge that we are often dealing with imponderables for which no one can legislate. All that one might safely say is that the task of leadership to which we have pointed is clearly a major one entailing gifts of imagination; intellect; political awareness; social conscience; understanding of the characteristic movements of the modern world; theological insight and, of course, pastoral concern and personal holiness. Such qualities, needless to say, are not likely all to be found in full measure in any one person. The plea, in other words, is for leadership which retains room for the widest possible representation of relevant gifts, and which maximises the chances of such gifts being deployed in mutually reinforcing and enriching fashions.

On a more severely practical plane, this seems to point in the direction of at least three possible conclusions. Firstly, it could be that the Church of England might re-examine its own recruitment, training, promotional and other institutional arrangements with a view to casting its net even more widely in the search after, and nurturing of, potential leaders. There may always be a danger of having unduly stereotyped, or culture-bound conceptions of appropriate leaders and the quest for an enriching diversity might seem in order.

Secondly, it seems possible that the demands of existing diocesan, synodical, and other bureaucratic structures make so many relatively routine administrative or managerial demands upon leaders that they are left individually and collectively lacking in appropriate opportunities for long-term thinking, and for the exercise of those more distinctive gifts, demanded by present circumstances. It might be argued that the studied attempts of the present Archbishop of Canterbury to share tasks and more carefully to allocate priorities might constitute an example that could be followed more extensively and systematically throughout the Church. It is obviously recognized that this might have implications for the allocation of resources but part of the relevant debate would obviously be about where the ultimate balance of advantages lies.

Thirdly, the pooling of diverse gifts at this level points to a continuing reinforcement of that general trend toward enhanced collegiality that we have already observed as a feature of recent times. Such collegiality is naturally not meant to imply colourless conformity or uniformity. Rather one looks for more collective forms of leadership that allow for the widest possible sharing of responsibility whilst honestly acknowledging, and even positively embracing, differences of outlook. There are already stirrings pointing in the direction of as yet incompletely fulfilled potentialities. It seems possible that the willingness to take risks in the more complete fulfilling of such potentialities could have significant implications for the life of the Church and of the wider society. It is a still open question whether the Church of England at large is prepared to run such risks. Part of the present task of the leadership is surely to lay down the challenge.

Chapter 5

THE GENERAL SYNOD AND POLITICS
Giles Ecclestone

5.1: Introduction

In this chapter, I consider the role of the Church of England's
central bureaucratic institutions in national politics. Impetus and
direction is given to the Church's life at the centre from three
sources: Lambeth Palace, the General Synod (within which I
include the Central Board of Finance) and the Church Commissioners. The reader has already seen how Lambeth Palace
contributes to the political process in Chapter 4. While the
Lambeth staff has in recent years expanded, and its functions
diversified, it is still essentially, in my view, a personal
secretariat serving the diverse needs of the Archbishop of
Canterbury in his very special episcopal ministry. By contrast,
the organisations of the General Synod and the Church
Commissioners are typically bureaucratic. They derive their
authority from statute; responsibility for policy-formation is
collective rather than personal; and there is a clear, conceptual
distinction between the development of policy, resting ultimately with elected representatives, and its implementation, the
responsibility of salaried officials. While the analogies ought not
to be pressed too far, it is not fanciful to see in Lambeth an early
modern Royal Household serving a personal monarch, and in
the twin bureaucracies of Church House and Millbank the
administrative and financial structures of a representative parliamentary indirect democracy.

As far as the General Synod is concerned, the fact that the
analogy can be drawn is not fortuitous. Its procedures, like those
of its predecessor body, the National Assembly of the Church of
England (the 'Church Assembly'), are closely modelled on those
of the House of Commons and there have rarely been times
when it has not had members (or staff) of one or other House of
Parliament among its own members. It has drawn senior lay

107

staff from the Civil Service (including the current Secretary-General of the Synod, and the author of the present chapter). Their presence, together with regular contact between Synod staff and civil servants in central Government departments, has reinforced the governmental model which is prevalent in the General Synod. The same is broadly true of the Church Commissioners. Both organisations drive home the message by the use of civil service grades and salary structures, and, from time to time, by evaluating the work of staff by reference to civil service parallels.

The analogy is an instructive one, but it must not be pressed too far. In relation to national and local politics, the subject of this volume, the Church of England's central institutions are for the most part more like pressure groups than organs of parliamentary government. This is dictated by the nature of the task. If we consider those activities of the Church's central institutions which impinge on the national political process, three different types of activity can be distinguished. First, there is the activity flowing from the Church's need periodically to update its own structures and processes, and requiring either political or statutory sanction. Examples include the negotiations with the State in the mid-1970s concerning the appointment of bishops, which led to the setting up of the Crown Appointments Commission,[1] and the legislative activity, dating back to 1919, by which measures passed by the Church Assembly, and now the General Synod, are presented to both Houses of Parliament for their approval. This activity, though it engages the attention of political analysts from time to time as evidence of the shifting relationship between Church and State, is essentially directed towards the institutional needs of the Church. Secondly, and similarly, there is that political activity carried on by or on behalf of the Church in response to proposed changes in national policies. Later in this book, Robert Waddington describes the way in which Church agencies have participated in the evolution of national educational policies

---

[1] For the statements to the Synod by the Standing Committee of the new scheme, see *Crown Appointments* (GS 304 and GS 313). See also the discussion of liturgical reform in Chapter 3.

from the vantage-point of the Church's practical involvement in primary and secondary education and teacher training.[2] When the Church of England and the British Churches sought relief from the provisions of the 1974–76 Labour Government's Community Land Bill it was the Churches' Main Committee (CMC) which took up the issue with Government; the same body has more recently negotiated with Departments on the application of VAT to charities in general.

It is the third type of activity with which in this chapter (and at points elsewhere in the book) we are principally concerned: the participation by the Church's agencies in a wider national debate on public policies, and the consequential activity of representations to Government, lobbying and parliamentary activity. From the standpoint of ecclesiology, 'the Church' is engaged in this type of political activity whenever and wherever any of its members are involved – as citizens, as public servants, as full-time politicians. In concerning itself with national policy issues through the medium of its own national institutions, the Church of England is acting independently of its own members. Nevertheless, it operates within the same conceptual structure of democratic citizenship which shapes the activity of individual politically-aware citizens. It proceeds from a concept of the public good (sometimes spelled out in theological terms) which values consensus and compromise rather than conflict and the pressing of partial interests. It is oriented to affirming the value of persons; in recent years it has urged the importance of human rights as an expression of this concern. It is, however, sensitive to the claims of institutions to act on behalf of their members, and is uncomfortable with formulations of political values which firmly set the individual over against the collectivity. Thus, in a protracted discussion in the Synod and its agencies in 1976–8 over the closed shop in industry, attempts to secure an outright condemnation of the principle of the closed shop as contrary to human rights proved impossible; instead the Synod coupled a commendation of active participation in trade unions with advice to Christian unionists to try to ensure that particular

[2] See Chapter 10. The other contributions in that section of the volume illustrate similar activities in other policy areas.

closed shop agreements were drawn up and applied flexibly.[3]

Of the three central institutions of the Church of England, the Church Commissioners are the least directly concerned with this wider national debate on public affairs. As John Sleeman shows in his chapter on the Church and economic policy, the Commissioners' contribution lies in the formulation of policies regarding the management of their own assets in the light both of Church thinking and prudent trusteeship. Their experience of straddling the two worlds of the institutional Church and institutional finance gives them an unrivalled capacity to speak with authority to both. While these distinctive functions give the Commissioners a special point of view on many of the public policy issues with which the Church is concerned, this point of view has also contributed to the formation of Synodical thinking, through informal contact between the staffs of the Commissioners and the Synod and by the overlap of membership between the Boards and Committees of the Commissioners and the General Synod.

5.2:   The Sources of Political Involvement

The Synod is only incidentally an agency for expressing opinions on political matters. Its primary function is as part of the central administrative structure of the Church, through which procedures are operated, goals pursued, and resources channelled, for the overall task of the Church. Nonetheless, its Constitution, after setting out the functions of the Synod in regard to these tasks, explicitly authorises the members of the Synod to 'consider and express their opinions on any other matters of religious or *public* interest' (my italics) (Art. 6b). In its turn, each of the Synods elected since the inception of Synodical Government in 1970 has agreed to establish a Board for Social Responsibility as one of its principal Advisory Committees. The terms of reference of that Board, as most recently stated, are 'to

[3] *Report of Proceedings* of the General Synod (February 1978 Group of Sessions), pp. 343-60.

promote and co-ordinate the thought and action of the Church in matters affecting man's life in society'. Thus concern for the public, political and social realm is firmly built into the Church's central structures, not simply as a means of securing the Church's own institutional interests, but as a particular and proper activity in its own right for the Church, its members and its agencies, an activity which, it is recognised, needs some specialised agencies and resources if it is to be effectively carried on.

This pattern has, in fact, characterised the Church of England's central structures since the setting-up of the Church Assembly. The Convocations of York and Canterbury, as well as the decennial Lambeth Conferences, had a tradition of discussing affairs of the day as well as more specifically ecclesiastical matters. The new Church Assembly continued this tradition; at its first meeting in 1920, it debated the League of Nations. Following a lengthy public discussion within the Church on the goals and methods of Christian social involvement, the Church Assembly set up a permanent Social and Industrial Committee in February 1923 which continued in various forms until the late 1950s when it was merged with the first Board for Social Responsibility.

The work of this Board now generates much of the political agenda of the General Synod. Much, but not all; there are some issues of public policy, notably broadcasting, where the Standing Committee of the Synod retains the initiative. More significantly for the ordinary business of the Synod, private members' motions have frequently initiated major debates on political issues (the example of the closed shop has already been cited), and representations by private members either to the General Synod Office or to the Board for Social Responsibility are a valuable indicator to those departments of members' priorities. Private members' motions, like Early Day Motions in the House of Commons, are for the most part 'ineffective orders'; they are put down on the notice paper more as an expression of opinion, and to test opinion, than with any expectation of their being debated in the immediate future, if at all. Unlike Early Day Motions, however, some private members' motions are actually selected for debate in the Synod, and for this purpose account is taken of the number of signatures a particular motion has attracted. This may on occasion create a problem, particularly when a political issue is the subject of a motion which has risen to the top of the list; for, in the time it has taken for the motion to rise in this way, the motion may actually have become 'stale'. A rather different problem arises when a private members' motion on a highly topical and contentious issue comes up for debate. Is it right to restrict the debate to the limited time provided for private members in the agenda for the Group of Sessions, when that may be inconvenient for adequate press reporting or otherwise fail to provide for the number of people who are likely to wish to speak? In such a situation, it is open to the Business Sub-Committee of the Synod's Standing Committee to decide to give such a motion a more prominent place on the agenda.

By these and other means, private members share in some degree in iniating political debate in the Synod on current issues. For most of the lifetime of Synodical Government, it has been the policy of the Standing Committee to ensure that each Group of Sessions (lasting 3-4 days and occurring 3 times a year) includes at least one 'outward-looking' debate, scheduled at a time of day when the press are likely to be able to report it. In the main, these raise issues of national or international importance, for the most part falling within the area of concern of the Synod's Board for Social Responsibility, and initiated by that Board. Unlike debates on financial or liturgical business or legislation, which occupy a substantial proportion of the Synod's time, political debates characteristically do not issue in decisions which can be regarded as determinative for the Church's institutions or its members. They are rather expressions of an opinion, a collective judgement by the members of the Synod acting as a 'corporate citizen'.

From the standpoint of the Church, this activity is one means by which it validates its claim to be concerned with the stuff of public and social affairs – the nation's life – as well as with the joys and sorrows of individual people. From the standpoint of the State it must be presumed to be at least as useful as any other collective voice reflecting on current policies. It may not say anything strikingly different from other voices, but it cannot be ignored simply because of the ramifying nature of the Church in society and its claim to speak for an undifferentiated public good over and against more partial interests and goals. In political terms it is not so much *what* is said in a Synod debate and in its resolutions that is significant, as that fact *that* it is said, in that setting and by that group of people. This accounts for the nervousness with which many politicians as well as Church leaders approached the Synod's debate on nuclear weapons in February 1983 (considered in greater depth elsewhere in this volume by John Elford).[4] For the central representative organ of the Church of England to express significant reservations about Government and NATO defence policy would be to give respectability to criticisms of those policies in a way that the Campaign for Nuclear Disarmament never could, precisely because the Church cannot be type-cast in a way that more straightforward pressure-groups can. It is arguable that Synod members' awareness that this is so injects a degree of caution and discretion into many debates where one might expect a much more forthright statement of judgement. Here we come up against one of the dilemmas facing a Church deeply rooted in the nation's life. If it is to retain its influence over the development of affairs, it cannot afford to step too far out of line with current thinking, yet it must be sufficiently distinctive, to be noticed and followed at all in a period when the practice of religion is a matter of personal choice.

From the standpoint of the Synod, a debate on a political matter is a self-contained, 'one-off' affair, not expected, in the ordinary course of events, to lead to further debates or otherwise return to the Synod's agenda. In recent years, it has become the practice for the Secretary-General to convey the text of resolutions adopted to the Minister of the Crown most nearly concerned, and on a number of occasions Ministers' replies have been circulated to Synod members (a recent example being the debate and ensuing correspondence concerning the Death Grant

[4] See Chapter 8.

in November 1982).[5] There the matter generally rests. Some topics, however, generate more substantial correspondence. Following one of the many debates the Synod had in the 1970s on South Africa, correspondence between the Secretary-General and the South African Ambassador in London became protracted, each exchange being made available to members as it appeared.[6] By this means it was possible to press home the Synod's concern, and to clarify misunderstandings, in a way which would not have been open to the Synod merely using the instrument of debate and resolution.

5.3:   The Creation of a Political Agenda

How do particular issues emerge as pressing political concerns for the Church and hence for its Synod? Manifestly not all issues on the Government's agenda appear on the Synod's agenda. Fiscal policy and the management of the economy have rarely figured, though it is arguable that these set the parameters for all other policy-formation.[7] Two different processes are, in fact, at work in shaping the Synod's political agenda. In the first place, there is the impact on the Church of England's thinking by its participation in ecumenical organisations and networks, notably the British Council of Churches (BCC) and the World Council of Churches (WCC). Secondly, there is the fact that Anglican social ethics characteristically place great emphasis on listening to the practitioner in a particular secular discipline and learning from him or her what the problems are. Thus, the Board for Social Responsibility channels much of its work through specialist standing committees or ad hoc working parties where theologians and Church administrators sit alongside lay specialists in relevant secular disciplines. A Church in ecumenical

[5] Proceedings of the General Synod (November, 1982 Group of Sessions), pp. 989-1006. See also Synod Documents GS 550 and GS 557 Annex.

[6] See Synod Document GS Misc. 72.

[7] See the discussion in Chapter 11. A wide-ranging debate on Economic Policy and the Christian Conscience took place in November 1984.

encounter; a Church in encounter with lay experts. In each case, the Church of England is sharing an exploration rather than working in isolation; in each case the responsibilities of partnership generate an expectation that the Church will make the shared concern its own, play its part in its own fora, and put its undoubted weight behind an issue.

Throughout the 1970s, the issue of apartheid in South Africa and the correct British response to developments there, was a particular concern of the BCC and the WCC. The General Synod debated the matter on several occasions, on one occasion at the instance of private members, more generally at the instance of the Board for Social Responsibility, the body with the closest links with BCC activity in this area. When, in the Spring of 1979, the BCC published a detailed statement of the case for disinvestment from South Africa[8] and scheduled a BCC Assembly debate on the subject for late November 1979, the Board agreed to mount a Synod debate on the same subject in the first half of November so that Church of England representatives at the Assembly would have the benefit of recent Synodical thinking behind them. The Board staff mounted a day consultation in the early Autumn, bringing together African nationalists, British academic specialists on Southern Africa, representatives of industry and others. The BCC report, the report of the consultation and lengthy discussions at a residential Board meeting in October, together formed the basis for a Board report to the Synod the following month.[9] Significantly, while the BCC Assembly adopted motions endorsing disinvestment, the Synod restricted itself to encouraging 'widespread consideration of the proposals for economic disengagement'.[10]

In line with this, the Board devoted part of its resources in the next two years to stimulating discussion of the issues at stake and in July 1982 the matter was again brought to the Synod. On this occasion the Board spoke with two voices. A report prepared by a working party of the Board's International Affairs Committee and presented by the group's chairman, Reverend

[8] *Political Change in South Africa – British Responsibility.*
[9] *Political Change in South Africa* (GS 424).
[10] *Proceedings,* November 1979 Group of Sessions, pp. 1169-96.

Peter Wheatley, strongly endorsed disinvestment.[11] The Chairman of the Board, the Bishop of London, while formally presenting the issue to the Synod on behalf of the Board, spoke against such a policy, as did the First Church Estates Commissioner, Sir Ronald Harris, who had studied the issue closely in a visit to South Africa. Despite these strong voices raised in criticism, the Synod adopted the case for disinvestment.[12] It should be noted that what was a issue was not primarily the location of Church investments but the policy which, if adopted by the British Government, industry and investors generally, would exert significant pressure on the South African Government to change its policies. As far as the Church's own investments are concerned, the response of the Church Commissioners to the successive debates has been to endorse their long-standing policy of avoiding investment in companies operating 'wholly or mainly' in South Africa but not abjuring all investment in companies with a South African connection.

This episode illustrates the interlocking relationship between the BCC and the Church of England's central institutions, characterised both by an Anglican readiness to collaborate with the ecumenical body and a different temper and tempo. The episode also indicates one of the dilemmas of ecumenical and denominational engagement with long-term political issues. When the option of economic disengagement from South Africa was first mooted in a British context, there was a good chance that the Labour Government, in power for most of the 1970s,

[11] *Facing the Facts: The United Kingdom and South Africa* (GS 529).

[12] *Proceedings* (July 1982 Group of Sessions), pp. 684–725. The Resolution ran as follows:

The Synod welcomes the Report *Facing the Facts: The United Kingdom and South Africa* for its contributions to understanding the origins and present character of the problems of South Africa, and Britain's role in relation to them; and commends it to the dioceses and parishes for study and appropriate action.

The Synod endorses the view expressed in the Report that progressive disengagement from the economy of South Africa and generous aid to the independent states bordering on South Africa, in order to promote their own economic and political development, is now the appropriate basic policy for this country to adopt as a contribution to bringing about peaceful change in South Africa and asks the Board for Social Responsibility to enter into discussion with Her Majesty's Government and other appropriate bodies about how this policy might best be implemented.

would be responsive to this approach. With the election in 1979 of a Conservative Government, it rapidly became apparent that the chances of the British Government and industry as a whole adopting a disengagement policy were dwindling rapidly. In ecumenical discussions which took place in 1980, it was acknowledged that the task must now be to keep the issue alive until such time as a new shift in British politics made it once more a live option. I draw from this the conclusion that on major issues where the choices are complex and there is no obvious moral imperative pointing judgement in one direction rather than another, there are great difficulties in getting the Church of England's institutions to arrive in time at a decision. Sensitivity to the attitudes of those in political authority and to those likely to be affected by a decision, coupled with a natural caution about adopting policies which may be characterised by critics as 'radical', predisposes the Synod to move slowly.

When the Synod expresses an opinion on a political issue, it is reflecting, at a particular moment in time, on what is essentially a continuous process, whether the subject is *apartheid* in South Africa or housing policy in Britain. This means that its interventions cannot avoid having an 'occasional' or 'episodic' character; it also means that, apart from those members of the Synod deeply engaged with the issue under examination, the question always has to be asked and answered: 'why *this* issue at *this* time?' 'Not South Africa (or abortion, or race, etc.) *again!*' is an instinctive reaction of many Synod members to a fresh instalment of these long-running serials. It is to the Board for Social Responsibility, for the most part, that such questions and reactions are addressed. For it is this Board which sustains, on behalf of the Church of England's institutions, the long-term grasp of particular problems in the sphere of public policy; this Board which must decide whether it is appropriate to bring an issue before the Synod for public debate rather than, say, continue a process of committee discussion, liaison with other organisations and representation to Government. The two courses are not alternatives; rather, a debate represents the point at which a process carried on by expert committees and staff is exposed to public view and the Church is, in effect, invited to endorse a particular style and direction for the next phase.

It is rare for the Board's own view as to what that style and direction should be (as expressed in a report to the Synod and motions for debate) to be rejected by the Synod, though not uncommon for it to be qualified by different emphases. The reason for this general willingness by the Synod to accept the Board's judgement must be sought in the processes followed in the Board itself, and to these I now turn.

5.4: The Board for Social Responsibility

The Board for Social Responsibility is one of four Advisory Committees of the General Synod, the others being the Board of Education, the Board for Mission and Unity and the Advisory Council for the Church's Ministry. It consists of eighteen members and a Chairman. The Chairman, currently the Bishop of Birmingham, has with one exception always been a Diocesan Bishop; he is appointed by the Archbishops of Canterbury and York acting as Presidents of the Synod. One major advantage of having a Diocesan Bishop as Chairman is that sooner or later he has a seat in the House of Lords. Past chairmen have made considerable use of this privilege both in conveying the Church's thinking on particular issues to that body, and in advising his colleagues on the Board on parliamentary sensitivities.

The membership of the Board is formally determined by the Standing Committee early in the lifetime of the Synod. It reflects three principal concerns. First, there is a formal requirement that a majority must be members of the Synod. Members of the Synod are invited to indicate whether they would be interested in serving on the Board and the Board chairman and staff are also consulted at this stage. Although 'party' groupings are significant for some aspects of Synod business, notably liturgy, they do not materially affect the choice of members of the Board for Social Responsibility. Secondly, the outgoing Board has a determining voice in the selection of those members who are not members of the Synod, and uses this power to bring onto the Board men and women with particular experience relevant to the Board's agenda. Finally, in recent years, the Board has sought to strengthen its links with specialist committees, and now provides that, in addition to the Chairman of each committee, one other member also sits on the Board. By this means, the risk of expert committees pulling in a radically different direction from the Board is, if not obviated, certainly lessened. This is an important consideration given the weight of reliance the Board places on subordinate bodies in investigating issues.

The predominance of members of the Synod on the Board is one means by which the Board is kept attuned to the demands of the Synod and to the sensitivities of Synod members as a whole. The Board gives high priority to requests from the Synod that it should do work in particular areas, though in recent years there has been a growing readiness on the part of Board Chairmen to resist demands on the ground that Board resources are over-stretched. This is in marked contrast to the 1960s, when the Church Assembly made few demands on the Board.

In subject-areas where specialist committees exist, the Board's principal function is to review the results of the work of those committees, notably by authorising reports for publication. In a number of areas, however, no specialist committee exists and then the Board retains a full responsibility for handling a matter. For many years, all issues relating to race relations came to the Board (though immigration was handled by the Board's International Affairs Committee). From the mid-1970s, however, the Board followed the lead of the BCC's Community and Race Relations Unit, and dealt with race relations and immigration together. Thus, a succession of major discussions took place in the Board on race, immigration policy and nationality legislation. Latterly, the setting up of an advisory group within the Board structure on race has meant that some matters do not come direct to the Board.[13] When dealing with substantive matters itself, the Board has frequently exercised its power to invite specialists to take part in meetings. Thus, it brought in MEPs and a Professor of Economics specialising in the Common Agricultural Policy to assist it in discussing the EEC's Food Aid Policy. The outcome of the

[13] For a detailed discussion of this subject, see Chapter 9 in this volume by Kenneth Leech.

discussion was a request to staff to prepare a discussion paper for publication. On another occasion in 1970, the Board invited a number of defence specialists, including senior civil servants and academics, to join members in identifying the questions to be included in a study of nuclear weapons which the Synod had earlier asked the Board to undertake. At the Board's request, a working party led by Canon John Baker (subsequently Bishop of Salisbury) engaged in this study; its report, *The Church and the Bomb*, is discussed elsewhere in this volume.[14]

One of the problems which the Board faces in handling detailed issues itself is the lack of continuity and expertise among its members. For that reason there has been a constant tendency for the Board to refer matters to one or other of its specialist committees for attention, and where necessary to create new committees or other second-tier bodies. From its inception in 1958, the Board had two subordinate committees, one dealing with moral welfare (social casework with unsupported mothers and their children), sex and the family, which had been the task of the Church of England Moral Welfare Council; and one dealing with industrial matters, in succession to the Social and Industrial Council. In 1965, the International Affairs Committee was established and in 1976 the Development Affairs Committee (dealing with questions relating to the 'underdeveloped world'). In addition, as already mentioned, there is now an advisory group on race, one on scientific and medical matters as well as, since 1982, an Environmental Issues Reference Panel.

These permanent committees have very considerable autonomy in regard to what they may do in their own subject-area. The Board retains the final decision as to whether a report from a committee (or a working party set up by a committee) may be published. That apart, it imposes few restrictions on its committees. A committee may, through its chairman, write to the newspapers; it may collaborate with other organisations in pursuing a particular task; it may make representations to Government or to parliamentarians. The Board exercises oversight through the requirements that committees report to the Board at every meeting. In addition, the choice of chairman

14 See Chapter 8.

of a committee rests with the Board chairman, and the Board or its executive must approve changes in membership. These have not hitherto been experienced as significant checks on the autonomy of committees. The reason is clear. The committees, once constituted, develop considerable cohesiveness around a shared concern and a common body of knowledge, and it is not easy for the Board, composed of people who are for the most part 'lay people' in regard to the agenda of a particular committee, to qualify or challenge its judgement. In addition, the requirement to respond quickly to developing events can be, and in practice has been, met more effectively by specialist committees meeting 4-5 times a year than by the full Board, meeting on average three times a year.

In consequence, the specialist committees of the Board for Social Responsibility must be seen as autonomous in their own fields. Over the years, each of them has developed characteristic styles of working, and of relating to the other statutory and voluntary organisations in its field. The Industrial Committee, which draws together industrialists, trade unionists, academics and industrial chaplains, has eschewed involvement in particular industrial disputes and has instead concentrated its attention on shifts in attitude to the organisation of industry, employment, technological development, economics and so on. It has published a number of studies in these areas.[15] In addition, it makes a point of studying new legislation (Green and White Papers and Bills) and making its own views known to Ministers. Like other committees of the Board (though not the Board itself), the Industrial Committee has on it serving civil servants, but it has not thereby been inhibited in expressing critical views to Government, notably regarding the increasing reliance on the criminal law in labour relations by Governments in recent years. While there have been occasions when the Committee has experienced in its own discussions the familiar conflict of interest between employers and employees, in the main it has been a forum for exploring the many areas of common interest that exist within industry. It is in no way surprising, therefore, that this Committee was able to agree on a report which broadly

[15] Its most recent study is Perspectives on Economics (1984).

endorsed the concept of the Closed Shop in industry – or that the Board by contrast was distinctly less enthusiastic.

The Social Policy Committee inherited the responsibilities of the former Moral Welfare Council and has added to them the oversight of social policy, broadly defined. This aspect of public policy has seen increasing controversy between the major parties in recent years, notably concerning the extent to which statutory services and benefits should meet personal needs and the choice between universal and selective provision. In the first decade of Synodical Government, this Committee (then styled the Committee for Social Work and the Social Services) did not find it easy to engage with these debates. The reasons for this are complex. The Committee was presiding over a fundamental reshaping of diocesan-based social work in response to the Seebohm Report and the Local Authority Social Services Act 1970. The Committee was oriented towards issues which it was still possible to engage with in non-political terms: relations between statutory and voluntary services, professional ethics in the social services and so on. Nonetheless, the Committee made its opinions known to public departments on a number of occasions. It monitored the passage of the Bill which became the Children Act 1975; it gave evidence to the Merrison Royal Commission on the National Health Service, and to the DHSS on priorities in the Health and Social Services. Following a long-standing concern with housing, the Committee in 1982 produced a report on housing and homelessness which was the subject of debate in Synod.[16]

The Committee has shared with the Board responsibility for abortion, for many years one of the most continuous issues of public policy in which the Churches have been engaged. During the passage of David Steel's Bill which became law as the Abortion Act 1967, the Board had identified itself with the case for moderate reform, and its report *Abortion: an ethical discussion* was influential in the parliamentary debates on the Bill. The Board subsequently gave written and oral evidence to the Lane Committee on the working of the Act, and at the instigation of

---

[16] *Housing and Homelessness* (GS 541). The debate is reported in Proceedings (November 1982 Group of Sessions), pp. 852-885.

members of that Committee was instrumental, with other Church agencies, in setting up a service at one of the London airports to divert overseas women arriving in the country for abortion away from unscrupulous commercial agencies. With the passage of time and further evidence of the working of the Act, the Board, like the Synod, has moved closer towards the Roman Catholic position on abortion. On two successive occasions, attempts to produce joint statements on abortion, with the Methodist Church and with the Mothers' Union, foundered. The very contentiousness of the issue has meant that the Board has been reluctant to leave the Committee with unfettered discretion in regard to it and has interposed its own judgement, at once more conservative and more sensitive to opinion in the Synod and the Church at large.

Foreign affairs, including development policy, has since the mid–1960s been the province of the Board's International Affairs Committee (IAC), though from the mid–1970s a separate committee on development affairs emerged, initially to energise the dioceses' concern with development education. The approach of the IAC to its task has been for many years shaped by two considerations: first, its links with Parliament and the Foreign and Commonwealth Office; secondly its ambivalent relationship with the Division of International Affairs of the BCC. The first of these predisposed the Committee to a cautious incremental approach to the issues with which it dealt. The second consideration has reinforced the first. Though there has been for many years an overlapping membership and sharing of concerns between the IAC and the BCC/DIA, the latter has been perceived by many Anglicans – unjustly in my view – as radical and irresponsible, in large measure owing to its policies in regard to South Africa. In fact, both agencies have for the most part operated according to the Niebuhrian philosophy of an earlier generation of ecumenical politicians, notably Sir Kenneth Grubb, who emphasised the importance of realistic and finite objectives, close contact with professional politicians and with the Christian community in the part of the world one was concerned with, and eschewed grand gestures. This style has been particularly apparent since the Second World War in the approach of the British Churches to issues of defence policy.

These have in the main been handled ecumenically rather than denominationally. The studies on which Church policies have been based have been characterised by judicious low-key analysis and detailed and practicable proposals.[17]

5.5:   The Staff of the General Synod

Consideration of the political role of the Synod and its agencies would not be complete without an assessment of the contribution of its staff. I have already referred to the links between the civil service and the staff of the Synod. It is possible that in the future fewer staff may be provided from this source than hitherto. There is evidence that the Synod, and particularly the Board for Social Responsibility, is looking for skills and experience among its staff, notably those working on issues of social ethics, that are more likely to be found among the clergy than among lay people. The civil service model is significant in the main because it reinforces a concept of Synodical Government which distributes responsibility between elected representatives and salaried staff. The analogy is perhaps weak in the field of the Church's political concern, given the 'occasional' character of the Church's political engagement and the fact that that engagement consists basically in the expression of opinions. By comparison with the areas of Ministry (where the necessity to recruit, train and maintain a sizeable nationally-deployed staff generates policies and resources), or Education (where, similarly, a material and human investment in the educational process by the Church calls out a long-term commitment to policy formulation and execution), the Church's commitment to the political process is basically at the level of ideas.

This has one important consequence for the management of the Church's political engagement. Its staff exercise a wide discretion, and are in general encouraged in this, in selecting

[17] For an examination of successive ecumenical studies of nuclear weapons policy, see the essay by John Elford, Chapter 8 in this volume.

areas of work and networks with which to associate. With the possible exception of industrial chaplaincy and diocesan-based community and social work   the Church does not have an institutional investment in most of the public policy issues with which the General Synod and the Board for Social Responsibility deal. Much, therefore, depends on the staff and the extent to which they are in touch, both with the 'public' political process and with other currents and influences in society. This typically requires of staff of the Board for Social Responsibility that they keep themselves informed, through meetings and reading, with a particular subject-area or areas, only some of which may be the remit of a Board Committee. For this purpose, the Board retains a corporate subscription to many specialist bodies, from the Howard League for Penal Reform to the Association of British Adoption and Fostering Agencies. These connections may on occasion provide the basis for quite detailed activity undertaken by the Church itself. For example, during the lengthy campaign against the British Nationality Bill, Board staff participated in the work of the Action Group on Immigration and Nationality, a coalition of bodies, Church and non-Church, which studied the Government's proposals and briefed spokesmen on changes. Without this body, it is unlikely that the significant part played by the Bishops in the Lords debates on the Bill would have been possible.

Staff-work of this kind is essential to the effective functioning of the Synod and the Board, whose members, including their chairmen, are only able to give limited amounts of time and attention to these bodies and their agenda. When a major political issue emerges, it is generally the staff to whom the press and broadcasters turn for instant Church comment, and it can be a task of some delicacy to summarise and apply such Church 'tradition' and current thinking as there is on a particular issue, to enquirers who may have little awareness of the Anglican style of social and political engagement. In general, Church staff working in these areas benefit both from the civil service tradition of impartial judgement and advice to elected representatives, and from a tradition within the Church of clergy attending to what lay people have to say, particularly when it stems from personal experience or professional engagement.

5.6: Conclusion

The General Synod and its associated institutions are involved in the political process at many points and in many styles. Because they are part of the governing structure of a major national corporation, their activity reflects assumptions about the relationship between Church and State which themselves require to be kept under scrutiny. In the Church Commissioners, the Church has long had an instrument by which its financial interests can be properly managed in a changing economic and political context, while the former Church Assembly represented a means of handling the increasing flow of legislation needed for an established church if it was to adjust to modern conditions. It is only with the inception of Synodical Government, however, that the Church's voice has been regularly and systematically heard in public on matters affecting society as a whole. In the Board for Social Responsibility, the Synod had an agency to hand with an already substantial record of low-profile work in this field. In the decade and a half it has existed, the Synod has had to contend with a number of underlying questions of method and choice, in regard to its public witness. In the first place, it has been working at a time of considerable national uncertainty over goals, values and hopes for the future. Is the Synod to be simply a barometer of the national mood, or is it the voice of a self-conscious Church, willing to set itself firmly over against those trends when it sees the need? The evidence is inconclusive. On a number of issues of secondary importance, the Synod has indeed gone against the current. On more substantial matters, it has on occasion been bold (*vide* the 1982 South Africa debate), on occasion cautious (its stance on nuclear disarmament in 1983).

Secondly, should the Church always speak with one voice? The Synod has, in my view, developed a considerable wisdom in determining those issues where it is right to promote, or contribute to, public debate, but ill-advised to seek to press the issue to a conclusion. In February 1981, it summed up a lengthy process of debate within the Church on homosexual rights by refusing either to adopt motions which would condemn homosexual people outright or to endorse claims for homosexual relations to be regarded as equally valid with heterosexual patterns. The issue is left open: in this as in so many other areas of social ethics, the Church has *de facto* adopted a pluralistic position, not out of indifference but out of respect for the diversity of testimonies and experience.

Finally, does it speak only to the converted? There is no doubt in my mind that despite the movement in the Church in recent years towards a greater sense of corporate identity, the Synod clearly intends that what it says on the nation's affairs should not be merely heard by people at large, but intelligible to them whether or not they are themselves Christian. The penalty it incurs in so doing is the accusation sometimes heard that it is 'insufficiently theological'. This criticism overlooks a necessary distinction between engaging, as the Synod does, in a common civic debate within the terms set by democratic pluralism, and the style appropriate to the intramural exploration of theological concepts. As one who has worked in the Synod for its Board for Social Responsibility, I am, however, in no doubt as to both the necessity of speaking a common language if we are to contribute to the common political process, and as to the undoubted problems this creates for members of the Church when it comes to giving a *theological* account of the hope that is in them.

Chapter 6

THE DIOCESE AND LOCAL POLITICS

Ronald Bowlby

6.1: The Nature of a Diocese

Dioceses vary greatly in size and character especially in the Church of England. I have served in four dioceses (Durham, Canterbury, Newcastle and now Southwark), in two of them as parish priest and in two as diocesan bishop. Newcastle Diocese, to a greater extent than any other, contained a mixture of everything from severe urban deprivation along Tyneside to severe rural depopulation in Northumberland. Southwark Diocese, by contrast, has some urban deprivation spread along the South Bank of the Thames and some countryside thick with commuters, but is composed mainly of well populated urban parishes covering several hundred square miles.

Some of the larger dioceses are now divided into 'areas', which can function as small dioceses for certain purposes (the five London diocesan areas are probably the best known). Since each diocese is made up of a number of deaneries, which in turn comprehend a much larger number of parishes, and since either deanery or parish (or both) may engage with the local community over a matter of political or social concern, it is clear that the 'diocese' can be seen as relating to local politics in a number of different ways.

Until the twentieth century, parishes enjoyed considerable legal and financial independence, an independence reinforced by the difficulties of travel and a slender theology about the primacy of the diocese.[1] The diocese lacked any organs for

[1]"But who exists for who's sake? All too often, it seems to me, local churches are made to feel that they exist for the sake of larger bodies. Talk about "the diocese" as the basic unit of the Church, while it may have a sound theological rationale, can seem very threatening to those whose actual experience of Christianity is rooted in a particular place and among particular people, and for some "the diocese" is an

128

taking corporate decisions or concerted action, though on occasion there would be a determined voluntary effort to rally support for a particular cause. A vast amount of day-to-day 'social work' was done by clergy and laity in the parishes until the end of the 1939–1945 war and the emergence of the 'Welfare State'. The fact that the clergy were resident in their parishes, for instance, meant they had an unusual knowledge of social conditions, and a few were prepared to campaign actively for improvement and redress. Katherine Lloyd describes one such example on Tyneside in William Moll, Vicar of St. Philip's, Newcastle, who became a Christian socialist and constantly engaged in battles with authority over such things as pensions, relief and housing conditions.[2]

Moll was not alone in such views, but Newcastle Diocese (founded 1882) was unusual in having regular Diocesan Conferences from its inception where a more general debate could and did take place. Thus, in 1884, there was a debate on the 'Housing of the Poor', much needed since Newcastle housing was particularly bad and the town councillors little inclined to act. Hopefully, this debate and others like it stirred a few consciences, though as with all such debates it is hard to detect the precise influence which they may have had. Motions demanding action by somebody else are easily passed, and may even act as substitute for action which those present might take in more modest ways themselves. Yet the continued place of such debates in diocesan conferences and synods suggests a need to face issues of political and social concern within the diocese, to listen to the experience and judgement of others, and to reflect corporately on some of the implications in the light of the Gospel.

A diocesan 'identity' may take a long time to develop, though even here it is difficult to generalise. Durham and Canterbury, for instance, with their roots deep in history and blessed with

abstraction.' John Habgood, *Church and Nation in a Secular Age* (London: Darton, Longman and Todd, 1983), p. 119.

[2]W.S.F. Pickering, *A Social History of the Diocese of Newcastle* (Stocksfield: Oriel Press, Routledge & Kegan Paul, 1981), Ch. XII, esp. pp. 194–200.

magnificent cathedrals and other reminders of their past, are both dioceses which still mean much to many inhabitants as well as to parish congregations. Newcastle and Southwark are both comparatively new (1882 and 1905). The former quickly established an identity through its association with a distinct region and a distinguished city, the possession of a particular history centred on Holy Island and the Northern Saints, and an unusual absence of division over churchmanship. Southwark, by contrast, has had to struggle with an absence of history and the comparative insignificance of being on the 'other side of the river' from the City of London and the West End, seen as the seat of national government and the centre of culture and commerce in so many other ways.

In the last decades there have been several significant changes in the relationship between the diocese and the parishes:

(i) In the first place, many parishes are no longer financially independent, and depend for the partial support of the clergy and lay stipendiary workers on the giving of parishes in other parts of the diocese. This inevitably leads to an increase of diocesan influence, since the diocese becomes in effect the agent of an interdependence between parishes which is slowly being recognised and accepted.

(ii) In the second place, demographic changes and a decline in the number of stipendiary clergy mean that hard decisions have had to be made at diocesan as well as local level about pastoral reorganisation, often involving the union of parishes and the closure of some churches.

Such changes have the effect of reinforcing the degree of diocesan involvement, which can now also be more directly expressed through synods. There is some evidence also to show that diocesan or area synods more frequently discuss matters of political concern than their predecessors, the diocesan conferences,[3] which may reflect this growing sense of needing to work together more closely. Deanery synods, which have replaced the infrequently held ruri-decanal conferences, offer similar opportunities at a more local level, and may sometimes

[3]See section 6.5 of this article.

correspond directly in area with that of a local authority (e.g. the Deanery and Borough of Greenwich).

6.2: The Diocese and Politics

Any attempt to reflect on Christian social engagement at diocesan level must, therefore, take account of both the complexity and variety of English dioceses, as well as the imprecision of the term 'local politics'. In a paper published in 1980, 'The Church of England and Politics', Giles Ecclestone argued that the Churches are caught up in politics 'by their sheer existence'.[4] He went on to suggest that there are three particular characteristics which have marked the style of political involvement by the Church of England since the nineteenth century: freedom, closeness to the seat of authority and a 'disturbed conscience'. 'It is non-authoritarian, seeking not so much to bind the state as to nudge it in particular directions by an appeal to a shared perception of what is desirable.'[5] He goes on: '....even when events prompt it to challenge particular policies, it is moral concern, rather than a worked out perception of an alternative social order, which has shaped its interventions'.

This accurate perception applies as much at diocesan or parochial level as it does at the national. It explains why the minute books of conferences and synods will produce little evidence of any consistent policy which might be labelled 'Diocesan', but considerable evidence of religious and moral concern over particular issues. For the same reason, while the issue under discussion may be a matter of wide political concern on which the parties are divided, there is seldom much evidence of a party political line being taken unless a clear threat to Christian values is perceived.

Occasionally a more specific response emerges. In April 1977, the Southwark Diocesan Synod set up a Diocesan Race Relations Campaign employing two workers. At the same meeting, it

[4]Giles Ecclestone, *The Church of England and Politics* (London: Church Information Office, 1980), p. 4.

[5]*ibid.* p. 5.

condemned a National Front march in East Lewisham as 'inconsistent with Christian commitment' and warned Christians in Southwark against association with the National Front. (Both motions passed *nem. con.* with six abstentions.) Subsequently, the Bishop of Southwark called on all the clergy of the East Lewisham Deanery to join him in a march from Hillyfields to St. Stephen's Church, Lewisham, where a Eucharist was celebrated in the forecourt of the church in the High Street. Almost all the local clergy and many others took part, and the event was generally regarded as marking a significant reverse to the acceptability of National Front activities in that area.

From 1977 onwards, it appears that the Southwark Diocesan Synod has spent more of its time debating issues which may be described as political and/or social. In July 1977, it was unemployment; in May 1978, the increase of violence, and a motion deploring the use of the Union Flag by the National Front; in May 1979, the subject was overcrowding in prisons, and in July the law on "Stop and Search" (sent to the General Synod). In January 1980, the Bishop of Southwark spoke on the Housing Bill before Parliament, and in July 1980, a motion was passed opposing the raising of fees for overseas students at British universities and polytechnics. In 1981, the Brandt Report was discussed, and a letter sent to the Foreign Secretary asking the Government to take a strong lead in implementing its recommendations.

The debate in March 1982 was about the Scarman Report. One of the most widely known reports of this century, it dealt mainly with the 'disorders' or riots which broke out at Brixton on the evening of April 11th, 1981. Brixton is in South London and the Diocese of Southwark; an area of much urban decay and deprivation, with an above-average proportion of young unemployed and a reportedly high crime rate. Contrary to a widespread view, it was not an area of particularly high racial tension, although there is a substantial black population. Hostility to the police, particularly among young people, constituted the main cause of growing tension during 1979–1981, rather than conflict between black and white neighbours. The latter, of course, existed, but it must be seen within a context which also included much friendliness and cooperation, and the emergence of several strong black-led Christian churches. (In fact, their congregations probably exceeded in numerical size those of the mainstream churches of the area by the beginning of the 80's.)

In 1979, the 'Borough Dean' (roughly equivalent to an Archdeacon) of Lambeth was invited to serve on a working party set up by Lambeth Borough Council to study relations between the police and the community in the Borough. The report, published in early 1981, was highly critical of police methods in 'L' Division. The disorders took place in April. Two weeks later, the Brixton Council of Churches issued a statement, which went beyond an analysis of the riots and events leading up to them, and pointed to some constructive steps that could be taken in the future. Christians took an active part in presenting evidence to the Scarman enquiry and in accepting leadership positions on the newly formed Police/Community Consultative Committee, formed later in the year. As Bishop, I visited the Railton Road area on the morning after the riots, and subsequently tried to make a brief statement in the House of Lords.

I have told this story at some length, not because the Diocese of Southwark made any obvious impact on events, but because it illustrates clearly some of the ways in which a diocese, along with other Churches and their leaders, may become involved in an issue concerning the 'polis' very directly. Not only are local congregations drawn in, but the Borough Dean, a senior member of the diocese, works closely with secular colleagues in trying to analyse the problem and make recommendations.

As Bishop, I try to express the concern of the wider Christian community, as do other Church leaders. Subsequently, our Diocesan Synod debated the Scarman Report, and endorsed many of its recommendations in specific terms. Most noticeable, perhaps, is the way in which the local churches are sufficiently in touch with one another to produce a united report, and to offer a small platform of reconciliation in a very divided community. Since 1981, the Diocese has deliberately appointed a number of black clergy to posts in the Brixton area.

It is sometimes suggested that it is only in recent years that the

Church of England has developed any strong concern about social and political issues and that the concern which has developed is the consequence of an upsurge of secular liberal attitudes since the 1939–1945 war. While there is clearly some truth in this,[6] it is important not to ignore the ways in which dioceses have been involved in social and political concern over a much longer period. The evidence for this in one diocese is well documented in Part II of *A Social History of the Diocese of Newcastle*.[7] It shows how the Diocese and its parishes were actively involved in education (especially the founding and maintenance of Church schools), in moral welfare (as it was later called), and in police court work (later merged into the Probation Service). In addition, there were repeated efforts to assuage the dire effects of unemployment and extreme poverty, and these led to the formation of several housing trusts and the setting up of a Tyneside Council of Social Service during the 1920's and 30's.

I now turn to some of the wider questions raised by this brief description of the ways in which a diocese can be involved in politics, and by the particular experience of Newcastle and Southwark.

6.3: 'Diocese' and 'Diocesan'

In a chapter entitled 'The Bureaucratic Church', the Archbishop of York examines some of the changes which have taken place in the organised life of the Church of England in recent years, and says that all are in the direction of making the Church of England a more centralised, exclusive and self-contained religious body.[8]

One aspect of these changes which is relevant to our theme is the 'struggle between two organisational patterns, backed by different systems of authority, which synodical government was supposed to bring together'. On the one hand there is the

---

[6]As K. Medhurst and G. Moyser recognise in their article 'From Princes to Pastors', *West European Politics,* Vol. 5 (1982), No. 2, pp. 172ff.

[7]Pickering, *A Social History of the Diocese of Newcastle*, pp. 193- 317.

[8]J. Habgood, *Church and Nation in a Secular Age*, Ch. 7, p. 116.

rational, administrative and representative system of synods, boards and committees. On the other hand there is the traditional, pastoral, hierarchical system, staffed by the clergy, and finding its fullest expression in the – largely undefined – authority of bishops. 'These two have never been fully integrated and probably ought not to be, for a good theological reason. . . .'[9] This reason lies in an understanding of the Church as a particular kind of organisation, in which the essential Gospel or message is embodied in people, so much so that they are part of the message itself. Further, both the potential impersonality of bureaucracy and the potential authoritarianism of hierarchy can be held in check when the two forms of government exist in a healthy tension.

This is an important perception when trying to evaluate the particular role of the bishop in relation to political and social issues. On the one hand, he is the spokesman for a diocese, and so will do well to heed what the diocese thinks; on the other hand, he is his own man, sometimes taking initiatives and exercising leadership which go beyond that which any civil servant or executive might deem proper in their organisation.

It must also be remembered that the personal influence of the diocesan bishop has a long history, most clearly expressed in membership of the House of Lords. There, bishops do not normally seek to sway votes, nor are they physically able to be present on more than a handful of occasions in the year. Owen Chadwick comments: 'Bishops are only acceptable as speakers in the House of Lords if they speak on the issues of moral life, or matters touching the churches, or a social evil like unemployment which touched the people of their diocese'.[10] He mentions this as backcloth to the decision of Hensley Henson, then Bishop of Durham, to denounce the government of the day for acquiescing in the invasion and occupation of Abyssinia by Mussolini. Cosmo Gordon Lang, Archbishop of Canterbury at the time, reluctantly supported the Government. (It could be claimed that moral issues were indeed at stake, even in a matter

[9]Habgood, *Church and Nation in a Secular Age*, p. 115.

[10]Owen Chadwick, *Hensley Henson* (Oxford: Oxford University Press, 1983), p. 250.

of foreign policy, and Henson's speech is described by one observer as 'scorching'.)

The point which concerns us here is that the intervention of the Bishop of Durham owed nothing to any decision of his diocese, however arrived at. Bishops today still feel free to speak their minds on issues of public concern without any specific synodical authority to do so, and frequently do. Indeed, some of them come under increasing pressure to appear on television or speak on radio, since instant comment by national leaders is preferred to the newspaper articles and letters of Henson's day.

But while there is a clear line of continuity between, say, the pronouncements of the Bishop of Durham in the '20s, and '30s, and the pronouncements of his successors in the '70s and '80s, there is also a perceptible change in style. Medhurst and Moyser make the point that most contemporary bishops expect to work with others in a more 'collegial' style, especially within their own diocese, and are less likely to see themselves as part of a small and privileged elite charged with government in Church and State.[11]

A particular and still unusual example of this more collegial style is that of the joint statement or appearance by several Church leaders. The Bishop of Liverpool, the Roman Catholic Archbishop of Liverpool, and the senior Free Church leader in that area meet regularly in order to reach a common mind or to speak on issues of concern on Merseyside.

It is clear, therefore, that a diocesan bishop may make his own contribution to local debate and decision about political and social issues, and frequently does. He may number political leaders among his friends, and be personally involved in the governance of local institutions. He may, if he wishes, develop the art of 'nudging' in many ways! But recognition of this should not be used to deny the existence of many other ways in which a diocese may exert its own influence.

Mention has already been made of synodical debates and resolutions. These are rarely of a 'party' political nature, and serve primarily to register a general concern for the well-being of society and as an opportunity to explore the central

[11]Medhurst and Moyser, 'From Princes to Pastors', pp. 178-9.

arguments of a particular issue. They have an educational value for the participants, which may spill over into the parishes and beyond, but they rarely cover the ground as thoroughly as a debate in the General Synod. They serve also to prevent the diocese from becoming exclusively preoccupied with its own internal problems and survival.

The Bishop will naturally listen carefully to such debates and sometimes contribute to them. They may give him the nearest thing to a 'consensus' that he is likely to get, as when the Southwark Synod passed a resolution in 1979 expressing concern at the deterioration of commuity and police relations in parts of South London, and calling on Christian people to campaign for an urgent review of the use of Section 4 of the Vagrancy Act (The 'Sus' Law). In some dioceses, he may also use the Bishop's Council, a smaller and more intimate body, to the same end. But he will also know that neither Synod nor Council are necessarily representative of the majority view in the pews of the parish churches (see section 6.5 for a further discussion of this point).

6.4: 'Issues' New and Old

To the best of my knowledge, no research has been made into the range and variety of issues which might be considered under the heading of 'local politics', nor of the frequency with which they have been publicly handled in all the dioceses of the Church of England. But on the basis of a limited amount of reading and enquiry, it seems likely that there are certain issues which have recurred persistently during the past century or so.

The first is education, not surprisingly, since the Church of England has been and still is closely involved in the provision of actual schools, the debate about religious instruction and the whole ethos of education.[12] Many dioceses are represented on Local Authority Education Committees, sometimes with voting

[12]The educational involvement of the Church, and the nature of the links with local and national government to which this gives rise, is discussed later in Chapter 10 of this volume.

membership. Until recently, the Church Colleges of Education were a substantial element in the provision of training for teachers.

The Church of England, along with others, pioneered many forms of care for children, unmarried mothers, court offenders, and so on. These have gradually been extended and often taken over, usually by local government, but there is still a strong sense of partnership between the statutory and voluntary arms. The fact of partnership can, in turn, affect policy; as when, for instance, a church-sponsored protest prevents a particular piece of work being closed down or leads to the establishment of a new project.

In recent years, attention has once again been focussed sharply on two issues which were dominant in the depressed areas of Britain earlier in the century: unemployment and bad or insufficient housing. Here it is difficult to be precise about the interaction of diocese and local politics, since both issues clearly have their roots in national conditions and decisions. But there is little doubt that a diocese and its parishes can focus concern about the consequences of such policies, perhaps unforeseen, and it is from this point of view that bishops and others most frequently speak.[13] In Liverpool, the Anglican and Roman Catholic Bishops, together with the Methodist Chairman of the District, joined a march through the city in protest against the threatened closure of Tate and Lyle's works, and were later involved in some public statements and in going to see the Minister concerned in London. As a Bishop of Newcastle, I was in close touch with those campaigning to ensure a future for the large firm of C.A. Parsons in Heaton (now part of Northern Engineering Industries) at a time when the order book was running out.

The new issue which has stood out most clearly in the last ten years or so, has been 'race relations';[14] even more recently, community relations with the police have emerged as a separate but connected issue. In both cases, the focus has often been quite local, as the examples from Lewisham and Brixton have already

[13]An interesting example is given in the following chapter.
[14]For further detailed discussion, see Chapter 9.

indicated (see section 6.2). The Bishop of Lincoln, for instance, found himself drawn into a dispute at Scunthorpe over the future of the Community Relations Council, at the request of the local churches.

Finally, mention ought to be made of the growth of industrial and community 'chaplaincies' since the 1939–1945 war. Established primarily in order to promote a theological critique of work and society, as well as to open the Churches' eyes to the moral and human questions this evoked, they have represented a powerful expression of diocesan concern in areas where the Churches are normally only present in individual lay members. The majority of such chaplaincies have been directed by 'industrial missions', but in the Durham Diocese especially, there have been some far-reaching and imaginative experiments: a chaplain for Arts and Leisure; several community development chaplains; and a chaplaincy to local government which included a direct and personal ministry to councillors and executives in Co. Cleveland. Diocesan "specialist staff" are sometimes appointed to advise on a particular social need, not only to help individuals and parishes take action to meet it, but also to raise issues and act as a bridge between the Church and other bodies, statutory or voluntary. An example of this in the Southwark Diocese is an adviser on Single Homelessness, whose expertise is now widely acknowledged throughout London. In almost all dioceses there are now Social Responsibility advisers who may specialise in particular fields such as young unemployed or race relations.

6.5: Theological Understanding

From all this it can be surmised that the average Church of England *diocese* is probably more closely in touch with many local issues of social and political concern than it has ever been before. But in many a parish (though clearly not all), the reverse may be true. The reasons for this are complex.[15] There can be little doubt that for many people, especially those at the end of a

[15]See the succeeding chapter in this volume and the chapter on 'Public Life and Private Life' in Habgood, *Church and Nation in a Secular Age*, Ch. 3.

long commuter line and caught up in a hostile, secular environment at work, church is one of the means by which you escape some of the pressures, renew personal values and safeguard your family against the corrosions of the city.

It may, therefore, seem strange to claim that there has been any significant shift in theological understanding of the Churches' role in society, or of the relationship of diocese to local politics. Nevertheless, I believe this to be true. In 1893, the Diocesan Conference of Newcastle debated whether socialism was compatible with Christian faith. Several speakers urged that it was, pointing to the morality of controlling the economic life of the country or city in the interest of justice and compassion. But the Bishop, in summing up, stated that 'Our Lord dealt with individuals, so must we'. Twenty years later, another Bishop of Newcastle upbraided a new curate (John Groser) for dabbling in political questions: 'I sent you down there to save the souls of those people, not to look after their bodies. Go back and do the work you were ordained to do'. Groser comments that he had no intention of doing anything else, and at that time had no idea that in feeding the poor or pressing for better housing, he was being 'political'.

Today, it is unlikely that many Christian leaders would make such crude distinctions as those two Bishops. We are more aware of the extent to which sin and evil infect institutions as well as individuals, thanks to the work of such men as William Temple or Reinhold Niebuhr. We are more aware that you cannot separate souls and bodies without undermining the doctrine of the Incarnation. This is not to be confused with that surrender to 'liberal' values which has been attacked by writers like Dr. Edward Norman and by some contemporary politicians, attacks in which the episcopate is often charged with being out of touch with the ordinary people it should be serving, meddling with matters beyond their concern, and so of being more interested in social causes than in transcendent faith. Recent international statements, including a notable evangelical conference at Lausanne in 1975,[16] make it abundantly clear that

[16]See, e.g., John Stott, *Christian Mission for the Modern World* (London: Inter-Varsity, 1975); David F. Wright, *Essays in Evangelical Social Ethics* (Exeter: Paternoster, 1978).

all the Churches are defining mission to include social responsibility as well as evangelism and teaching.

Activists in Church life tend to be more aware of this than others. And since they are more likely to find their way on to the Diocesan Synod, its boards and committees, to this extent it is possible to speak of a significant shift of theological understanding. It is less easy to say how far the recognition of social responsibility as part of mission is understood to carry with it a political dimension. As suggested earlier, there is rarely any overt identification with a particular party, either among the bishops or among synod members.

"Political Theory" is little studied outside the ranks of the clergy or ordinands, and not much there as yet; nor is it easily applied to the British situation. One way in which political and social issues may be discussed in a Christian context is through the work of those concerned with in-service training, lay training and the like. This, in turn, gives rise to training courses at parish level, and sometimes members of a congregation will be challenged directly to look more closely at the needs and realities of the community of which they are a part. (Churches where the majority of members live outside the parish will, I find, normally resist such a development of their theological understanding or practice more strongly.)

More important is the process by which a local church may decide to become closely involved with the local community, and in the process (or 'praxis', to use the recent term) discovers a theology of the Kingdom which is still rare in parish or diocese. The chapter by Gerald Wheale is a vivid description of how this happened in Moss Side, Manchester, but makes clear how difficult it is to generalise about the diocese in local politics, since dioceses vary so much; this Chapter has been written out of a similarly limited experience.

6.6: Diocese and Local Community

There are at least four ways by which members of a diocese may express active concern for the life of the community, and may in consequence find themselves caught up in issues which touch on the political dimension of local government.

The first is through direct individual influence, scarcely mentioned so far and yet in some ways the most important. In every diocese there are many hundreds of lay Christians who serve as councillors or ward members, for instance, and many more who play some part in organisations which act as pressure groups in the political arena: chambers of commerce, trade unions, voluntary service bodies, and so on. Even today, it is surprising how often there is a clear Christian motivation for political service. Anglicans thus involved will not often relate such political responsibility to their diocese in any formal way, nor to the parish where they live and worship, and in practice the diocese usually does little to recognise them or support them in their vocation. The Roman Catholic Church, through adult colleges and the training methods used by movements like the Young Christian Workers, has done much more to encourage and foster lay vocation of this kind. If dioceses wish to stimulate a stronger awareness of social and political responsibility for the community, they will need to listen carefully to those already so engaged among their own members, and then to use them and others to develop sensitive forms of training and mutual support.[17]

The second is through the parish. There are, for instance, a number of ways in which a parish can influence local opinion, or act as a focus for local feeling, despite its relatively small active membership. It was reported recently that the Rector of a Billingham parish was leading local opposition to the proposal to use a former anhydrite mine for disposing of nuclear waste. Members of a church in south London campaigned vigorously for improved pedestrian crossings. The parish magazine or newsheet often has a wide circulation and may offer a platform for views which might not otherwise find expression in local newspapers. It is almost impossible to quantify such activity or to measure its 'political' impact, yet one suspects that

---

[17]See William Temple Foundation, *Ministry in the Town Hall*(Occasional Paper No. 6, 1982), especially the essay by John Williams.

a large gap would emerge in the fabric of local community life if it was all withdrawn.[18]

The third way by which a diocese may affect local politics is through the various synods. It has already been made clear that diocesan synods can and do debate matters of pressing local concern, such as unemployment or race relations, though these are often also part of a national problem. Deanery synods, which also came into existence in 1970, replaced the 'Ruri-Decanal Conference', which was usually a large and unwieldy body and met seldom. After thirteen years, it is possible to draw rather different conclusions about the strength of this relatively new dimension in synodical government. In some places, deanery synods have begun to address themselves to genuinely local issues, and to find that they represent an area of convenient size to do so effectively, an area which corresponds approximately with a large town, or with a borough or district. Deanery synods, or groups of parishes, often organise a common platform for candidates at a general election in the local constituency – the only people to do so. The ensuing meeting sometimes produces genuine debate and serious questioning. In other places, deanery synods still have great difficulty in working out appropriate common tasks or in establishing sufficiently strong trust and representation from the parishes to carry them out. Nevertheless, there are enough signs of improvement in some places, reinforced by the work of centres like St. Georges, Windsor, to suggest that the deanery synod could become an increasingly important arm of diocesan concern for local politics in future years.

The fourth way is that of the Bishop himself, or perhaps more accurately the episcopate (which may number four or five in large dioceses) and immediate senior colleagues. I have already discussed aspects of this at some length in considering the relationship between the diocese and the 'Diocesan'. Bishops represent a wide constituency, and it is still possible for them to be regarded as relatively impartial. Certainly most of the bishops

[18]This whole theme of parish involvement in local politics is developed very concretely in the next chapter

I know will make it their business to get to know political leaders regardless of the party to which they belong.

In the Southwark Diocese, the previous Bishop (Mervyn Stockwood) inaugurated an annual social event at his house for all the newly-elected Mayors of London Boroughs and Chairmen of Surrey districts, attended also by the chief executive of the authority concerned. Not only has it proved popular and enduring, but it proved to be almost the only occasion when such an intermingling occurred. In a number of London boroughs, the Archdeacon or 'Borough Dean' (who carries out similar duties), is particularly charged with keeping in close and regular touch with civic leaders of his own borough. The model has sometimes been copied by other Church leaders, such as the Methodist superintendent, which then makes possible the kind of cooperation practised at city level in Liverpool.

This kind of personal contact is important for the trust it can breed, especially if a crisis should develop, but also for the witness it gives that the Churches care about the quality of local government. Even more important, perhaps, it can occasionally provide a genuine resource and support for individuals whose lives are often stressful and confusing. This is well demonstrated in the pioneer work of John Williams on Teesside as a chaplain to local government, which was exceptionally well planned and thorough. From time to time a bishop, archdeacon or rural dean has 'stood alongside' some particular politician in a time of need, and by prayer and sensitive friendship been able to provide a detached support which no other politician could easily give. How often this happens is impossible to say, though I fear it happens far less often than it could or should. The sheer scale of the demand in a large diocese is daunting.

6.7:   Conclusion

One thing which strikes me again and again is that there is seldom a discernible diocesan policy in relation to local politics. The reasons for this are not far to seek: a long history of parochial independence, a lack of organs to formulate a clear policy or carry it through. Gradually, this situation is changing, as dioceses make more use of their boards for mission and social responsibility, and there is greater recognition of the need to take certain issues seriously and persistently. But there is still a long way to go, and meanwhile many pressing internal problems capture the energies and attention of diocesan leaders and members alike. Here, in the sphere of what is often described as 'Kingdom Theology', is surely where local ecumenical cooperation can prove most fruitful in the next decade, strengthening and extending the influence of the diocese and other Churches in their proper concern for the 'polis' to which they belong.

Chapter 7
THE PARISH AND POLITICS
Gerald Wheale

7.1: Introduction

To write about the parish and politics from the standpoint of a
parish priest is a fascinating task for it requires an unravelling of
the various strands of a ministry which has extended over a
period of 21 years. I will describe the context and the content of
a ministry in an inner-city parish set in a largely urban diocese.
The results of reflecting upon that ministry are offered as a
contribution to the current debate about the nature of ministry
in a rapidly changing world.

7.2: The Challenge of the Inner City

The parish of St. James' with St. Clement's, Moss Side, is an
inner-city parish in Manchester. In the last 20 years, half of the
Moss Side area has seen its housing cleared and redevelopment
take place. The remaining half has been subject to considerable
activity in the field of housing improvement and rehabilitation.
A new district centre has been built, complete with shopping
precinct, indoor market and leisure centre. In the years before
the redevelopment process got under way in Moss Side, every
indicator of social decline was already high. My description of
the characteristics, based on the 1966 Census, stated that they
included a substantial proportion of housing falling below
minimum standards, a disproportionately high degree of mobil-
ity, a disproportionately young population (30% under 15) and a
disproportionately high immigrant population.[1]

[1] G.A. Wheale, *Citizen Participation in the Rehabilitation of Housing in
Moss Side East, Manchester*, unpublished Ph.D. Thesis, University of
Manchester, 1979, pp. 91-92.

A city-wide survey of Manchester was drawn up in 1975 in order to select areas on which to focus efforts in the tackling of urban deprivation. It identified three factors as indicators of deprivation. These were stressful housing circumstances and large and often over-crowded families. The study stated:

'There are four enumeration districts which are in the extreme 10% of all three factors, all in Moss Side. Family life in these enumeration districts, with extreme poverty, lack of social cohesion and a high percentage of young children often living in overcrowded rented accommodation must be a considerable ordeal. Moss Side emerges as the part of the city most deserving of the label of 'multiple deprivation'.'[2]

By 1975, the proportion of black faces in the community was rising and this is indicated in a report to the City Council prior to the declaration of an area of Moss Side for housing rehabilitation. It stated that 'between 30% and 40% of all residents in the area are either first or second generation immigrants'. This was an area in which there were only a few black faces in 1962. The report also drew attention to a long-standing problem in the area, a problem which pre-dated the advent of significant numbers of black immigrants, when it said:

'Prostitution is the most visible social problem in the area and one which many, particularly the long standing residents, complain about bitterly.'[3]

Although redevelopment is complete and the rehabilitation of property well under way by the 1980s, problems still remain. 1981 Census material revealed that 26.4% of the population were under 15; Moss Side residents tended to be poorer and overcrowding tended to be worse than in other areas of the city; 650 households still lacked a WC; 24.9% of residents were born

[2]City Planning Department/Social Services Department, *Social Information Study*, City of Manchester, September 1975, p. 25.

[3]Director of Housing, *Informatory Statement, Greame Street HAA*, Manchester City Council, 17 November 1975, p. 3, para. 3.

outside the UK (this figure does not include 2nd or 3rd generation immigrants); the overall unemployment rate was 24% and youth employment (16-19) was 39.4%.[4] On the basis of information drawn from unemployment figures for Moss Side, a local community worker observed in January 1982, that the local unemployment register had increased by 80% over the last two years and that youth employment had increased by 90% in the same period. On the 10th November 1983, there was still a minimum of 6,906 persons unemployed in Moss Side. Vacancies unfilled at the Moss Side Job Centre totalled 185.[5] Riots took place in Moss Side on the 8th. and 9th. July, 1981.

This picture of Moss Side has formed the context of my ministry for the last twenty years. My initial understanding of the situation when I came to the area in 1962 led me to the belief that such conditions were an affront to the God-given dignity and integrity of Moss Siders as human beings and as a community. My commitment as a priest required me to preach the gospel and administer the sacraments but also carried a moral imperative to identify with and to struggle alongside my parishioners in their search for true humanity. Attempts to grapple with the implications of impending redevelopment of the area quickly led our church council and congregation to ask fundamental questions about the nature of the parochial system and the role of the Church. Requests to the City Planning Officers and to Diocesan officials for information on strategic planning for the future, revealed the powerful influence of the institutions of our society upon the quality of life of individual citizens. The failure of both institutions to engage in a dialogue to plan for the future, resulted in frustration, disillusionment, aggression and even conflict between local congregations and the Diocese and the Moss Side community and the Town Hall.[6]

[4]R. Morris, *A Social Survey of Moss Side Based on the 1981 Census*, unpublished project whilst on placement from the Northern Ordination Course, July 1983.

[5]Department of Employment, *North Western Region, Unemployment and Unfilled Vacancies Figures, November 1983*, Press Notice, 1 Dec. 1983.

[6]The story of these unhappy events in the history of Moss Side has been documented in G.A. Wheale, *Citizen Participation in the Redevelopment of Moss Side, Manchester*, unpublished M.Ed. Thesis, University of Manchester, 1974.

This powerful institutional dimension and the relationship of the Church to it, was discussed into the early hours of many mornings with a long-standing friend, Brian Cordingley of the Manchester Industrial Mission team. The Kingdom of God became a more important concept in my theology and was strengthened, developed and related to community involvement in a fruitful relationship with the William Temple Foundation.[7] A visit to down-town churches in Toronto, Canada, in 1978, served to sharpen my understanding and at the time I referred to the striking similarities between their experience and ours in Moss Side:

'Whether a local church survives or not seems to depend almost entirely upon a small group finding the ways and means of keeping the doors open despite the demands of an over-large and increasingly expensive set of church plant. Clergy feel threatened by the apparent lack of Diocesan interest. Laity feel unsupported in their attempt to be the local church and either opt for the most conservative kind of non-involvement or move to more affluent churches which do not have the same problems of survival. In circumstances such as these it is little wonder if the down-town church feels that it suffers the same fate as the poor in an affluent society, namely that they are unwanted and unloved. I must emphasise that I sense both here and in Canada a sadness rather than a bitterness that this is so. Sadness because we expect more of the Church of God; bitterness only because it seems a betrayal of God's love by those who charge us to preach in His Name. However, I do want to push the analysis one stage further for at a wider level I believe there are quite worrying consequences to contend with. Just as the poor are a critical testing point of the objectives a society sets itself so, too, the down-town churches are a critical testing point of the performance of the Church in living out the gospel it proclaims. Both test whether we believe that self-sufficiency and the numbers game lie at the heart of democratic society on the one hand and

[7]*Involvement in Community, A Christian Contribution*, a Report by the Community Development Group of the William Temple Foundation in collaboration with the Community Work Advisory Group, British Council of Churches, 1980.

the Kingdom of God on the other. State and Church often act as if they do! If they do then let the poor parish and the down-town churches disappear. I cannot recognise this picture as an adequate description of either democracy or the Kingdom of God. My Jesus demands a special place for the poor in both the democracy and the Kingdom of God. Furthermore, that place is to do with dignity as much as dependency and inter-dependency as much as individualism. If acting in accordance with a principle of self-sufficiency or the numbers game suggested a lack or inadequacy of theology it would be worrying enough. What worries me more is that such a view may be to do with a lack of faith.'[8]

I have tried to describe the context of my ministry in Moss Side and the development of my thinking about the ministry over a twenty year period. I have done that in order to make clear that a particular style of ministry has evolved in relation to a particular situation. I believe it to be a ministry based upon word and sacraments. It has also been, and still is, a ministry which has attempted a reconstruction of community in Moss Side as part of God's purpose to bring in His Kingdom. Ministry for the ordained must be the living out of faith in the place where they find themselves just as it must be for the laity. A worshipping and supportive base is essential for the people of God. The base, in my case the parish, is an observation post on society; here we pick up and test the attitudes of society to the poor. At this margin of society we are more than a church unit with an internal self-contained and self-interested life; we are in the forefront 'doing theology' by working out our faith in the realities of a disadvantaged and poor community. Our witness is at many levels; proclaiming the gospel and celebrating the sacraments and expressing the power of Christian love in our community. By these means we seek to enable man to discover his true humanity.

To put it another way, the parish is the testing ground for true humanity and the arena for the living out of faith. Man

[8]G.A. Wheale, "Reflections on a Visit to Canada: May/June 1978", in *The William Temple Foundation Bulletin*, No. 7, October 1978, pp. 13-14.

cannot be fully man in church alone. Church should not simply be the vehicle of receiving man's gifts of time, money and talent to sustain and enhance its own structure and life, but a means whereby mankind is enabled to discover its salvation and fulfilment in God in daily living. Neither is the parish an end in itself, it is an integral part of the process of living out the faith in the universal brotherhood of man. Every parish is set in a world context within the eternal purposes of God, so the ways in which it lives out faith are relevant to, and significant in, that wider context.

7.3: The Church's Response

I see this style of ministry for both priest and laity as theologically justifiable and necessary in practice, but it has drawn a wide range of responses from both the Church and the secular world. In the Church, there are a few kindred spirits, and more, who wish this style of ministry could be accepted, but who speak of the 'dead weight' of many of the laity or the 'diocesan establishment'. There are many others who would find this style 'too radical' and compare it to 'a proper ministry'. From the secular world there has been a variety of response. Within the local community many have said that it is 'good to see someone standing up for Moss Side' and that our Church and particularly our Church-sponsored Housing Association, has shown that 'things can be made better in Moss Side!'

Some of our more radical leaders in Moss Side would see my efforts as typical "sloppy liberal" establishment, conscience-salving, activities which only reinforce an already repressive system. After many years of building relationships and establishing credibility, there is a good deal of evidence to show that politicians and officers at both city and national level regard our efforts, particularly in housing, with approval and support.

7.3.1: The Housing Association

Since its formation in the 1960s, the Housing Association sponsored by the churches in Moss Side (Mosscare Housing Limited) has grown steadily to its present holding of nearly

1,000 properties. Its main efforts have been concentrated into areas of housing need and physical decline. There are strong indications that regeneration is occurring in some sub-areas where private buying had collapsed some years ago. Families in housing need have been given rehabilitated homes with a further 30 year life span and, more importantly, confidence in the future has been regenerated as near-derelict and denuded communities have been reconstructed. The 'tenant-intensive' style of management and the community base of the Association have led a number of community organisations to Mosscare's door with requests for housing projects to help those in special need, for example Polish Catholic elderly, single West Indian homeless and families with mentally handicapped members. The Deputy Director of Mosscare is Chairman of the North West Regional Council of the National Federation of Housing Associations and the Association had two representatives at the Department of the Environment consultations held during 1983 on inner-city regeneration through Housing Association involvement.

The community base of the Housing Association has been symbolised by the staff of the Association working from the Moss Side Pastoral Centre. This Centre, opened in 1973, replaced the old St. James' church hall in Moss Side and was designed by, and is still managed by, a group drawn from the local Council of Churches. Its purpose was to provide an accessible point at which the Church could be seen to have a working base from which to show its commitment to the community of Moss Side. It was designed to be an open and accepting building into which people could come with confidence and without embarrassment to share in the various activities of the Centre or simply to seek help with any problems. Happily, the experiment has worked and the building provides a home for parish functions (including worship during the winter), church council meetings, the Housing Association, a community project, residents' group meetings, the local carnival committee, advice bureaux for the MP and local councillors, a dancing school, the Methodist Brownies and many other activities.

Because it is a 'multi-use' centre, all files and the records of daytime users are stored away at night and all furniture is multi-purpose. As parish priest, I am at my desk by 8.00 a.m. so that 'the church' may be seen at work as people go about their daily business. The Centre gives Moss Siders ready access to the Church and its ministry and to other caring agencies. It also gives to the Church, and to me as parish priest, a most significant point of entry into many community activities as well as an enormous number of contacts with local people.

7.3.2:   The Community Project

Three workers of the Longsight/Moss Side Community Project work from the Pastoral Centre. This project was founded by the local churches in the late 1960s and two major aspects of its work in Moss Side deserve mention here. The first concerns its work with residents' groups. This has been a long-term piece of work which began with resident response to the redevelopment process. Response in the early 1960s and early 1970s was particularly volatile as larger areas of Moss Side were cleared and new housing was built. Participation in planning for the future was very much a live issue and the Moss Side Social Council (later the Moss Side Peoples' Association) enjoyed a quite spectacular career as it confronted the City Council with the undesirable consequences of its housing policy, which many felt was leading to 'the destruction of the Moss Side community'.

The Community Project committee felt that a professional community worker could be of service to the community in expressing this kind of concern and resources were allocated to this work. The lessons learned in the work on redevelopment issues were then used in ongoing work with residents' groups in the area who tried to encourage a change in City Council policy towards the rehabilitation of housing. When such a change did take place and improvement, rather than demolition, was adopted as a Council policy, one of the most significant factors in the choice of areas for improvement in Moss Side was the high degree of resident commitment to the new policy. I believe that that confidence was well-founded as there has been a considerable improvement in the physical fabric of the Moss Side area. Many houses have been improved by the City Council and by the Housing Associations active in the area. The confidence generated by this activity has led in recent years to one or two of the major financial institutions, as well as the City Council, funding the improvement work of owner-occupiers. Central Government policy on "New Initiatives in Housing" was also intended to encourage regeneration of this kind, but the experience of our Housing Association, formed for this purpose, seems to suggest that the exercise is not financially viable in Moss Side. This view was expressed to Sir George Young at the Pastoral Centre during his visit to Moss Side in October 1983.[9]

The work with the residents' groups still continues and currently covers issues such as street cleaning, the continuing problem of prostitution, the use of vacant buildings and land in the area and road widening proposals for a major road into the City through Moss Side. These and other issues are also taken up through the Inner City Partnership Committee.

At a wider level, the Parish Church, the Housing Association and the Community Project are all represented on the Moss Side Consultative Committee set up by the City Council. Strong local councillor representation on this body makes it a significant vehicle through which the community can make its voice heard on Moss Side issues. This body, with City Council backing, mounted extensive consultations with the community through the Moss Side Conference after the riots of 1981. Following a large conference with many community representatives present, a series of smaller conferences was held on specific issues and an encouraging number of initiatives have been mounted as a result.

In the present economic climate, two factors stand out as major stumbling blocks to progress; the first is the time taken to put together the proposals and to get them through the various levels of the decision-making process and the second is the availability of funds to finance any initiatives. There is often a package of resources to put together which may be compromised if any one supporting agency fails to deliver.

These difficulties were most dramatically demonstrated in a project mounted by our Housing Association, Mosscare. In

[9]G.A. Wheale, Memo of visit of Sir George Young, Resume of points made (Under Secretary of State, Department of the Environment), Mosscare Housing Ltd., Development File, Programme July 1982 to November 1983, 4 October 1983.

1981, Mosscare had sixty vacant properties awaiting rehabilitation for which there was no funding available through the
mainstream housing programme. Through the Inner-City
Programme, and in partnership with the City Council, Mosscare secured the promise of £1 million support for the capital
improvement work. In conjunction with the Construction
Industries Training Board, two contractors were recruited who
would undertake the contract work as a training scheme for
unemployed young people in Moss Side. A full course for
recruits was reserved at the Manchester College of Building and
a major contractor was prepared to set up a training compound
in Moss Side. Both sources would provide recruits to gain
experience on site with the main contractors during the period of
the contract. The local Job Centre was prepared to handle
applications for places on the scheme, and local schools and
community groups were contacted to publicise the scheme. This
was to be a major training initiative in an area of high unemployment.

A crucial element in the scheme was the provision of funding
for the training element in the main contract work. This was
being negotiated between the Construction Industries Training
Board and the Manpower Services Commission. With contractors ready to move on site, and 18 months investment by all
concerned, the Manpower Services Commission, at national
level, was not prepared to commit the funding for the training
element. Despite strenuous intervention by Manchester Town
Clerk's Department, the scheme collapsed and the opportunity
of training many unemployed youngsters was lost. When, at a
later date, mainstream funds became available, the contractors,
as a gesture of goodwill, did recruit some Manchester youngsters.

The second major aspect of the work of the Longsight/Moss
Side Community Project which deserves mention here is its
work with co-operatives. An Asian community worker with the
project team drew attention to the exploitation and isolation felt
by Asian women who were involved in the 'outwork' system in
the textile trade. So that they could supplement their family
income, many women spent long lonely hours at home
producing garments on hired industrial sewing machines. With

children at school, they were cut off from social contact, with little chance to learn the language of the host community in which they lived. An action/research team of two workers was appointed. It took years to investigate and put together the elements of a co-operative venture. The workers' reports to the Project Management Committee amply demonstrated the incredible complexity and frustration involved in trying to secure premises, machines, funding for supervisors, designers, cutters and the co-operative worker members in the training period as well as the difficulties of ensuring a constant flow of work from suppliers and guaranteed market outlets. It is a tribute to their tenacity as well as to their skill that they succeeded at all and that they sustained the interest of a nucleus of women during the many months of preparations.

The project is quoted in a recent Department of the Environment publication as an example of the Government's determination to overcome racial disadvantage. The report states that, since its foundation in 1981, the workshop:

'....has developed very rapidly. Under the guidance of three skilled supervisors – one experienced in designing and cutting – the trainees have learned to machine various kinds of light garments. The speed and quality of their work have shown steady improvement and some are making their own patterns or doing quality control. The trainees have learned to work as a unit and have a better command of English.'

The report continues,

'The project has increased the all-round confidence of the trainees. They feel they can make an important contribution to family and community life, enjoy better relationships with their children and consider themselves better equipped to come to terms with their new country. Two are hoping to study part-time to expand their skills.'[10]

[10] The Urban Programme: Tackling Racial Disadvantage, Department of the Environment, 1983, p. 8.

7.4: The Political Dimension

Have I been involved in politics? The way in which I have described the context of my ministry, the development of my theological understanding and some of the work undertaken by myself and others in the name of ministry, could well raise that question. The question also implies a further question as to whether it is appropriate for a priest to be so engaged.

It is difficult to answer these questions directly but my mind goes back to theological college days when Mervyn Stockwood, who was then Vicar of Great St. Mary's in Cambridge, gave a series of talks on ministry. One of these talks was about whether the parish priest should be involved in politics. I remember very clearly two of the points which he made. One of these was that the exercise of ministry in itself generated a personal political stance on the part of the priest, and the other was that the activities undertaken in the parish are themselves a commentary upon the outworkings of the political system as expressed in the life of the local community. In his opinion, this meant that every priest ought to work out an explicit political stance and should be sensitive to the political implications of parish activities.

At the time I did not understand the implications of what he was saying, but now, with twenty five years of experience, twenty one of them spent in a disadvantaged community, I can bear witness to the force of his argument. The exercise of power and the control of resources by the institutions of our society have a very powerful effect upon my life and the lives of those I minister to. Decisions made by such bodies as Central or Local Government either enhance my dignity and integrity as a human being and a child of God or they impair and restrict it. So, too, they enhance or impair the life of the local community of which I am a part. In short, these institutional activities either enable or block the coming of the Kingdom of God. A very large part of the exercise in power and the control of resources is, in fact, the political process of the society and world in which we live. It seems to be that, whether I like it or not, both I and my parishioners are bound up in a political process which we cannot avoid. We cannot ignore it; although in my experience, many try to by compartmentalising 'faith' and the other dimensions of life. Grappling with the political dimension presents us with untold difficulties and dilemmas but must be undertaken if we are to be fully Christian and if I am to exercise my ministry to the full.

At this point I would wish to enter a rider on behalf of those of us who would plead that the Church should take the structural/institutional dimension of life more seriously than it does at the moment. We are often attacked as somehow lacking compassion in the exercise of our ministry to the individual. The criticism seems to be that the pastoral ministry is neglected so that political activity can be pursued. I would wish to respond by saying that in my experience compassion is a quality which is strongly exhibited by those of us who share this standpoint and that a significant proportion of our ministry is expressed in pastoral care. I would also raise the question of whether, in some areas, the view that the priest is constantly in demand for pastoral care is a myth in these days. During the last three years I have come across an increasingly large number of clergy who have talked of a running down in demand for traditional pastoral care. I am sure that there is no less need but perhaps it is now being met by social workers, community workers or advice bureaux workers, who are all particularly active in areas of disadvantage.

In case the reader is beginning to feel that I am advocating out and out overt party political activity for the parish priest, let me say that in some situations I think that that may be the appropriate course of action but in Moss Side that has not seemed to be the right answer. I believe that the priest must be political for the reasons which I have mentioned earlier and yet he must be above party politics. I say this because loyalty and solidarity can be divisive and can compromise the dignity and integrity of fellow human beings in a way I would oppose as a Christian. Loyalty is often seen as unswerving and uncritical allegiance. If I am critical of the Church, people sometimes respond as though I do not love it as the Body of Christ, or as though I have lost my sense of vocation.

Similar views are taken in the political sphere. Some years ago, a number of Moss Side ministers attended a political meeting of a prospective MP in order to question him on overseas aid and attitudes to immigrants. The questioning was critical of the views of the candidate. The chairman of the meeting became more and more agitated as the questioning proceeded until he at last sprang to his feet with puce face to put an end to the persecution of his candidate. He bellowed at the audience and said that he wished the questioners to know that he, the candidate, most people present, and in particular his party, were 'damn proud to be British', had fought wars to prove it and would tolerate no more questions from 'communists'!

Those who try to generate solidarity also present a problem for they often call for sides to be taken in an 'us' and 'them' sense. For example, when the community wants to take action over a particular issue and the demand is made to join forces against the enemy. The enemy is made out to be oppressive, to have devious motives and to be capable of dirty tactics to maintain the *status quo* or to enhance their own power and status at the expense of the disadvantaged in society.

This was certainly the position adopted by certain members of the militant wing of the Moss Side Housing Action Group in conflict with the Town Hall over the issue of redevelopment. The Moss Side Rehousing Charter drawn up by the Group gives both direct and indirect expression to this view when it states:

'It is a basic human right to live in fit and uncramped accommodation. The intention of slum clearance and council house building should be to ensure that all citizens are given this right.'[11]

and again in Section 6 of the Charter when it states that:

'Everyone be given a decent house – whatever their wage or house 'standards'. The Council must stop the inhuman practice of grading us by looking at our rent books and other personal documents to see whether we can afford 'their' houses, and by

[11]The "Charter" of the Housing Action Group (Moss Side Peoples Association), a Draft for the revised version as recorded in "Which Community, What Fight?", C. Duncan, 1970, unpublished, duplicated paper of the Housing Action Group.

looking at the upkeep of the house, to see if it is up to 'standard' (and whether we are 'respectable' or 'problem' families).'

As might be expected there is also a sting in the tail of the Charter. It demands that the Council should:

'(a) Show the profit being made out of housing – and who it goes to. As people soon to be rehoused, most of us, whether tenants or owner-occupiers, will be paying a higher rent in council accommodation than we are paying now, and

(b) give us a written statement of where the money for council housing comes from and to what companies the loans are repaid (and at what interest).'

I find it hard to express solidarity with those whose ideology, analysis and tactics demand an identifiable enemy which acts in the way described above. Yet it was that same 'enemy' who acted equally indiscriminately in response to the determined efforts of Moss Side residents to participate in planning the future of their area. Within a few days of the publication of the Skeffington Report on Pubic Participation in Planning,[12] the City Planning Officer was quoted in the Press as supporting his Committee Chairman who had broken off contact with the Moss Side People's Association. He was recorded as saying:

'All I can say is that if my Chairman hadn't taken this action I would have done so myself. These people proved to be anti-Council, anti-Town Hall, anti-Establishment, a little group of revolutionaries, out to stir up trouble.'[13]

It is an interesting comment on the situation that this 'little group of revolutionaries' published a local newspaper which sold 1,000 copies a month and that a Housing Action group

[12]A. Skeffington, People and Planning, *Report of the Committee on Public Participation in Planning*, London, 1969.
[13]H. Pendlebury, *"Anti-Council, Anti-Town Hall, Anti-Establishment Revolutionaries", City Planning Chief Hits Out at Moss Side Militants, Daily Mail*, North West Extra, Manchester, 14 August 1969, p. 1.

candidate in the local election of May 1970 polled 767 votes. In the previous election, the Labour candidate had polled 450 votes and the Conservative 1,700. At this election, they polled 950 and 1,450 votes respectively. An additional 1,000 voters turning out when housing was an issue! By any standard, the performance of the independent candidate was remarkable.

As a member of the General Purposes Committee of the Moss Side Peoples Association, I found myself in an interesting position. To the City Planning Officer I was a revolutionary and to the militant element of the Peoples Association I was a member of the Establishment. At the same time I polled the second highest number of votes in the election to the General Purposes Committee of the Association. These issues of loyalty and solidarity certainly arise if you attempt to identify with, and are committed to, the disadvantaged and they raise deep theological problems about our understanding of the Gospel.

The ethos of my life, training and ministry, is Western, liberal democratic and Protestant. My theology supposes that love as found in Jesus is capable of bringing reconciliation between God and man and between man and his fellow man. Reconciliation is the key-stone of faith and I celebrate the death of Jesus on the Cross as the 'full, perfect and sufficient sacrifice, oblation, and satisfaction for the sins of the whole world'.[14] I am, however, faced with a world in which there are many examples of those in positions of power exercising their power and controlling the associated resources in a way which is both obdurate and repressive. Criticism by the disadvantaged is interpreted as disloyal or as expressing unhealthy anti-Establishment feeling and solidarity with the disadvantaged and repressed is treated as subversive. Reconciliation between the disadvantaged and the oppressor does not seem possible and some Christians respond by opting for confrontation, conflict and revolution.

I have spoken to Christians from abroad who speak of suspending their theology until the revolution is over. I do not find that an acceptable solution, although I must also face the

[14] *The Prayer of Consecration*, Book of Common Prayer, 1662.

fact that I am not in the same situation! Archbishop Runcie accurately describes the position for me as a priest working in England when he writes:

'I believe, however, that the Christian seriousness brought to government by an establishment in which laity as well as clergy have always held positions of responsible leadership, has contributed greatly to the growth of a corporate sense of obligation towards the needy and a respect for justice which has softened conflict and enhanced the life of every citizen. It is, of course, easy to detail what still needs to be corrected and where welfare provision is not sufficiently generous, or not applied with enough compassion, but it would be foolish to let proper indignation blind us to the achievements of our society in recent centuries or cause us to forget what a rare and fleeting experience in the history of the world it is to live in a society which is secure, reasonably just and moderately prosperous.'[15]

Even though I accept the position adopted by Archbishop Runcie, I am conscious that I do not suffer the harsh realities of the life of the disadvantaged as they do themselves. Commitment to, and identification with, the disadvantaged is not the same as being disadvantaged oneself. A Moss Sider expressed it to me in the following terms – "You say 'we this' and 'we that' and 'we the other', but you are not the same as us; you can walk out at any time, we are stuck with it!" It is easy for the liberal Christian to overlook the urgency in the plight of the disadvantaged. When the liberal Christian neglects the urgency for reform, the militant in society responds by adopting the view that almost any tactics are legitimate in attempting to alter an intolerable *status quo*. To pontificate that two wrongs do not make a right may result in being accused by the radical of making a facile moral judgement from the comfort of a middle-class armchair.

I remain critical of the Church as an institution because of its failure to recognise and significantly engage the political dimension of life but I also believe that the Church of England

[15]Robert Runcie, *Windows onto God*, (London: S.P.C.K., 1983), p. 63.

can no longer be labelled the Tory party at prayer! There are now many parish priests for whom a life spent in ministry to the disadvantaged is the living out of a faith which has in it a more 'left wing' political stance than hitherto. They live close to the realities of disadvantage as they are experienced in their own parish. They are often politically to the left of their laity, although not to the left of many of their parishioners! The professional job of living out the imperatives of faith means that they have to work out a faith stance in the context of disadvantage in which they work. It is not difficult for them to recognise the paternalistic authoritarianism of our own democratic society for the Church itself has been, and still is, guilty of this style of management in its affairs.

7.5: The Ecumenical Dimension

To write as I have done about the nature of ministry is bound to raise questions about whether my views would be shared by ministers in other denominations. As one would expect, reaction is mixed, although I am delighted to record that there was a most significant ecumenical moving together of local churches in Moss Side during the troubled years of the 1960s and early 1970s. Baptist, Methodist, Church of Christ, Congregational and Church of England congregations were concerned about the quality of life in the community during the redevelopment process. Working together on this issue led them into fruitful co-operation and eventually to a formal covenanted relationship. The Longsight/Moss Side Community Project and the Mosscare Housing Association were both founded in that era by representatives from the various churches and much joint work and witness was undertaken to demonstrate our unity in Christ and to live out the faith in deed as well as in word. Tragically, unilateral reorganisation of manpower and buildings by each of the denominations in a declining situation was a major factor in the collapse of the ecumenical group. It is interesting to find a new ecumenism abroad in Hulme and Moss Side at the present time, when the added disadvantage of unemployment is hitting the area so hard. The new Fellowship of Churches, including the Roman Catholic Church, is engaged in trying to mount a major initiative to provide some additional employment in the area.

At the ecumenical level, two things are particularly striking. First, that there has never been any significant or widespread co-operation or ecumenical activity on the part of the black churches in Moss Side, although one or two black churches are now associated with the Hulme Fellowship of Churches. Many seem to be small bodies rent by internal disputes over belief or leadership and resistant to ecumenical overtures by what are seen as 'white churches'. The local Fellowship of Churches, however, was prominent at a service in 1983 held at one of the black churches to commemorate the 150th anniversary of the abolition of slavery in the British Empire. Second, that the theology of the black churches seems to be 'other worldly' and, therefore, involvement in community or political issues is not regarded as a corollary of faith.

Despite the reluctance of the black churches to be involved in ecumenical activity or community issues, the mainstream denominations have a long history of involvement with each other and in community affairs. As indicated earlier, this has led to the formation of the Community Project, the Housing Association and, more recently, the Youth Employment Scheme. Over the years, regular support has also been given to Third World needs through collections for Christian Aid, to the local Alexandra Park Carnival and to the provision of facilities for youth work. The Hideaway Youth Club, started by the Baptist Church, has become a showpiece of youth work in the inner-city. Each of these activities has raised questions about the relationship of the Church to powerful institutions in the secular world. The Church has won credibility in the political arena of decision-making by a high level of commitment and the willingness and ability to learn sophisticated operating techniques. It has not been a story of unqualified success, there have been many problems along the way but there is an impressive record of skilled community work and a growing pool of informed community leadership.

7.6: Implications and New Directions

When we turn to the question of training for the ministry and the strategic use of the resources of the Church, there are encouraging signs that there has been some recognition of the need to meet a rapidly changing situation. For example, I was involved in teaching on the North West Ordination Course, now known as the Northern Ordination Course, for thirteen years. On this course, men and women receive training whilst remaining in full-time work. They attend evening sessions during the week, weekend conferences and a ten-day summer school during each of the three years of training. Apart from the usual academic training for the ministry, the members of the course receive training in 'community studies' which aims to make them sensitive to the issues raised by ministry in an urban technological context. This element of the course has included visits to inner-city areas like Moss Side and a study of ministry in a disadvantaged area. Our congregation at St James has been most generous in sharing its experience and insight. In the course of the last year we have had visitors from Canadian churches, from the University of Manchester, from South Africa through the British Council and students on placement from Bradford College, Stafford Borough Council, as well as the Northern Ordination Course. This two-way traffic enables us to share our experience and also keeps us alert and in touch with a wide network of agencies who share our interest and concern.

Manchester Diocese has recently prepared a report on ministry in the inner-city and in it reference is made to establishing 'centres for urban ministry'.[16] I have long nurtured the hope that we would be able to share our experience on a more regular basis and this new thinking in the Diocese may represent a possible way forward. The Diocesan Board for Social Responsibility has now established a Churches Urban Community Council to try to set forward the ministry and to draw the Churches into a partnership in which meagre resources will be

[16]J. Atherton, *Supporting Church Life and Mission, The Report of the Inner City Urban Areas Working Party*, Appendix 4.

used strategically to the greatest advantage. A recently established Diocesan Board of Ministry has also set up a working party on leadership in priority areas. This working party is concerned with leadership in working class communities and has been asked to make proposals about the most effective types of leadership for the Church in such communities. It is due to the report in June 1984 and I see it as an imaginative attempt to get to grips with contemporary forms of ministry.

These are only small examples of a current desire within the institutional Church to act more strategically in matters of ministry and I am encouraged that they are happening. One of the most encouraging events to take place in the Manchester Diocese is a recent conference involving all the clergy of the Diocese in an attempt to evolve a strategy over the next five years. Account was taken of the contemporary context of ministry in an urban diocese and to relate the mission, buildings and manpower policy to the patterns which emerged in discussion. Inevitably, the tensions inherent in parochial structure and the complexity of strategic planning in a situation of diverse and conflicting interests were revealed. Deanery consultations were held in conjunction with the exercise. In our own Deanery of Hulme, the consultations revealed a wealth of imaginative thinking about contemporary ministry and I am convinced that it is worth pursuing as many possibilities of strategic planning as possible within the Church for in doing so we may discover more strategic ways of planning the Church's relationship with the world we are all part of.

At a Deanery level, the local Anglican churches have also been able to discuss a number of issues which relate to the wider aspects of life in society, such as housing needs in Greater Manchester, issues of unemployment, 'the Church and the Bomb' and relationships between the police and community. The latter issue is, of course, a most sensitive area for the Church to be involved in and it would not be helpful here to comment in detail but I would like to record my own appreciation of our diocesan Bishop's pastoral care and concern which is expressed in personal counselling and consultations with community leaders, clergy and senior police officers involved in this problem.

At the time of the Moss Side riots in 1981, the support of senior Anglican staff in the Diocese was most striking. On the night of the riots I had an offer of emergency accommodation from the Diocesan staff, on the morning after, a visit from the Archdeacon to offer support and a personal visit from the diocesan Bishop after he had made a tour of the area. I was inundated with telephone calls and letters of support from friends and from clergy I had never even met. I also hope that it was significant that there was no damage whatsoever to either the church or our Pastoral Centre, although the area was a scene of devastation the morning after the riot. We did suffer from the attention of the media who seem to appear like vultures to feast upon any unhappy events which occur in the life of Moss Side. No one was interested in filming or writing about the three hundred or more West Indians who came to a funeral service at St. James' the morning after the riots to mourn the loss of one of their community who had died a few days previously. They did not require police supervision and ordered themselves in their usual quiet and dignified manner. The contrast with the events of the previous night was obvious but the media showed no interest. Normality, even in a disadvantaged inner-city area, is not headline material.

7.7: Conclusion

In a ministry in Moss Side which stretches over more than 20 years, I have been most concerned to see that our people are treated as God's children and that they are enabled to develop their full human potential and true dignity. Over issues such as the maintenance of roads and pavements, the siting of industry, educational provision, police-community relationships or planning issues, there has been a patronising attitude, a "we know what is best for you" attitude by those in authority which robs people of their dignity and calls in question their integrity as human beings. A constant questioning of motives and attitudes is necessary if the situation is not to resolve itself into a 'them and us' conflict in which local people express themselves in questions like 'who cared before the riots?'; 'who wanted to listen to the voice of Moss Side before the violence?' or 'are job creation schemes just a move to keep the lid on?'!

I believe that the role of the Church is to enable and sustain the ministry of love with the poor and disadvantaged who are at the margins of society. The disquieting and discomforting thing about this view is that the poor and disadvantaged challenge the understanding and living out of the faith at its most vulnerable point. It is too easy to dismiss the poor as undeserving and to send them away in self-righteous indignation and pride. To succeed, we must penetrate, with humility, to the heart of the problem of interdependence and to develop an appropriate style of ministry and suitable training to achieve it. This brings us to the paradox that the great strength of the parish system is also its greatest potential weakness, for 'parochialism' can sound the death knell of vision. We wish the poor parishes would 'go away' for they challenge the values of comfortable self-sufficiency. Like the poor, they will not go away for it is there that the pursuit of true humanity in the name of God is to be found, at least until the Kingdom comes.

Part Two

THE CHURCH OF ENGLAND AND PUBLIC POLICY

INTRODUCTION

This section of the volume concentrates on the specific contribution that the Church of England makes in four particular areas of public policy. Collectively they illustrate in concrete terms the extent to which the Church can and does exert political influence, the manner in which that influence is brought to bear and the consequences discernible in political and governmental actions. Obviously, four case studies cannot necessarily be taken as definitive – there is no discussion of the fields of family and sexual law for example. Nevertheless, they do as a group depict the differential leverage and involvement of the Church in public policy. To that extent they can be considered to sketch in outline the nature of the Church's political entanglements at a very practical level.

The first of these contributions is by John Elford on nuclear defence policy, a subject recognised by many as raising perhaps the most pressing issue facing the world today – its very survival. As he points out, in 1945 the Church 'found itself with a very different attitude towards political and military matters from that which it had often previously held', an attitude both more outspoken and more critical of the use of force. The specific matter of nuclear weapons came onto the Church's own agenda in 1946 partly as a result of a British Council of Churches' initiative, but it was not until 1948 that a full debate took place. As on later occasions, the result was a division of opinion in the Church Assembly. In 1963 a further report was called for, again in collaboration with the British Council of Churches, but to little apparent effect.

Part of the problem, as one contributor to a subsequent debate in 1974 pointed out, was that the issue was being dealt with at too abstract and anodyne a level. Only specific, concrete but potentially divisive contributions would have any discernible influence on the decisions of Government. In recognition of the point, an expert and ecumenical committee was set up in 1980 to provide the basis on which the Church might 'participate more effectively in public debates on these issues'.

171

The result was the now famous 'Church and the Bomb Report' debated in the General Synod in early 1983 and carried live on television – the first time that had ever happened. Unfortunately, the consequence of it attempting to be highly specific in its analysis and recommendations was a deep division in the Synod and, indeed, the rejection of the Report. However, merely by producing a document close to (though not actually endorsing) the unilateralist position, the Church has played an influential part in opening up a serious dialogue between Government and its critics where little had taken place before. But the price for the Church was to clearly demonstrate the lack of any internal consensus on the issue and therefore the urgent need for the development of a political theology that would command the united support of its adherents. Nevertheless, at least the Church was seen by Christians and non-Christians alike as attempting to grapple very seriously with something right at the top of the nation's political agenda.

The chapter by Kenneth Leech on Immigration and Race Relations Policy makes the observation that in this area too the Church did not until recently try to work out its position and then take a stand. Until late in the 1960s, he says, it was virtually a non-issue to the Church even though the matter had first been raised as early as 1910. So when in the late 1950s immigration from the Commonwealth sharply increased, 'many West Indians testified to the coldness or positive hostility which they encountered in Anglican Churches'. The leadership of the Church in his view, had allowed 'the issue of racial prejudice' . . . to be 'passed over or trivialized'. Very slowly, however, the size of the problem forced the subject up the Church's agenda until, in 1977, 'the first major debate on race in the (General) Synod' took place. Even so, as the writer wryly notes, 'during the debate, an observer noted that there were only two non-white faces in the Synod itself and seven in the packed public gallery'. In the following year, Margaret Thatcher also raised the issue of immigration controls stressing 'the need for a clear end to immigration'. This was then reiterated in her 1979 election campaign speeches. For once, a significant minority within the Church's episcopal leadership publicly rebuked her. 'It was an important stage in the developing rift between

Anglican thinking on race and the Conservative Government'
and, indeed, is an example of the latent tensions between the
Synod and the Parliamentary Conservative Party which was so
forcibly vented on the proposals for liturgical reform.

As a culmination to the Church's debates about race, in 1980
the appointment of a Race Relations Field Officer was approved
and funded, to be connected with the Board for Social
Responsibility (BSR). The first holder of the post is, in fact, the
writer of this chapter. Since then, a variety of activities has been
initiated from this bureaucratic base. These have been aimed at
the local level of the Church, at other Christian and interested
secular groups and, not least, at public policy, most notably the
British Nationality Act of 1981. But, despite intense pressure both
in the House of Lords and in other quarters, 'Government policy
has not essentially changed'. On the other hand, as Leech points
out, measured in other terms there have been some tangible
effects and some less easy to measure. Thus, through the
Church's auspices a fund has been set up to help pay for the legal
expenses in naturalizing immigrants and it has also been
involved in deportation cases with some success. Yet, interestingly, he argues that 'probably the principal value of the
Church's witness . . . has been that it has helped to increase
consciousness in the nation ... which will in time help to bring
the present racist legislation to an end'.

Valuable though this is, he concludes by calling for more
'positive action' both structurally and individually. Part of the
problem he feels, is that 'theology in the Church of England . . .
reflects the values and asumptions of a white, middle-class, male
clerical culture'. What is required, in short, is a theology
through which a broadscale attack on social injustice can be
mounted. But even with this, 'the Church is likely to fight shy
of open confrontation' with the 'powerful forces' such action
might generate. It is at this point that the dilemmas of consensus
and division, prophecy and support may become particularly
acute. The next chapter by Robert Waddington on educational
policy may appear to lack the immediacy of the moral challenge
presented to the Church in the field of race relations, but its very
substantial historical investment in education has led it into a
more continuous and entrenched contribution than in any other

field of public policy. With 6,000 schools, the Church 'cannot escape a degree of political debate, encounter and sometimes confrontation with those (who) . . . organize publicly-funded education'. At the same time, he rightly recognizes that there are moral issues to be faced in this area 'what is our vision of human maturity? . . . what kind of model of society have we in mind? and . . . what is the place of the educational process in providing answers?' The big difference, however, is that, in education, 'the Church actually implements policy through its own involvement as a partner in the system'. It is not (as often the case with social policy in general) merely a commentator or critic acting from the side-lines. This position gives the Church very considerable potential and actual influence over educational policy, but it also imposes on it the obligation to exhaust all these private channels of representation before 'becoming publicly vocal on difficult issues'.

This chapter also well illustrates the difficulties facing the Church in taking advantage of these opportunities. As Waddington points out, there is a relatively diffused authority within the Church over its educational efforts. The Board of Education itself may try to represent the Church to the Department of Education and Science but its internal role is principally advisory. Actual operational control is exercised by the schools themselves in consultaion with their respective diocesan education committees. And then there is the National Society itself which, although moving into close collaboration with the Board in 1975, formed more of 'a marriage . . . than a merger'. The consequence of all this is sometimes to create misunderstandings with the Church's secular partners when binding decisions have to be made.

Even so, the Education Committees in local government welcome a wide-ranging participation of the diocesan Education Directors in shaping their educational policy. This illustrates very concretely what can be done by the Church in a very important sector of governmental action. As Waddington says, the Church can bring vision and idealism to an otherwise pragmatic, incremental and bureaucratic process. But even this contribution, if properly sustained, in turn may entail a reallocation of, or a strain on, existing Church resources, the potential for compromise with secular norms, a certain loss of distinctiveness and possibly being party to the side-stepping of awkward issues.

Several of the themes raised about education also appear in the chapter by John Sleeman on economic policy. He points out that in matters of general economic doctrine the Church has not one view but several – encouraged by its non-authoritarian ethos and the diversity of its membership. At a general philosophical level he calls these views respectively, the social-catholic, individualist-evangelical and conservative perspectives. The first of these he traces back through Ronald Preston and William Temple to F.D. Maurice and the Oxford Movement. Their aims are to derive 'middle axioms', a set of principles specific enough to provide a policy for practical issues yet not so specific that God is spuriously claimed to be on the side of one very particular option rather than another. Thinking of this sort influenced Anglican debates in nuclear defence issues as John Elford pointed out in Chapter 8. As in that case, this tradition is 'often . . . shared by many with a broad humanist background'. It is presumably for this reason, as well as for its collectivistic and socially critical emphases, that a 'conservative' reaction has arisen. But, as Sleeman points out, all perspectives, including the conservative, are never 'based solely on pure theology, since the way we look at God and his purposes is influenced' by background factors not necessarily entirely of Christian prove-nance. This question of social constraint is, of course, a fundamental issue which must be tackled head on if the Church is to form an effective consensus around prophetic pronounce-ments on public policy that are themselves specific enough to make any difference.

So far, he finds few instances in which Governmental action has been changed but, at the same time, the Church has had a 'pervasive effect' on the 'prevailing ... ethos', not least in its contribution to the construction of the post-war consensus on social welfare and a mixed economy. As that consensus has now to some degree broken down, there is hardly room for complacency. But, he concludes, 'the Church is alive and thinking . .. the voice of its spokesmen is heard and respected, even if not always agreed with'.

Chapter 8

THE CHURCH AND NUCLEAR DEFENCE POLICY

John Elford

8.1: Introduction

Members of the General Synod of the Church of England have no better reason for looking upwards than when they meet in Church House, Westminster. There, glittering above them, is the haunting sentiment: 'Holy is the true light and passing wonderful, lending radiance to them that endured in the heat of the conflict'. In matters of defence and disarmament, many of those who have to so endure sit in their own chamber across the road from Church House. The upward gaze thus raises the fundamental question about the relationship of the true light to political responsibilities.

In 1945, the Church of England, along with other British Churches, found itself with a very different attitude towards political and military matters from that which it had often previously held. This attitude, for example, had been succinctly expressed through the writings and ministry of William Temple. In a broadcast address in August 1939, when he was Archbishop of York, Temple expressed the view that :"No positive good can be done by force; that is true. But evil can be checked and held back by force, and it is precisely for this that we may be called upon to use it." With such words, Temple spoke not only for Christians, he also showed himself to be a national leader who spoke for others. In 1942 he published *Christianity and the Social Order*, just before he was translated from the Archbishopric of York to that of Canterbury. In this widely read and immediately influential work, Temple vigorously urged the Churches to enter spheres of social, political and economic thought where, previously, religion had been regarded as a trespasser. Temple's work ended tragically with his

176

unexpected death in 1944, but it had the effect of preparing both the Churches and the political establishment for a much closer Christian engagement with political and military issues than had often previously been the case. One result was that, with the dawn of the nuclear age, the Churches were at least initially prepared for a thorough-going engagement with the issues it presented. It is a commonplace today to view questions about the morality of nuclear defence and disarmament as being of paramount importance. But such a view has been taken by the Churches, along with others, with varying degrees of intensity since 1945. In this chapter, I will examine the nature of its debates about the issue and will also consider their relation to historical and technological developments as well as something of their wider influence on, and reaction to, public opinion and government policy.

In its debate about nuclear defence policy, the Church of England has brought a number of specific approaches to bear. It has invariably, but not exclusively, been ecumenical. This has meant that it has worked closely, both with other Christian bodies (particularly the British Council of Churches) and with individuals from other Churches whenever they have been thought to have specific spiritual, theological or technical advice to offer. It has also availed itself of secular opinions particularly when, as in the debate about nuclear defence policy, much revolves around the nature of thermonuclear weaponry and the manner of its deployment in the strategies of its possessors.

8.2: The Origins of the Nuclear Debate

The sense of relief and jubilation which followed the end of the Second World War was clouded by a ghastly realisation: that the nuclear bombs used at Hiroshima and Nagasaki had, in the words of Professor Oliphant, "blown to pieces the world of disinterested science". The power they unleashed heralded the dawn of a new age which offered a blessing and a sword. The blessing was the promise of the use of nuclear energy for peaceful purposes and the sword was its use in weapons of war. There was urgent need to understand them both.

Hence, in 1945, the British Council of Churches (B.C.C.) appointed a commission to consider the problems created by the discovery of atomic energy. Under the chairmanship of Dr. J.H. Oldham, the commission published its findings in *The Era of Atomic Power* in May 1946. The Church Assembly of the Church of England debated this in June and tentatively approved of its findings, but expressed the view that more information was necessary before it would make up its mind about problems arising from the military uses of atomic power. A new commission was appointed, to obtain this information, by the Archbishops of Canterbury and York. Under the chairmanship of Dr. E.G. Selwyn, the Dean of Winchester, it published its findings in *The Church and the Atom* in 1948. Its aim was to achieve an 'other worldly worldliness' which had been called for in the previous B.C.C. Report. It recognised, bluntly, that 'civilisation is confronted today with the possibility of its own self-destruction' and it aspired to understand this fact in the light of 'the distinctive approach of Anglican thought and theology'.[1]

Arguing that any attempt to understand the present dilemmas must be put in an historical perspective, the Report claimed that secular history and Biblical theology complemented each other. It held that this is the foundation of the Biblical view, common to both the Old and the New Testaments, that God is the Lord of history and that its events reveal the nature of his judgements. It concluded this by noting Arnold Toynbee's insight that the causes of the decay of civilisations were invariably internal ones and by claiming that the present generation 'should come to interpret its misery as God's wrath, and to realise that this wrath is the index of its own desperate need of the Spirit of Love'.[2]

Against this background, the Report discussed the ethical problems raised by the discovery of the atomic bomb. The morality of the laws of war are discussed in Chapters 2 and 3, in an attempt to show just how closely Christian theology has engaged itself with questions of war and peace. The Report concludes that atomic weapons must be considered in the same category as all the weapons of modern warfare; conventional bombs, chemical, bacteriological and biological weapons.

[1] *The Church and the Atom*, (Church Assembly, 1948), p. 6.
[2] *The Church and the Atom*, p. 22.

Claiming that military opinion supported such ethical insight, the Report argues that weapons which are indiscrimate and disproportionate in their use are not only wrong from a moral point of view, they are also bad weapons. So understood, it is not admissable to use atomic bombs in attacks upon military objectives in inhabited cities. However, the Report did allow that they 'may be used in circumstances that do not oblige to the same discrimination – for instance, against an isolated armaments plant, a fleet at sea, a system of fortification or a concentration of armour'.[3] Necessity might permit this as the militarily most efficient and morally acceptable means to a desired end.

Drawing heavily on a discussion of natural law, the Report concludes that '. . . a lawyer would not be justified in giving it as his professional opinion that the use of atomic bombs or other highly destructive agencies is positively forbidden by the laws of war as they stand today'.[4] This does not mean, however, that Christians are obliged to participate in any act of war which they believe to be morally wrong. Applying these conclusions to events in the recent (1939-45) war, the Report concludes that 'the "obliteration" bombing of whole cities with high-capacity and incendiary bombs, the success of which is measured by the number of acres devastated, must be condemned. . . (as) an act of wholesale destruction that cannot be justified'.[5]

As to whether the atomic bombs dropped on Hiroshima and Nagasaki could be justified, members of the commission were divided. A majority did not accept the apologies for their use which were put forward by Mr. Henry Stimpson, the U.S. Secretary for War from 1940-45, in an article in *Harpers Magazine* which was printed in an abridged form in *The Daily Telegraph* on February 14th 1947. They, therefore, implicitly held that the bombing was immoral and ought not to have taken place. Others, however, felt that they were not in a position to pass such a judgement and refused to do so without qualification. They were unsure about rejecting the reasons given by

[3] *The Church and the Atom*, p. 45.
[4] *The Church and the Atom*, p. 71.
[5] *The Church and the Atom*, p. 43.

Stimpson for the military and technical need for not giving warnings before the attacks.

The Report made passing reference to the deployment of atomic bombs as deterrents to attack, on the grounds that 'such warning might go far to prevent the abuse of atomic weapons'.[6] The unanimity of the commission's findings was challenged by the dissent of one of its members, the Ven. P. Harthill, the Archdeacon of Stoke-on-Trent. In a Minority Note he explained that he did not wish to dissent from much of the Report's content, particularly the findings on the historical and Biblical background. His principal objection was that Chapter Two on the 'Morality of Warfare' was too preoccupied with legal questions and paid insufficient attention to Christian tradition, ignoring much of Christ's teaching particularly the Sermon on the Mount. He also believed that the Report lacked realism in the sense that it did not fully recognise the implications of the present situation, in relation to which the Report was too academic. He held the view that the enquiry should have started not from the point of view of tradition and the Just War, but with 'the actual facts of modern war and consider them *de novo* in the light of the New Testament revelation of the character and will of God'.[7]

As a tract of its time, *The Church and the Atom* reflects the uncertainties and perplexities of its age, but it does show that, with scholarly care, Christianity has the resources to produce an 'other worldly worldliness' in which it is able to ignore neither its spiritual and moral resources, nor the worldly events which challenge them. Much of its discussion still stands as a model of its type and it was perspicacious in identifying issues which were later to assume far greater importance; that of nuclear deterrence, that of the relation of atomic to conventional weapons and that of subjecting scientific technology to social policy.

The Church and the Atom was published only under the authority of the signatories of the commission which produced it. Before it could be described as the view of the Church of England it had to be debated and this took place in its General Assembly on the 9th and 10th of November 1948. Dr. Selwyn

[6] *The Church and the Atom*, p. 52.
[7] *The Church and the Atom*, p. 115.

opened the debate. After outlining its contents and making attempts to counter some criticisms which had been made since its publication, he pleaded that the Assembly should face the facts, ugly as some of them were and in so doing enable the Church to make a contribution to both the defence of the country and the peace of the world. Archdeacon Harthill followed this with a presentation of the reasons for his partial dissent. The debate was then divided between those who, like the Report, acknowledged the evils of such indiscriminate and disproportionate weapons of war, yet allowed that some uses of some atomic weapons might not be among them and others, like Archdeacon Harthill, who rejected the possibility of giving the assent of the Church of England to their use, claiming that it could never be in accord with the will of God.

Bishop Bell of Chichester included himself among the latter, arguing that the Report's willingness to allow the manufacture and deployment of atomic bombs, as well as their use in dire necessity, added up to the unacceptable paradox that necessity knew no law. Whilst he hoped that the Report would be received as a valuable essay in history and politics, he urged the Assembly not to approve of its findings since they were both unreal and alarming. Other speakers followed Bell in his further claim that the Report had laid too much emphasis on law and not enough on the Christian ethic, claiming that the latter prohibited what the former allowed. One speaker, Dr. Bryn Thomas, said that, since the publication of the Report and of the fact that he was to speak in the debate, he had received no less than one hundred and eighty three separate petitions from individuals and corporate bodies who had urged him to make sure that the Report's findings did not become the official opinion of the Church of England. All such opposition focused on paragraph six of the Report's conclusion which advocated '. . . that in certain circumstances defensive "necessity" might justify (the use of atomic weapons) against an unscrupulous aggressor'.[8]

In the outcome of the debate, it was decided by a remarkably small majority of 211 votes to 209 'that the Assembly commends

[8] *The Church and the Atom*, p. 111.

the Report to the earnest attention of the Church together with the Report of the British Council of Churches Commission entitled *The Era of Atomic Power*. Since the alternative to so commending it was to refer it back, the indication of this vote was that the Assembly was evenly divided. What is not clear from the records of the debate is whether this close division of opinion was solely over the issue of approving the possible use of atomic bombs in carefully defined circumstances. Towards the end of the debate, some contributors had objected to commending the B.C.C. Report along with *The Church and the Atom*. This might have caused some to vote against the motion who would otherwise have voted for it, thereby approving of the limited use of nuclear weapons.

8.3: The Nuclear Debate and its Context in the 1950s and 1960s

It is, of course, important to remember that, in spite of the then recent uses of atomic bombs at Hiroshima and Nagasaki, there were no foreseen circumstances which portended their further use. The U.S.A. was the only state which possessed them and, as a result of its Atomic Energy Act of 1946, it was reluctant to share its nuclear technology with other countries including Britain, in spite of the previous collaboration between the two countries in the Manhattan Project which produced the first atomic bomb. The Baruch Plan, under which the U.S.A. proposed to destroy its atomic bombs and place nuclear energy under international control, was approved by the U.N. but rejected by the U.S.S.R., which carried out its first atomic test explosion in 1949.

In 1954, the repeal of the U.S. Atomic Energy Act began a new period of collaboration with Britain. Britain had already tested her first atomic device at Monte Bello in Australia on 3rd October 1952. The first British atomic weapons were free fall bombs carried by the medium-range jet V-bombers: Victor, Valiant and Vulcan. These were later equipped with Blue Steel 'glide bombs'. The planned replacement of which, by the Blue Streak missile, was eventually cancelled because of rapidly escalating costs. Instead, Britain collaborated with the U.S.A. on the Skybolt missile system which was intended to extend the strategic life of the V-bomber force.

In 1962, the U.S.A. decided unilaterally to scrap Skybolt much to the consternation of Britain. This was soon overcome by an agreement, reached at Nassau in December of 1962, between President Kennedy and Prime Minister Macmillan, which effectively settled the nature of Britain's nuclear defence policy for the next three decades. It provided for cooperation over the Polaris submarine-launched ballistic missile system (S.L.B.M.). Britain was to manufacture, with American help in design, the submarines and the warheads and America was to manufacture the delivery systems. The political difficulty which this agreement exacerbated was that America was seen to be giving Britain preferential cooperative opportunities just when it was denying its other allies any right to independent nuclear forces of their own. How independent was the British Polaris force to be? Mindful of this difficulty, Macmillan secured an agreement at Nassau that Her Majesty's Government would not use Polaris, even against American requests to do so, if it thought that its supreme national interests were at stake. This agreement revived the public debate about the wisdom of Britain's continued possession of an independent nuclear deterrent.

In April of 1963, the British Council of Churches resolved to study the question as a matter of urgency and within six months of doing so it published *The British Nuclear Deterrent*. It was debated by the B.C.C. immediately. The outcome was the approval of a resolution which called for the limitation of the control of nuclear weapons by independent nations in the hope that 'more effective machinery can be established for shared control of the deterrent in any part of the world and so the proliferation of national nuclear forces can be halted'.[9] The resolution also supported the view that it was intolerable that there should be any question of the West using thermonuclear weapons first. Finally, the Report was commended to the member Churches for further study.

[9]*The British Nuclear Deterrent*, (London: S.C.M., 1963), p. 6.

The Church of England undertook this in a debate in its Church Assembly a few weeks later, when it amended a somewhat general resolution about the need for Christians to work for peace in the nuclear age by including an intention to debate the issue more thoroughly in its Spring session in 1964. In that debate, the Bishop of Chichester argued that all Christians should repudiate nuclear warfare even though they might disagree about how best to do so. He hoped, however, that they might achieve a sufficient consensus of opinion on this which would enable them to make an effective impact upon public opinion and government policies. To achieve this, they would not only have to approve of general principles, they would also have to consider what their application would mean in some detail. The Church should not only will and pray for peace, it should also evaluate and support the particular political measures which could be expected to bring this about. The outcome of the debate was the approval of a motion which endorsed the conclusion of *The British Nuclear Deterrent,* along with an amendment which claimed that 'the use of indiscrimate weapons must now be condemned as an affront to the creator and a denial of the very purposes of his creation'.

The Church of England addressed itself, briefly, to the question of nuclear weapons in *International Morality an Agenda for the Churches* which was published in February 1969. This was originally prepared by the Committee on Migration and International Affairs of the Board for Social Responsibility, to assist the Bishops attending the Lambeth Conference in 1968. It accepted nuclear deterrence as an accomplished fact which it neither analyses nor evaluates. It is simply noted that such weapons have the effect of preventing their possessors from engaging directly in local conflicts such as the Arab/Israeli war of June 1967. It stressed, however, that it was in the interests of all 'to cease the development of nuclear weapons, to stop the trend in the direction of the proliferation of ownership of these weapons'[10] and to reduce their numbers. The Report called for a ban on the testing of nuclear weapons and for the creation of

[10]*International Morality: an Agenda for the Churches* (London: C.I.O., 1969), p. 13.

non-proliferation agreements which included proper safeguards provided by regular inspection. It further approved of Britain's signing of the Non-Proliferation Treaty in 1968 and called for international consultation 'concerning the potential use of these weapons, leading to international control of them'.[11] However, this Report does little more than express what were then the common hopes of most people about the deployment and control of nuclear weapons. It is not at all critical of specific policies and it was never officially debated by the Church of England.

8.4:   The 1970s

In 1974, the Board for Social Responsibility of the Church of England published *Force in the Modern World*. It included the texts of two recent British Council of Churches Reports: *The Search for Security* and *Non-Violent Action*. It was debated, along with the World Council of Churches' statement *Violence, Non-Violence and the Struggle for Social Justice*, on 6th November 1974. As would be expected with such a rich agenda, the debate was wide-ranging to the point of being bland. Issue after issue was raised and none of them was analysed.

The outcome was the approval of a motion which commended the various documents for further study and expressed support for those engaged in the European Security Conference and the Strategic Arms Limitation Talks (S.A.L.T.). With this, the Synod clearly felt that it had done its job, but there was one voice of protest. It was that of Professor A.T. Hanson of the University of Hull, a member for the Province of York. 'We', he bluntly but correctly interjected, 'are wasting our time and making ourselves look foolish. . .we are only showing ourselves totally out of touch with reality if we think that by passing motions of high moral content with which we can all agree we shall affect anything whatsoever.'

This interjection was totally ignored in the debate, but it summed up the situation. Specificity of resolution in the Synod

[11] *International Morality: an Agenda for the Churches*, p. 13.

would be sure to lead to divisions among its membership. To avoid this, unanimity was sought but at a price: that of rendering the Synod virtually irrelevant as a forum for serious debates about nuclear defence. No one doubted the integrity of its concern. No one could fail to observe its moral awareness. But no one took other than polite notice of what it said.

The reason why it was capable of acting as it did in the early 1970s was probably because, like the British public at large, it tacitly supported the nuclear defence policies of successive British Governments. The Campaign for Nuclear Disarmament was, by then, past what many thought until recently to be the peak of its impact.

But three things then happened to trouble this quiescence in the minds of many. The first was the early failure of the Mutual Balanced Force Reduction talks. They had not resulted, as they still have not, in any perceivable reductions in the levels of nuclear weapons deployed, and official claims that if those talks had not taken place then more weapons would have been deployed than there actually were could not be verified. The second was that new generations of nuclear weapons, particularly tactical ones, for use in battlefield engagements and theatre ones for use over areas of up to 2,000 miles, had a use credibility which made it increasingly clear that although they were deployed as deterrents, the possibility of their use was clearly contemplated. Talk emerged about thinking the unthinkable, about fighting and winning nuclear engagements. The third was the related fact that previous distinctions between types of nuclear weapons, which had been thought to entail the fact that the limited uses of battlefield ones would not automatically lead to an escalating and uncontrollable nuclear war, were being blurred.

The result was that many believed that the N.A.T.O. policy, of the early first use of tactical nuclear weapons in the face of an uncontainable attack on Central Europe by Warsaw Pact conventional forces, had the effect of lowering the nuclear threshold which presented the danger of inaugurating an escalating nuclear conflict and which would then lead to all-out nuclear war. Concerns like these lay behind the resurgence of peace movements such as C.N.D., and helped to prompt the rapid politicization of issues about peace and disarmament in public discussion. It was against such a background that the Church of England was prompted to undertake its own first major consideration of the issue since 1948.

In January 1978, the International Affairs Committee of the Church of England's Board for Social Responsibility rejected the view that nuclear unilateralism was the required response of Christians to the growing dilemma. In order to explore the implications of such a view, it set up a working party to examine the issue. Under the Chairmanship of Admiral E.F. Gueritz, the Director of Studies at the Royal United Services Institution, twenty one participants set to work. This was immediately made difficult by bad weather, a rail strike and the General Election, which coincided with a planned residential meeting which was cancelled. The group met on very few occasions and always in plenary session, except for one occasion when some of the theologians met for a separate discussion. This was prompted by the fact that they were concerned that the working party was not giving enough time or attention to the theological issues in the plenary sessions.

The outcome was published in July 1979: *Christians in a Violent World: Defence and Disarmament*. This was written ably but not consultatively by the secretariat to the working party. Members of the working party were not given adequate time to comment fully on the drafts in preparation, partly because the Report was urgently required for a debate in the General Synod in the month of its publication.

The Report itself stated, bluntly, that the view that the Church has no business concerning itself with political issues 'reveals a lack of comprehension'[12] and thereby presumed that a direct engagement with such issues was its proper concern. It overlooked in this presumption the fact that, granted the Church's right to so engage itself, there remains a wide area of debate about what form it should take. This debate was considered by a subsequent working party and will be mentioned below. The general aim of the Report was to clarify the issues at stake so that Christians, who neither accept uncon-

[12]*Christians in a Violent World*, p. 4.

ditionally the arguments for the escalation of the deployment of nuclear weapons nor advocate renouncing them unilaterally, could decide on proper courses of action in the hope of guiding their representatives in secular government.

Christian pacifism, which was vociferously represented in the meetings of the working party, is briefly considered as requiring the adherence of all Christians to the power of self-giving love. This, in turn, requires the outright rejection of the view that political power depends upon military power and the acceptance of the consequences of such a rejection. No consideration is given in the Report to the fact that Christian pacifism takes a number of forms which include differing attitudes towards the status of non-pacifist Christianity, as well as differing attitudes to the way in which the ultimate aim of pacifism should be pursued. Pacifism, as the Report briefly defines it, is rejected as being inapplicable to the real world. Against this, it is accepted that a government's first duty is to provide the means of securing and maintaining the freedom of its people, not only by reacting militarily against aggression when it occurs, but also by preventing such aggression from occurring at all. The Report notes, in support of this view, the consequences of the failure to do this of previous British governments in 1914 and 1939. Armed preparedness through the collective security of N.A.T.O. is approved and its success at keeping the peace in Western Europe since 1945 is cited as evidence of its rightness.

Frequent claims that such an argument leads inevitably to the desire of non-nuclear states to become nuclear, are not even considered. Furthermore, the doctrine of nuclear deterrence is cited as being the best way to implement the spirit of the pronouncements of the Lambeth Conference of Bishops which claimed in 1930 (endorsed in 1948 and 1968) that 'war as a method of settling international disputes is incompatible with the teaching and example of our Lord Jesus Christ'. The Report adds that such a rejection of nuclear unilateralism leaves no room for complacency since, although it acknowledges that some progress has been made in the disarmament of biological and chemical weapons, as well as in the atmospheric testing of nuclear weapons, it recognises that no effective nuclear disarmament had yet taken place. On the contrary, it recognises that the relative velocity of the arms race is now getting completely out of hand.

It is at this point of its argument that many later claimed to detect its main weakness. It turned from this discussion, ignored its implications, and distinguished disarmament from peace. It argued with some cogency that peace must precede disarmament because it alone can create the milieu in which disarmament can take place. This, it added, is a fundamental point which has for too long been neglected. Paradoxically, however, it is then claimed that the way of creating peace is the way of 'arming to parley'. Difficulties which some Christians have when such arming includes nuclear weapons are, at this weakest point of the argument, only alluded to. The discussion then turns to an evaluation of the international trade in conventional armaments and a consideration of the peaceful uses of military forces. In both cases constructive suggestions are made, particularly about the need for non-proliferation treaties in the world-wide arms trade. What the Report fails to do is to examine the moral and theological issues which relate to the deployment of nuclear weapons as deterrents and to the possibility of their use in war fighting.

The Report was discussed by the General Synod of the Church of England, the successor to the National Assembly, on 5th July 1979. It came under criticism for not giving adequate attention to the moral and theological issues arising from its admission that any use of British nuclear weapons would inevitably cause the deaths of innocent civilians. The ostensible reason given in the debate for this failure, was the speed with which the Synod itself had required the Report to be produced. But two further reasons lay behind this failure. The first was the Report's general tone which arose from the fact that it was written to support conclusions which the International Affairs Committee had previously and separately arrived at. The second was that the working party did not create the means whereby drafts of the Report could be adequately criticised and amended. The result of this, as the Bishop of Birmingham pointed out in the debate, was that the Report defended the *status quo* by simply pointing out the inadequacies of pacifism as an alternative, when it should have tackled the very real complexities which are encountered in attempts to relate Christian moral and theological insights to the political and military institutions of a fallen world. At the end of the debate, the Report was simply 'taken note of ', which meant that the Synod, whilst finding it inadequate, did not reject it.

Two issues then arose, both of which were to be taken further. The first was the question of the international trade in arms. In a Synod debate in February 1980, a motion was passed by a large majority of 192 to 23 requesting more public information about the trade; that arms not be sold to governments which deny basic human rights and that studies be made about the possible redeployment of those currently engaged in the manufacture of such arms. The second issue was a call for a further study of 'how the theological debate relating to discipleship in this field might be more effectively and purposefully conducted throughout the Church of England in the light of the witness and insight of the whole ecumenical movement'. This was approved and the way lay open for a further study of nuclear weapons and of the manner of their deployment.

8.5:   *The Church and the Bomb*

The General Synod resolved in February 1980, that the Board for Social Responsibility should '. . .explore how the theological debate relating to discipleship in this field might be more effectively and purposefully conducted.' The result was the setting up, in July 1980, of a small working party under the chairmanship of the Rev. John Austin Baker, then the Rector of St. Margaret's Westminster and Chaplain to the House of Commons, who subsequently became the Bishop of Salisbury. It had five other members and a secretary who also contributed to its work. Membership of the working party was ecumenical, it included a Quaker, a Roman Catholic and a member with no particular Christian affiliation, but they were invited more for their expertise as for their non-Anglicanism. Its brief was: to study the implications for Christian discipleship of the acceptance by the major military powers of the role of thermonuclear weapons in their strategy; to consider the bearing of this on the adequacy of past Christian teaching and ethical analysis regarding the conduct of war, and to advise the Board for Social Responsibility on ways in which members of the Churches can be helped to participate more effectively in public debate on these issues. The concern of the working party was to produce a Report, of some length if necessary, which met this brief by doing three things: producing an outline of the nature of thermonuclear weaponry and of the manner of its deployment in the strategies of its possessors; setting out the Christian theology in the light of which it could be evaluated, and assessing the acceptability or otherwise of various policy options for peace. It was realised that, in fulfilling the third part of this intention, it would not be possible to ensure unanimity of agreement among all Christian people and that this regrettably was unavoidable if the Report was to achieve the level of specificity required of it. What mattered was that views and opinions which were rejected should be represented and evaluated thoroughly and fairly.

To assist this, the working party received evidence from individuals and organizations which had either expertise – scientific, military and political – or who represented particular views as to what Christians ought to think about the problems. Each member was given the task of drafting material for the final text and it was by no means clear at the beginning what the conclusion would be. Two members were well-known pacificists, two others had previously at least supported the need for a nuclear element in defence strategy and the remainder were uncommitted. In the course of the study, all showed a willingness to respond to the accumulating evidence and information.

As the work progressed, a conclusion was arrived at which received unanimous agreement, namely that the use of nuclear weapons in war fighting could not be justified from a Christian point of view. Principally, this was because, unlike conventional weapons, they caused deaths from radiation a part of which, after a nuclear explosion, went into the upper atmosphere and was subsequently distributed in a manner which could not be predicted, causing further deaths as well as long-term genetic damage to human beings and virtually unalterable harm to the environment. This scale of destruction meant that the explosion of nuclear weapons would be *indiscriminate* and, therefore, unsuitable for use against specific military targets. In addition, they would, in all probability, be *disproportionate* in scale to the good of any end which might be sought by using them. 'It is in our view proven beyond reasonable doubt that the Just War theory, as this has developed in Western Civilization and within the Christian Church, rules out the use of nuclear weapons.'[13]

The next question which was faced was: does this conclusion rule out the possession of nuclear weapons as deterrents to nuclear war? The working party believed that this was the crucial question, since many well-informed and sincere people believed that the answer to it was 'no' and that such deterrence was the *only* way to secure peace in the nuclear age. After much deliberation, the working party disagreed with this conclusion, largely because any deployment of nuclear weapons as deterrents could not rule out the possibility of their use. This meant that nuclear deterrence theory could not leave out of account a contemplation of the consequences of its failure, especially in view of the fact that modern generations of nuclear weapons were designed and deployed to deter because of the credibility of their use. Because of this, it was concluded that 'the nuclear element in deterrence is no longer a reliable or morally acceptable approach to the future of the world'.[14]

It was at this stage of its enquiry that the working party could have settled for the putting forward of a general conclusion which would have expressed their view and indicated the direction in which they hoped the defence policy of nuclear weapons states might go. An example would be a statement like: 'Because it is believed that both the use and the possession and deployment with an intention to use nuclear weapons is unacceptable to the Christian conscience, governments are urged to dispose of them.'

To have done this would have been to accord with a view about how the Church should exercise its political witness which has been advocated by Dr. J.H. Oldham and others ever

[13] *The Church and the Bomb* (London: Hodder & Stoughton, 1982), p. 143.
[14] *The Church and the Bomb*, p. 154.

since the Oxford Conference on 'Church, Community & State' in 1937. What the Church must do, it claimed, is not to engage itself in discussing the rightness or otherwise of detailed policy options. It should, rather, confine itself to general statements which express its views relating to them. Such statements are described as 'middle axioms'. Although they have much to commend them and although claims about their rightness have recently been made again, the working party eschewed this option on the grounds that Churches should concern themselves with the means as well as the ends of their statements of policy.[15] This meant that policy options for peace had to be evaluated in the hope of finding one which could be supported as that which, if acted upon, would be most likely to bring the moral conclusion to bear on the situation. If it had not faced this question the working party would have failed in its obligation to comment on the ways in which Christian discipleship in the field might be more effectively and purposefully conducted.

Pacificism was considered as a policy option and an attempt was made to do its complexity and subtlety the justice it deserves. Types of pacifism were outlined and separately evaluated. Against the held views of two members of the working party, it was agreed, eventually with them, that pacificism should not be advocated. The force of certain objections to it were thought to be compelling. Briefly, it was held that all forms of pacificism overlook the theological insight that, this side of the Kingdom of God, the exercise of constraint and even, under carefully controlled circumstances the constraint of war, was necessary for the preservation and furtherance of justice and peace.

It was then argued that the notion of deterrence is not itself immoral. It is not morally wrong to deter someone from doing something which it is believed, in all conscience, it would be against their interest and the interest of others for them to do. In spite of this, however, the moral case against nuclear deterrence stood. The policy option of attempting to reduce the levels of nuclear weapons deployed by negotiating from strength and seeking mutual balanced force reductions was considered. It was

[15]Cf., R.H. Preston, *Church and Society in the Late Twentieth Century* (London: S.C.M., 1983), pp. 141-156.

rejected for two reasons. First: because it inevitably leads to leap-frogging and must, therefore, be considered to be at least one of the causes of the nuclear arms race, and second: because the superfluity of nuclear power which results from it makes 'negotiation more and more difficult, and the consequences of a failure of deterrence even more catastrophic'.[16] It was further noted that, although this was the policy pursued by all the major possessors of nuclear weapons, the results which have been achieved by it are meagre to the point of being non-existent. The subsequent ending of both the Intermediate Nuclear Forces negotiations and the Strategic Arms Reduction Talks in Geneva have served, sadly, only to confirm this judgement although their starting again on a new basis is still thought, by many, to hold the prospect of achieving results by multi-lateral means.

The radical alternative to this policy was then considered: that of the total renunciation of all nuclear weapons whatever the consequences. This was thought to be too politically and militarily destabilising to merit serious consideration. Furthermore, it was thought, for this reason, to lie in the realm of fantasy, as no political party in the United Kingdom showed any sign of adopting it as a serious policy option. The Labour Party did advocate it, although not without the demur of some of its senior members, in the 1983 General Election, but its resounding defeat at the polls undoubtedly had something to do with the fact that public opinion did not support such a view. It is still a contentious issue in Labour Party politics.

The next policy option to be considered did, however, receive the unanimous support of the working party and it may be construed as a via media between negotiating from strength and unconditional renunciation. This is the policy of pursuing unilateral disarmament by phasing unilateral stages into it. 'A nuclear weapons state may decide to try to stimulate progress towards multilateral disarmament by getting rid of some of its own nuclear weapons without requiring (as a prior condition) corresponding action from the other side.'[17]

Details of how such an approach might be taken by the British Government are set out among the twenty two policy

[16] *The Church and the Bomb*, p. 132.
[17] *The Church and the Bomb*, p. 133.

recommendations in the working party's Report, *The Church and The Bomb* (Hodder & Stoughton, 1982). It was stressed that the timetable for such a staged withdrawal should be a matter for negotiation between Britain and her allies, but it was stated that the decision to undertake the process should be taken in one political operation. Time did not permit the working party to consider how long it might be before such a programme of staged withdrawal would lead to a nuclear weapons free British defence policy. It is, furthermore, likely that it would have found it difficult to reach agreement on the question. Such opinion as was expressed varied from those who thought it should take place within the lifetime of a Parliament and those who thought it could take up to perhaps fifteen years to complete during which time conventional forces could be strengthened and the terms of the British contribution to the defences of N.A.T.O. be re-negotiated. The working party advocated the continuation of British membership of N.A.T.O. and was mindful of the so-called "Free Rider" objection to its becoming nuclear free.

With this conclusion, the working party believed that, although it would have liked more time to complete its work and although the Report could have been much better than it was, it had, nevertheless, fulfilled its main obligation. It did not claim that the policy option favoured was entirely risk free, but did claim that it was arguably less risky than either continuing as we are, or pursuing wholesale and unconditional nuclear renunciation.

8.6:   The Reaction to *The Church and the Bomb*

The Church and the Bomb was published on 15th October 1982 at a press conference attended by all its contributors. To enable responsible preparation for this, copies were previously circulated to the press and broadcasting agencies. The result was a leak about the conclusions which had been reached which generated considerable public interest and publicity up to two months before publication. During this period, the Report was repeatedly misrepresented as advocating 'unilateral' disarmament, in the sense of total and unconditional renunciation. This was totally incorrect, but it was used, even if unwittingly, to support a then prevailing view that the Church of England was, in several respects, showing itself at odds with the political establishment. In fact, as has been explained, *The Church and the Bomb* wholeheartedly supported the vigorous prosecution of multi-lateral negotiations making this the first of its twenty two policy recommendations.[18] It now remained for it to be seen what the Church's General Synod would make of its recommendations when they were debated in the Spring of the following year.

The debate attracted wide public attention following the publicity given to *The Church and The Bomb*. It was clear from the outset that the favoured policy option, of phased unilateralism within a multilateral framework, would be unlikely to receive overwhelming support. The Bishop of London, then the Chairman of the Board for Social Responsibility, spoke bluntly against it, reflecting reservations which had already been expressed by members of the Board. He did not address himself to the vitally important distinction between phased unilateralism and an all-out total nuclear renunciation whatever the consequences. His argument simply defended the rightness of nuclear deterrence as the only alternative to the way of renunciation, claiming that these were the only two alternatives. 'In the face of this dilemma, there are ultimately two alternatives. One is the way of renunciation. This is the way of the pacifist who endures whatever befalls him rather than use force. . . the alternative way is that of deterrence.' In developing this theme, the Bishop failed to do justice to the fact that *The Church and The Bomb* had based the argument for phased unilateralism on a *rejection* of both pacifism and total unconditional renunciation. In so doing, he introduced into the debate a confusion which ought not to have existed. Phased unilateralism is, as *The Church and The Bomb* makes clear, not in any sense a pacifist policy, in the sense in which he was using the word.

In an influential speech, the Archbishop of Canterbury added his opposition to the Report. He did not believe that phased unilateral gestures, of the kind suggested, would have the

[18] *The Church and the Bomb*, p. 154.

desired effect of getting multilateral disarmament moving. This belief was tersely stated without argument, and was followed by the statement of a fear 'that the kind of action being advocated will actually undermine the negotiations now taking place in Geneva'. He did not note, as he might have done, that British nuclear weapons were, in fact, not a part of those negotiations, which meant that the effect he spoke of would, at the most, be an indirect one. The Archbishop concluded with a plea for the Synod to support the ongoing multilateral negotiations and those engaged in them.

The Bishop of Salisbury then proposed an amendment which gave the Synod the direct opportunity to express its opinion on the conclusion of *The Church and The Bomb*. In speaking to it, he rehearsed again the arguments in favour of phased unilateralism and, in particular, pointed to two fallacies which he believed were distorting the discussion. The first was the fallacy of believing that the prevailing mutual nuclear deterrence created a stability which would continue indefinitely. 'The overwhelming evidence', he added, 'is that mutual nuclear deterrence is becoming less stable year by year and so less plausible as a means of keeping peace.' The second fallacy he attacked was that of supposing that effective deterrence demanded parity. This, he said, was a view which was derived from incorrectly applying to nuclear deterrence a truth which was only applicable to deterrence with conventional, i.e. non-nuclear, weapons. Nuclear weapons functioned as deterrents not because of their parity with the opposing nuclear forces, but because they were capable of inflicting an unacceptable degree of damage if they were used, of being delivered to their targets and of being launched after a pre-emptive first strike by the other side.

He concluded, '. . . once these principles are grasped, it is clear that both East and West have many times more weapons than they need for deterrence, and that either side could cut many systems unilaterally without jeopardising its security in the least. Nor will it be until one side does cut in this way that the other will realise that it is wasting its resources on a mass of technological clutter which gives it no advantage.' He stressed that his amendment was essentially a multilateral one and that it was his belief that the modest unilateralism he was proposing was the most desirable policy option for Christians and others to support.

The Bishop of Birmingham then intervened in the debate out of an awareness that the Synod might respond to an alternative between these two positions. He proved to be correct in this. His amendment made a number of points, the chief of which express support, *pro tem*, for nuclear deterrence and insisted that under no circumstances should N.A.T.O. use nuclear weapons first in any engagement, even on a limited scale. The Synod did not discuss this amendment in detail. If it did so, it would have realised that the N.A.T.O. doctrine of "flexible response" depended upon the early, and possibly first, use of tactical nuclear weapons and that to qualify it by denying such a first use was, in effect, totally to call it into question. At the end of what was for the General Synod a long debate, this amendment was supported by 275 votes to 222 and the Bishop of Salisbury's amendment was defeated by 338 votes to 100. Whereas the Synod had not supported the *status quo* in the way the Bishop of London and the Archbishop of Canterbury, among others, had requested it to do, neither was it ready to endorse the argument of *The Church and The Bomb*.

8.7: The Outcome and the Future of the Debate

The outcome of this debate probably reflects the current state of general opinion in the Church of England about nuclear defence policy. It is opposed to the unilateral renunciation of all nuclear weapons whatever the consequences and it is also uneasy about supporting without qualification the present state of affairs. The subsequent failure of the two sets of talks in Geneva (notwithstanding the prospect of new talks) and the introduction of Cruise missiles into Greenham Common will, doubtless, have caused further unease about supporting the *status quo*. It now remains to be seen what will happen. The General Synod apparently has no firm intention of debating the matter again, although it remains under considerable pressure to do so. If the Government's policy of multilateralism continues to fail to produce perceivable results, and if the nuclear arms race continues, then it would doubtless have to review its position, as the already rapid politicization of peace continues to play a growing part in the influencing of public opinion.

That opinion about nuclear defence and disarmament in the Church of England is shifting away from a tacit and unqualified support for the *status quo* towards a more critical position which brings pressure upon it, is indisputable. This is in line with the recently expressed opinions of other Church bodies. In 1979, the British Council of Churches recommended that the Government should not adopt the Trident missile system and soon after the Methodist Church made a similar recommendation. More recently, the British Council of Churches has made further recommendations which specifically include emphasis on the importance of the nuclear powers adopting "no first use" agreements on nuclear weapons. An ecumenical consensus is emerging which is, to say the least, critical of the nuclear defence policies of the present British Government and N.A.T.O. This is not, as we have seen and as some have wrongly supposed, a consensus which is totally in support of the renunciation of all nuclear weapons whatever the consequences. For the most part, as in the Church of England, it is seeking a via-media between a multilateral approach to disarmament and a totally unconditional unilateral one. It has a politically practical orientation which seeks to find ways of checking and reversing the nuclear arms race by means which lie, by argument, within the realms of feasibility. A lot has been done to realise in this area something of the vision of William Temple which we noted at the beginning of this chapter.

All this is taking place within the wider context of what may be described as the rapid politicisation of peace within British democracy. At the beginning of the 1983 General Election campaign, the Prime Minister admitted bluntly that two issues were paramount: unemployment and peace. That the latter should be placed so high or her campaign agenda was due, no doubt, to a complex set of factors some of which we have already noted and which are associated largely with the present failure of the Government's nuclear disarmament policies. But it is due, also in part, to the recent resurgence of the peace movements such as C.N.D. In 1980 it had 3,000 paid-up members in the U.K., it now has 25,000. Furthermore, it now receives much more media coverage than it did previously and is recruiting among a wider cross-section of the community than it used to do. Much of its activities are at grass roots political level and this alone will ensure that critical thinking on peace and nuclear disarmament will feature in political discussion.

It may be observed that the debate about the morality of the deployment and use of nuclear weapons – which began with the British Council of Churches in 1946 and which has, as we have seen, now amassed, to its credit, an impressive amount of detailed critical analysis both theological, technical and political – is now influencing public opinion. It is to be hoped that within this general concern, and even demand, for peace in the Christian Churches, there are to be found politically realistic recommendations, such as those concerning phased unilateral disarmament, which will yet play their part in the future strategies of the British and other Governments. Dialogue between the British Government and the Churches is always discretely taking place and there is much goodwill on both sides. This leaves open the possibility that, although the Churches have yet to be successful in changing the Government's nuclear defence policy, they will eventually succeed, with others, in bringing this about; thereby furthering the complex political debate about how to make the world a safer place in the future than it is in the present.

Chapter 9

THE CHURCH AND IMMIGRATION AND RACE RELATIONS POLICY

Kenneth Leech

9.1: The Historical Background to the Issue

There is little evidence that the Church of England took seriously the questions of racial justice and racialism until late in the 1960s. In a sense, there is nothing surprising about that. Concern had been slow to develop in the labour and trade union movements too, while it can be shown that both organized religion and political groupings played their part in the growth of racist ideology.[1] However, on a world scale, Anglicans had been presented with much evidence of the challenge and threat of racially discriminatory policies to the Christian faith many years before. In 1910, Bishop Azariah told the missionary conference in Edinburgh that "the problem of race relationships is one of the most serious problems confronting the Church today".[2] It is doubtful if many British Christians made connections with the anti-Irish feelings in 19th. Century England, or with the anti-Jewish campaigns which had led to the Aliens Act of five years earlier.

During that campaign, Anglican clergy had played a not insignificant role. The Dean of Norwich had "urged the working men of England to rise in all the majesty of their manhood and all the strength and purity of their glorious cause

---

[1]For some of the evidence, see my Tawney Memorial Lecture for 1982, *Religion and the Rise of Racism* (Christian Socialist Movement, 1982).

[2]Cited by Philip Potter in *Your Kingdom Come: Mission Perspectives* (World Conference on Mission and Evangelism, Melbourne, May 12-25 1980, World Council of Churches, 1980).

to reject the dumping of alien paupers in their midst".[3] Back in the middle years of the 19th Century, the Christian Socialist clergyman, Charles Kingsley, had written to his wife after a visit to Ireland:[4]

'But I am haunted by the human chimpanzees I saw along that hundred miles of horrible country. I don't believe they are our fault, I believe there are not only many more of them than of old, but that they are happier, better, more comfortably fed and lodged under our rule than they ever were. But to see white chimpanzees is dreadful, if they were black, one would not feel it so much, but their skins except where tanned by exposure, are as white as ours.'

Such sentiments were by no means uncommon in the period.

The year 1924 has been regarded as a turning point in Christian concern in Britain with race. In that year, J.H. Oldham's *Christianity and the Race Problem* was published. In his review of Oldham's book, William Temple said that race was the greatest of all practical problems facing mankind.[5] Temple went on to argue against the view that racial antagonism was innate and inevitable. On the contrary, he claimed:

'Racial antagonism is not grounded in human nature, but in conventions of thought and conduct, so that by a change in those convictions it could be removed.'[6]

Kendall has suggested that both Oldham and Temple recognised the existence of institutional racism though the term was not known at the time.[7] However, after Oldham's study, there seems to have been little attention paid to race in the thought of

---

[3]Cited in Caroline Adams, *They Sell Cheaper and They Live Very Odd* (London: British Council of Churches, 1976).

[4]Cited in L.P. Curtis, *Anglo-Saxons and Celts* (New York: New York University Press, 1968), p. 84.

[5]*International Review of Missions*, 13:51 (July 1924).

[6]Cited in R. Elliott Kendall, *Christianity and Race* (London: British Council of Churches, 1982), p. 10. Kendall's booklet is a useful description of the background to Oldham's book.

[7]*Ibid.*, p. 11.

Anglicans in England. The 1950s saw the courageous witness in South Africa of the late Michael Scott and Trevor Huddleston, both priests who had been ordained in the Church of England; and their activities received considerable publicity in this country. But few made connections with England itself.

It was during the late 1950s that the numbers of migrants from the Caribbean to Britain increased, and indeed migrant labour was recruited to maintain the health service and London Transport. Anglicans in a number of localities were involved in ministering to these new arrivals. Important work was done, for example, by Bernard Ball, then a member of the Brotherhood of the Holy Cross, in Moss Side, Manchester; by the Society of St. Francis in Cable Street, Stepney; and in other districts. But there was a feeling that no serious problem existed which could not be solved by a certain level of goodwill. Not that the goodwill could be taken for granted. Many West Indians testified to the coldness or positive hostility which they encountered in Anglican churches in this period. Under the leadership of Archbishop Fisher, the issues of racial prejudice were passed over or trivialised. Fisher believed that racial divisions were similar to the social class divisions which led to differing patterns of Church worship in East and West London. "I think that the Bishop of Stepney would say that people who live in the East End would rather worship with people in the East End than with 'blokes' in the West End", he cheerfully told a dinner for bishops.[8] Nothing much to worry about there!

During these years, along with the lack of seriousness about race questions, there was a general reluctance to deny entry to "dark strangers".[9] The campaign to restrict coloured immigration pioneered by Sir Cyril Osborne, Norman Pannell and other MPs, did not receive widespread support. Enoch Powell, who was later to attain notoriety for his anti-immigrant views, was silent at this time, or, as Minister of Health, involved in recruiting Caribbean labour. His fellow Anglican, Philip

[8]*Daily Telegraph*, 17th June, 1955.
[9]The title of Sheila Patterson's study of Brixton (London: Tavistock, 1963).

Mason, first Director of the Institute of Race Relations, wrote in 1956:

'Only if there was such an influx of people wholly different from ourselves in way of life as to threaten the whole character of our existence would we limit immigration by British subjects, and then, consistently with our professions, only by a system which ignored race. It would not be easy to devise: but in any case, no one with a sense of proportion could maintain that the need has yet arisen, nor is anywhere near.'[10]

By 1965, however, the same Philip Mason, presumably still possessed of a sense of proportion, and, therefore, one assumes, confronted by a threatening influx, was insisting that "we are determined to cut down sharply the numbers of fresh entries until this mouthful has been digested".[11] The shift in attitude corresponds to a shift in the level of acceptability of racist language over the decade. It was this decade, from the mid-50s to the mid-60s, which was central to the growth of institutional racism in Britain. What were the factors which led to the change?

9.2: The Growth of Racism in Britain and the Church's Initial Response

Of central importance were the disturbances in Notting Dale in late August and early September 1958. The disturbances spread out to Shepherds Bush, as well as pockets of Notting Hill, Kensal New Town, Paddington and Maida Vale. They occurred in areas containing very few black people and the offenders came from areas which were wholly white. Sir Oswald Mosley's Union Movement and other racist groups were active in the area in the period immediately prior to the outbreaks.[12] However,

[10]Philip Mason, *Christianity and Race* (London: Lutterworth Press, 1956), p. 150.
[11]Philip Mason in *The Guardian*, 23rd January, 1965.
[12]See Ruth Glass, *Newcomers* (Centre for Urban Studies and George Allen and Unwin, 1960), pp. 133-4.

the disturbances were followed by immediate demands for control of "coloured immigration". In the preceding months there had been a series of press reports claiming that the Ku Klux Klan were active in Britain, and there was a media build-up of racial feelings.[13] The general assumption seemed to be that the presence of black people was directly related to the outbreaks of violence. If the numbers increased, so would the incidence of violence. The solution, therefore, was immigration control. Over the following years, the support for such control spread from the small organized racist groups so that, with massive support from the media, it became the majority view in the country.

There is no reason to doubt that it was also the majority view in the Church of England. Certainly the Church press showed little sign of any significant opposition to controls from Church members. After the 1958 riots, the *Church of England Newspaper* described the demands for control as "cowardly" and "wickedness".[14] However, by 1963, after the Rachman affair, the same paper was demanding that 'the coloured problem must be tackled'[15] and was supporting the controls which had been introduced. The Commonwealth Immigrants Bill was rightly denounced by members of the Labour Party as a racialist measure though within three years the same party was to renew and strengthen its provisions.

There is no evidence that any comparable opposition came from the Church of England, and it may reasonably be assumed that most Anglicans supported the 1962 legislation. During the Lords debate, the Archbishop of Canterbury, Michael Ramsey, described the Bill as "lamentable", but it was not clear if he meant that it should not have been introduced, or that it was

[13]On the KKK, see, for example, reports in *Birmingham Post,* 29th April, 1957; *Yorkshire Evening Post* and *Newcastle Evening Chronicle,* 3rd May, 1957; *Times,* 4th May, 1957; *Manchester Evening News,* 6th May, 1957; *Lancashire Evening Post,* 7th May, 1957; *Empire News,* 2nd February, 1958; and *Manchester Guardian,* 27th February, 1958.

[14]*Church of England Newspaper,* 5th September, 1958.

[15]*Ibid.,* 2nd August, 1963.

necessary and this necessity was lamentable. The moral aspects of legislation based solely on colour do not seem to have caused much debate in the Church although isolated voices were raised against it. Michael Ramsey's chairmanship of the National Council for Commonwealth Immigrants (which preceded the Community Relations Commission) and the establishment of chaplains to immigrants in Coventry, Birmingham and London were significant moves. It was not, however, until the 1970s that a nationwide network of community relations chaplains was established.

In the early period there was little writing about race relations from a Christian perspective. In 1958, there were short accounts by Clifford Hill [16] and Richard Gray, [17] while in 1960 the Board for Social Responsibility of the Church Assembly issued a booklet *Together in Britain: A Christian Handbook on Race Relations*. [18] This seems to have been the first semi-official publication from the Church. It included a section entitled "Towards a Theological Understanding of Race Relations". [19] It emphasised that Britain was not a plural society. "Britain is not a 'plural' society. . .into which distinct communities can be built" (p. 27). The statement was not explained or justified, and the author went on to warn, cautiously, against anything resembling "positive discrimination".

'Some thoughtful people are worried lest much special treatment of coloured people and the granting of privileges and giving of help over and above the normal entitlement of ordinary citizens may lead to the existence of a permanent group whose members will have interests vested in keeping it going. (p. 28)'

In contrast to the United States where a considerable amount of literature was appearing at this time, dealing with such issues as race and church renewal, the biblical material, and the pastoral aspects of racial justice, the British dearth of serious writing is

[16]Clifford Hill, *Black and White in Harmony* (London: Hodder and Stoughton, 1958).
[17]Richard Gray, "Race Relations and the Church in Britain", *Dublin Review*, Winter, 1958-9.
[18]Church Information Office, 1960.
[19]*Ibid.*, Chapter 4, pp. 13-19.

very striking.[20] Yet these were the years of riots, of crudely racialist campaigns, and years which saw the flowering of a wide range of racist, fascist and anti-semitic movements.[21]

However, the Christian supporters of control of non-white immigration were militant in these years. The devout Baptist, Sir Cyril Osborne, can claim the credit for the 1962 Act, for he had been pressing for it for years. But by 1965, the Labour Government, having moved away from Gaitskell's principled opposition, had produced a White Paper which strengthened the controls. Michael Foot desribed it at the time as "the most pathetic and craven departure from principle on an issue which has world-wide implications".[22] Few, if any, Anglican voices of opposition were raised in that year.

The voices of Anglican racialists, however, were not restrained at this time. The Rector of Linton in the Diocese of Hereford, Stephen Pulford, warned that any equality between black and white would lead to violence and segregated communities. "Once given equality, they will start bossing us around. We will have Smethwicks, Sharpevilles and Harlems all over the country."[23] An Anglican layman from Worthing, in the heartland of Christian racism, wrote to the *Church Times*:[24]

'There is no economic, social, moral or political justification for the presence of Coloureds in England, and nearly every Christian with whom I have discussed this subject would

[20]Among many studies of race and Christianity in the USA, see T.B. Maston, *The Bible and Race* (Nashville: Broadman Press, 1959); C. Herbert Oliver, *No Flesh Shall Glory* (Phillipsburg: Presbyterian and Reformed Publishing Company, 1959); Will D. Campbell, *Race and the Renewal of the Church* (Philadelphia: Westminster Press, 1962); Daisuke Kitagawa, *Race Relations and Christian Mission* (New York: Friendship Press, 1965) and *The Pastor and the Race Issue* (New York: Seabury Press, 1965); Kyle Haselden, *Mandate for White Christians* (Richmond, Va.: John Knox Press, 1966).

[21]See George Thayer, *The British Political Fringe: A Profile* (London: Anthony Blond, 1965).

[22]*Tribune*, lst October, 1965.

[23]*Guardian*, 14th December, 1964.

[24]Robert Clark, letter in *Church Times*, 10th September, 1965.

support a repatriation scheme....No Christian dislikes Coloureds as such, but most resent their presence here.'

A well-known Anglo-Catholic clergyman was equally hostile to
the new black presence. He resented the "constant anti-white
and pro-coloured propaganda" which, he claimed, was the
norm in Christian circles. He went on to attack (in 1964, two
years after the Commonwealth Immigrants Act) "the curse of
virtually unlimited immigration". There was a need for "a
definitely Christian 'Keep Britain White' campaign". Mis-
cegenation, he claimed, was "a grave sin". He concluded by
saying that "there are plenty besides the Dutch Reformed
Church who feel that some sort of *apartheid* will soon be
necessary in *this* country if it is not already too late".[25] When
this clergyman celebrated his ordination anniversary some years
later, the National Front was officially represented at the Mass.
Of course, it would be ridiculous to suggest that such people
were typical of the Church of England as a whole. But, in a
climate of widespread apathy and lack of awareness of any real
issues, it was sentiments such as these which were to win the
day.

9.3:   The Development of the Issue Inside the Church in the 1960s and 1970s

The 1960s saw both a worsening of race relations and the
"gentrification" of racist groups and racist ideology. A well-
informed commentator on the British scene wrote sadly in May,
1968:

'The deterioration of race relations in Britain could have been
prevented. Ever since 1958, the course has been predictable (and
has predicted) ....At every step prejudice has been encouraged.'[26]

Only a few weeks earlier, on April 20th – ironically Adolf
Hitler's birthday – the devout Anglican, Enoch Powell, had

[25]The Reverend P.E. Blagdon-Gamlen, letter in *Church Times*, 11th
September, 1964.
[26]Ruth Glass, letter, *The Times*, 4th May, 1968.

delivered the first of a series of major speeches on race, each one of which was to further the deterioration and give respectability to the growing racist movements. It was in 1968 that the term "racism" first entered popular vocabulary, partly through the writings of Stokley Carmichael in the United States. For the Churches, however, it was the meeting of the Central Committee of the World Council of Churches at Canterbury in 1969 which introduced the concept of "institutional racism" and called for the setting up of a worldwide programme to combat racism. This meeting followed the Assembly of the WCC in Uppsala in 1968 where racism had been a major item on the agenda.

The year 1971 saw a new Immigration Act and the setting up of a Community and Race Relations Unit (CCRU) at the British Council of Churches. CRRU became a major education resource for material on race and racism within the British Churches, and soon its Projects Fund established itself as one of the main sources of grant aid to multi-racial projects throughout the country. One of the first pieces of work undertaken at CRRU was a working party on the use of Church property by community groups. Two reports were published on this question.[27] But it was the appearance in 1976 of the Report, *The New Black Presence in Britain*, which brought CRRU into the field of controversy.[28] This Report was the first by a Christian body to bring the issue of racism before a large section of the British churches, and it did so in a way which shocked and angered many people. Meanwhile, the World Council of Churches was pursuing its Programme to Combat Racism (PCR). At the Central Committee in Addis Ababa in January 1971, there was a call for "a thorough review of existing parish education materials and programmes to eliminate overt or covert racist content" and for "a new creative effort to develop parish education materials and programmes designed to contribute towards the elimination of racism and racial discrimination, and to develop the conscientization of children, youth and

[27] *The Use of Church Properties for Community Activities in Multi-Racial Areas: An Interim Report* (BCC/CRRU, October 1972); Ann Holmes, *Church, Property and People* (BCC/CRRU, 1973).
[28] *The New Black Presence in Britain: A Christian Scrutiny* (BCC, 1976).

adults". [29] But the implementation of educational programmes to combat racism was slow to take place in the Church of England.

However, in 1971, the first meeting of the Anglican Consultative Council took place in Limuru, Kenya. The meeting commended the statements against racism issued at Uppsala in 1968 and subsequently commended in Resolution 16 of the Lambeth Conference later in that year. It called upon Anglicans to re-examine their life and structures, and, with dissenting voices from the Archbishop of Capetown and the Bishop of Mashonaland, commended the PCR in these words:

'With regard to the WCC grants, in our judgement no public action of the Churches during the past twenty-five years has done so much to arouse public discussion on a moral issue. It has given to ordinary people an indication of the fact that the Churches are ready to stand by the oppressed and exploited even when there is some risk to themselves. It has compelled Christian people to recognize that the Church is not necessarily on the side of the wealthy and the powerful. This recognition has been disturbing and cleansing. From the point of view of the total witness of the Church in the world, the majority of us find this action of the WCC to be the most important thing it has done in its history. Therefore we endorse and commend to Anglicans everywhere the WCC Programme to Combat Racism as set forth in Canterbury, England, in 1969 and as further outlined at Addis Ababa in 1971.' [30]

Resolution 17 of the Council proposed that all the Churches of the Anglican Communion should urgently seek ways of implementing the PCR (p. 28). This was reaffirmed when the Council met again in Dublin in1973. [31]

But the years that followed in England were the years of

[29]World Council of Churches, Central Committee, Addis Ababa,. 10-12th January, 1971; Document 55, 18th January, B4.

[30]*The Time is Now*, Anglican Consultative Council, lst Meeting, Limuru, Kenya, 23rd February–5th March, 1971 (SPCK, 1971), p. 18.

[31]*Partners in Mission*, Anglican Consultative Council, 2nd Meeting, Dublin, 17th–27th July, 1973 (SPCK, 1973).

Archbishop Coggan, a kind and caring man who showed no comprehension of the issues. He told the General Synod in York in 1976 that he supported a "clearly defined limit" to immigration, apparently unaware of the restrictive legislation since 1962.[32] However, the following years saw two important debates in the Synod which were to have abiding consequences. On July 6th 1977, the Synod debated a Board for Social Responsibility Report on *Britain as a Multi-Racial and Multi-Cultural Society* (GS 328) and *The New Black Presence*.[33] This was the first major debate on race in the Synod. The Bishop of Liverpool proposed a Church of England fund for race relations work on the lines of the fund established by the General Convention of the Episcopal Church in the USA in 1967. His proposal was rejected, but the issues raised were to become part of the ongoing agenda of the Synod. During the debate, an observer noted that there were only two non-white faces in the Synod itself and seven in the packed public gallery.

On November 9th 1978, the Synod returned to the question of a "Church of England special fund for race relations".[34] "We want the Church to make an effective and realistic response to the challenges identified in that debate", said Professor J.D. McLean, then Vice-Chairman of the Board for Social Responsibility, referring back to the debate of 1977. The main concrete result of the November 1978 debate was a proposal by the Bishop of Ripon in which the dioceses were invited to support the CRRU Projects Fund, and a figure of £100,000 per year for at least seven years was suggested. This was passed and the Bishop of Liverpool stressed that such a financial commitment was to put a "sharp edge" on the educational programme. There was no suggestion that the giving of money should be an alternative to, or substitute for, educational work. The Bishop of Truro, as Chairman of the BSR, told the members:

'Frankly, members of the Synod will simply be going back on their decision if they do not now put it into effect. They have

[32] *The Guardian*, 16th July, 1976.
[33] General Synod, *Reports of Proceedings*, 8:2 (1977), pp. 513–564.
[34] *Ibid.*, 9:3 (1978), pp. 1144–1160.

before them the chance to do something positive and concrete to show that when they spoke, as the Synod must speak, for the Church of England in the debate on *The New Black Presence*, they meant what they said.'[35]

The Synod was meeting at a time when organized fascism was on the offensive, when groups such as the National Front and the British Movement were vigorous in stirring up racial hatred, and when anti- racist and anti-fascist committees were springing up at local level throughout the country. The formation of Christians Against Racism and Fascism was a direct response to the NF threat. But at the beginning of 1978, Margaret Thatcher, the Conservative leader, spoke on television about the fears that the British race might be "swamped" by the "alien" influx of black people. She stressed the need for a clear end to immigration.[36] It seems likely that the effect of this interview, and of the feeling it conveyed that the Conservative Party was now firmly committed to a racist position, did much to undermine support for the NF and transfer it to the Conservatives. While a press report suggested that the Bishop of Truro had welcomed Mrs. Thatcher's words, feeling among many Christians, especially those who had been struggling against intolerance and hatred at a local level, was of disgust and horror. The Thatcher interview of 1978, like Enoch Powell's first speech of ten years before, was a crucial landmark in the transformation of racism into a respectable element within mainstream politics. Ethnic minority groups became more and more convinced that they could expect little help from political leaders. When, in the summer of 1978, there was an epidemic of racial attacks, including several murders and orchestrated violence against the Bengalee residents of the East End of London, these groups saw that they must themselves organize as a force against racism.

However, the combination of NF activity and the growth of the new Tory racism had one good effect on Anglican leaders. A number of bishops, not all of them well known for their involvement in radical politics, issued a strongly worded

[35] *Ibid.*, p. 1160.
[36] World in Action, Granada TV, 31st January, 1978.

statement in which they accused political leaders of having made racism respectable. The bishops pointed out that while "the National Front and similar organizations are crudely and blatantly evil, and must be totally resisted, Christians must resist even more strongly the institutionalised racialism which some highly placed politicians have made respectable and which they exploit for electoral benefit". They went on to refer to Mrs. Thatcher, who was now Prime Minister:

'Since more people have left this country than have entered it since 1970, the Prime Minister's remarks about "being swamped", first made last year, and repeated during the election, and her calls for "a clear prospect of an end to immigration" have in practice the effect of fanning racial prejudice. '

The letter was signed by the Bishops of Birmingham, Bristol, Chelmsford, Lewes, Lichfield, Lincoln, Liverpool, London, Manchester, Namibia in Exile, Newcastle, Ripon, Southwell, Sherborne, Stepney, and St. Albans, and Bishop Michael Ramsey.[37] It was an important stage in the developing rift between Anglican thinking on race and the Conservative Government. A well-known evangelical clergyman, a leading figure in the Evangelical Race Relations Group, wrote, also at the end of 1979:

'How far the National Front's poor showing in the election was due to Mrs. Thatcher having stolen their thunder is uncertain, but very certainly at the last party conference, the unacceptable face of Conservatism was visible at its most naked and embarrassing in some of the hysterical speeches on immigration.'[38]

So, as 1979 drew to its close, there was evidence that more Anglicans were coming to see racism as something far greater than prejudice, tense relationships, or the street violence associated with small political movements. Racism was in-

[37]The letter was printed, among other places, in the *Church Times* on 30th November, 1979.
[38]John Root, in *Third Way*, December, 1979, p. 4.

creasingly recognized as institutional, embodied in the structures of society and in its legislation. In September 1979, a conference on Combatting Racism in the '80s met at Loughborough, and sought to identify priorities for the struggle of the next decade.[39]

9.4:   Racism and the Church in the 1980s

On July 8th. 1980, there was a further General Synod debate, based on a BSR document *Pluralism and Community*.[40] This document proposed the establishment of a Resource Group to advise the BSR and the Synod, and the appointment of a Race Relations Field Officer. The main purpose of the group and the new officer would be, according to the Bishop of Truro, "to assist in the work of adult education in the sphere of race relations".[41] Funding had been assured for three years by a number of voluntary church societies, and during the debate, Mrs. Jean Mayland expressed regret that the Synod itself had not been able to finance the entire project.[42]

The field officer was appointed and began work at the beginning of 1981, and within a few months the Race, Pluralism and Community Group was set up within the BSR. The General Synod itself held two further debates on race questions. In November 1980, there was a debate, arising from a diocesan motion, on police-community relations,[43] and in February 1981 a private member's debate on the forthcoming Nationality Bill. A motion that the Bill "may lead to treatment of individuals which is not in keeping with Christian teaching and which could be racially divisive or socially inequitable" was passed by 198 votes to 1.[44] By this time, the work for racial justice within BSR was well under way, the Board itself maintaining a concern with national issues, while the Field Officer and the new resource

---

[39]For a summary of its proceedings, see *Racism and the World Church* (British Council of Chuurches, 1979).
[40]GS 450. See *Reports of Proceedings,* ll:2 (1980), pp. 524–538.
[41]*Ibid.,* p. 525.
[42]*Ibid.,* p. 529.
[43]*Ibid.,* ll:3 (13th November, 1980), pp. 936–953.
[44]*Ibid.,* 12:1 (24th February, 1981), pp. 176–187.

group were mainly involved with educational activity. This was in line with the summary of the Field Officer's work as given in the job description for the post: "To give support to, and where necessary to develop, work in the dioceses and parishes of the Church of England, directed to enabling church members and congregations to make an informed Christian response and contribution to a multi-racial society based on a plurality of cultures and religions and in that context to develop means of promoting the Projects Fund of the Community and Race Relations Unit of the British Council of Churches."

Six principal accountabilities were identified for the Field Officer: making contact with Church-based race relations and inter-faith groups, diocesan race relations chaplains, and so on; bringing proposals to the resource group; speaking at meetings; taking part in staff consultations; advising the BSR and other groups within the Church on specific issues; and consulting with the Church on important issues. Throughout, there was a strong emphasis on education. The key document, *Pluralism and Community* (GS 450) had stressed that "this task of adult education is of greater urgency than that of raising money for projects in the field of race or community relations" (p. 4). So the aims of the new resource group were seen as including the production of educational materials, information-gathering, advisory work, drawing the BSR's attention to specific issues, the formation, where necessary, of sub-groups, and the raising of funds for further work.

In October 1981, the first major event to be organized under the new unit took place. This was a consultation held in Holy Cross Priory, Leicester, on the theme "The Church of England and Racism". Some sixty people, drawn from various parts of the Church of England, as well as a number of supportive non-Anglicans, met in a series of workshops over a weekend. The aim was to assess priorities for the struggle against racism by the Church of England during the 1980s. Five workshops took place, concerned with Church structures (including the re-presentation of ethnic minorities, equal opportunity and positive discrimination policies, the role of black clergy, the relations between inner-city and suburban churches, and theological education); race and attitude changing; education (including church schools); penal, legal and police issues; and international aspects (including support for the PCR, attitudes to South Africa, and so on). The recommendations of the consultation were published and circulated within the dioceses, and they were followed up a year later by a series of commentaries on the resolutions.[45]

These recommendations and the ensuing process have run parallel with strategies and developments in other Churches and groups. A Joint Christian Group on Race Relations has been meeting quarterly since 1981, consisting of representatives of BSR, CRRU, the Catholic Commission for Racial Justice, the Evangelical Race Relations Group, CARAF, the Zebra Project and others. One of the most interesting examples of cooperation between denominational race relations groups was the opposition to the British Nationality Act of 1981. This began with a statement by the Roman Catholic bishops which was then approved by the BCC and by the General Synod House of Bishops. There was regular briefing of the hierarchies of both Churches and very close collaboration with the Joint Council for the Welfare of Immigrants (JCWI) and the Action Group on Immigration and Nationality (AGIN). So great was the opposition, that the Government seemed to find it difficult to understand that Church leaders had not been "got at" by sinister political forces. Since the Act became law, on 1st January 1983, the campaign has continued, and further material appeared from the BSR in 1983.

How much impact has this campaign made on Government policy and action? It is possible both to exaggerate and to underestimate the effects. That the Nationality Act is racist both in intention and in effect was stressed by speakers, including the Bishop of Birmingham, in the General Synod debate on February 28th, 1984. Members were told of case after case where applications for registration were refused after lengthy delays; of families divided for years through the operation of the immigration rules; and of the seriously damaging effects of this legislation on race relations. Supporting documents demons-

[45] *The Church of England and Racism* (BSR, 1981); *The Church of England and Racism – and Beyond* (BSR, 1982).

trated this in detail.[46] The Synod voted overwhelmingly in support of a motion highly critical of the Act. Significantly, the two Conservative MPs who are members of the Synod, John Selwyn Gummer (the Chairman of the Conservative Party) and Sir William van Straubenzee, were both absent for this major debate. Yet Government policy has not essentially changed. The appalling case of Zola Budd, the white South African athlete, who was given British citizenship in *ten days* in April 1984, stands in bitter contrast with the majority of individuals whose applications have taken around two years to process. Most of these people are black or Asian; some of them are refugees from racism in South Africa.

However, there is evidence that in specific campaigns against deportations, the support of bishops has not been without effect. The experience of the Diocese of Leicester is interesting in this connection. Here the Bishop and others have set up a Nationality Fund which helps to pay the exorbitant fees required of those applying for registration and naturalization. There have also been some successful appeals against deportations. These campaigns on behalf of individuals will no doubt continue, but the long-term struggle must be for new legislation.

Probably the principal value of the Church's witness against this racist legislation has been that it has helped to increase consciousness in the nation, among people not directly affected, and has helped to build up a well-informed and committed body of opinion both inside and outside the Church which will, in time, help to bring the present racist legislation to an end.

9.5:   Racism and the Church – The Current Agenda

Currently, the issues facing the Church of England in its concern for racial justice are formidable and complex. Only the briefest sketch of them can be made here. The first issue arises from the urban riots which occurred in the Spring and Summer of 1981. In many ways, the results of these conflicts were positive. While

[46]See Anne Owers, *Sheep and Goats: British Nationality Law and Its Effects,* and *Families Divided: Immigration Control and Family Life* (Board for Social Responsibility, 1984).

their effects should not be exaggerated, they did bring home to national leaders the reality which countless reports and surveys had revealed and had met with no response. The conditions which intelligent and supposedly well-informed persons found so shocking in Liverpool 8 and Brixton and elsewhere had, in fact, been documented for years in a succession of detailed studies. Conditions in Liverpool 8 had probably occupied space in more published papers than had occurred in any comparable area of Britain. There was nothing in Lord Scarman's Report on Brixton[47] which was new except the date. It seemed, sad and depressing though it might be, that it took riots to arouse the establishment even to minimal awareness of the need for change. The Church of England came out of the disturbances rather well. In most of the areas affected, the Church's presence was characterized by dedication, informed critique, close and detailed knowledge of events, and a high level of trust and credibility within the community.[48] It is essential to build on this experience and to develop the Church's prophetic and diacritical task in the urban cores.

Secondly, a major area which the 1981 events highlighted was the growing gulf in comprehension and experience between inner-city and suburban churches. The statistical strength of Anglicanism lies in the mainly white suburban areas where people are often inclined to rely on the view of the world and of Christianity offered in the pages of the *Daily Telegraph*. Insufficient attention has been given by the Churches to the strength of prejudice in the suburbs and to the urgency of the need to overcome the gulf between these communities and those in the urban cores. Many years ago, Lewis Mumford described the culture of suburbia as "a collective attempt to live a private life".[49] How does a Church which is committed to corporate values and the interdependence of the human community minister to this culture?

Thirdly, the Church needs to emphasise the importance of

[47] *The Brixton Disorders* (London: HMSO, 1981; Penguin, 1982).

[48] For the Church's response in Southwark and Moss Side, Manchester, see Chapters 6 and 7 in this volume.

[49] Lewis Mumford, *The Culture of Cities* (London: Secker and Warburg, 1946 edn.), p. 215.

positive action in the structural area against racial disadvantage and discrimination. Attitude change, consciousness-raising, race awareness training, may be helpful but will be of no avail so long as no serious attempt is made to reverse the inequities which are built into our institutions. The often-cited fear that "positive discrimination" or "affirmative action" may lead to a "white backlash" does not seem to be supported by the American experience where such action has led to considerable progress.[50] The Church needs both to press the need for such action, and to ensure that its own structures provide an example of such action. So far there is no evidence that this is taking place.

Fourthly, the question of theology and theological education needs to be grappled with. Theology in the Church of England does not, for the most part, reflect the insights of a multi-racial, plural society; it reflects the values and assumptions of a white, middle-class, male, clerical culture. There is no evidence that issues of race and pluralism were taken seriously in the study of Christian social ethics until very recently. Indeed, when the textbook *Teaching Christian Ethics* was being prepared in 1973, the contrast between the amount of space devoted to such issues as medical ethics and the almost total by-passing of race was striking. In the final draft, the treatment of race consisted of some eight lines including a recommendation of an out-of-date Penguin book published in the 1950s! Only after strong protests were references to more recent work added at a very late stage.[51]

A recent study of theological education has suggested that candidates for the ministry are not being prepared for the experience of a multi-racial and multi-faith society.[52] The most recent publication from the Advisory Council for the Church's Ministry (ACCM), a study of the ministry between 1963-2023, suggests that, on the issue of race, they have learnt little over the past decade. Apart from a passing reference to "black and coloured people" in a list of "losers in the urban race", the existence

[50]See Ronald Dworkin in *The Times,* 12th December, 1981.
[51]The final version was published as *Teaching Christian Ethics* (London: SCM Press, 1974), p. 104.
[52]Kenneth Cracknell, David Jennings and Christine Trethowan, *Blind Leaders for the Blind?* (Birmingham: AFFOR, 1982).

of black people, black Christians, black Anglicans, is ignored. The "strategy" offered is one for a white Church.[53] There is, then, an urgent need to develop a theological tradition which is more open to insights from beyond the narrow English culture of academia. The Church of England cannot remain indefinitely shielded from the blossoming theological movements of the Third World without serious consequences for its spiritual health.

Fifthly, it is vital that the attention of Christians is directed to the ideological shifts in the Conservative Party and to the growth of a "new racism" which draws on sociobiology and on ideas of the unity of the nation.[54] In recent years, many of the racist tendencies within the Conservative Party which had been kept in check or marginalised in the years of Macmillan and Heath, have resurfaced, finding the Thatcherite climate more amenable.[55] But more significant than this reappearance of crude racist groups is the discernible growth of a philosophical tendency marked by authoritarianism, nationalism and intolerance, a tendency which provides a strong ideological support for racism.[56] If this tendency gains ground, the gulf between the Church and the Conservative Party must become wider and increasingly unbridgeable. Yet the Church is likely to fight shy of open confrontation with these powerful forces and it may fail to see how serious are the issues involved. Nor can the Church ignore the fact that the development of this philosophical tradition derives a good deal from Christian sources.

Finally, it must be said that the growing awareness in the Church of the importance of combatting racism needs to be seen as on facet of a wider and developing concern for social justice as a whole, and for a theological critique of the present system. Such a critique is urgent and long overdue. The struggle against racism may well be a sieve through which a whole range of impurities in our society may be purged.

[53]John Tiller, *A Strategy for the Church's Ministry* (London: Church Information Office, 1983), p. 38.

[54]See Martin Barker, *The New Racism: Conservatives and the Ideology of the Tribe* (London: Junction Books, 1981).

[55]See Francesca Klug and Paul Gordon, "Boiling into Fascism", *New Statesman,* 10th June, 1983, pp. 12-13.

[56]See David Edgar, "Bitter Harvest", *New Socialist,* September-October, 1983, pp. 19-24.

Chapter 10

THE CHURCH AND EDUCATIONAL POLICY
Robert Waddington

10.1: Introduction

Any nation-state before it constructs or re-constructs its educational policy must face three basic questions. First, what is our vision of human maturity? Second, what kind of model of society have we in mind? And, third, what is the place of the educational process amongst the means used to achieve that vision for humankind or that model for society? The questions may not be faced head-on but they will lurk behind every educational debate. Answers to them may be assumed by educational practitioners.

In nations where the answers are part of a state-authenticated ideology, education will be highly centralised and teachers may be expected to behave as obedient public servants. Such a model for educational process one expects to find in Marxist quasi-totalitarian states. Yet, Queensland, like many of the Australian states, has had in the past (less so more recently) a highly centralized "free, compulsory and secular" educational system in which the status of teachers was very much that of public servant. But, as a democratic state favouring private freedom and initiative, it is not surprising to find there, alongside State schools, a large and healthy independent sector of schools. By far the largest proportion of such institutions are run by Christian Churches, for Christians have their own answers to the three fundamental questions. Their yardstick for the measurement of human potential is not a biological model, nor a tortuous theory from psychology, useful though both may be, but it is the "measure of the statue of the fullness of Christ". Their ultimate vision for corporate life is the Kingdom of Christ. Inevitably, Christians are drawn into the process of nurture, whether it be individual, social, cultural or political. They set the

221

partial models of the politicians, or the opportunist policies of bureaucrats, alongside the deeper theological insights that the vision of faith provides. They will offer a critique, therefore, and often find it received as unjust criticism. They may feel driven to try their own hand at the educational process only to find themselves accused of obscurantism or isolationist policies. Christians in states new and old find themselves caught up in the tension between vision and practice, for all educational planning generates heady philosophical debate alongside a brisk pragmatism.

The Church of England today, then, on the one hand adds its own insights to the continued search for an answer to the question, what are schools for? and on the other is also busy with the practical demands of six thousand schools. Inasmuch as the Church articulates theological visions alongside politicians' ideological paradigms, and within the framework of educational law encourages distinctive styles in its own schools, the Church cannot escape a degree of political debate, encounter and sometimes confrontation with those whose authority via the democratic process gives them power to organize publicly-funded education.

This chapter is a personal and, therefore, subjective account of the relationship between the Church and that apparatus of State which plans and resources education. It is also selective, salted from recent experience, as well as, perhaps, spiced by that slight recklessness (abandon would be too strong a term) which stems from the realization that I have just left the 'educational desk' of the General Secretary of the General Synod's Board of Education. It is consciously subjective, even idiosyncratic, because it draws on three very particular areas of my experience. First, international comparative observation of the English educational scene whilst a Headmaster in Queensland. Second, five years' experience as one of the 43 Diocesan Directors of Education in England during which time, in my area, five local authorities merged to become the new shire County of Cumbria. In this period I also served as a member of the Taylor Committee on School government (an interesting personal first sight of governmental thought and process). Third, the responsibilities since 1977 of Joint General Secretary of the General

Synod's Board of Education and the National Society (the famous voluntary society which, from 1811, established the first national schools for the poor and has maintained a role as the base for Anglican work on behalf of church schools). It is experience of this latter set of responsibilities that has taken me into the offices both of the Secretary of State for Education and Science himself, and his Ministers as well as his senior officials. It has also provided direct observation of, and discussion with, leaders of other partners in the educational service – Local Education Authorities, teachers and their union leaders, trainers of teachers, parents, schools, other Churches, employers and community interests.

Although the remit of the General Synod Board of Education is a wide one, including Higher Education (and Chaplaincy provision within it), the Youth Service, Adult Education and all aspects of voluntary 'in-church' education, since this Chapter represents a personal view, I have restricted my discussion to primary and secondary education.

10.2: The 1944 Education Act

In Britain, the Christian Churches had an historic role in establishing national schools for the public education of the poor who would receive knowledge (including religious instruction) and be able to develop a number of social and vocational skills. This historic innovatory role of the Churches is acknowledged and continued within the Education Act 1944 by the provision of Voluntary Schools. The precise formulation of the Church of England's involvement through Voluntary Schools was to be the subject of long, detailed and sometimes heated debate. The actual provisions of the Act are so precise that they reflect the hard-bargaining process. Butler's grand design included a recasting of schooling from nursery provision to Higher Education, and extended compulsory education to 15 years. The Act refers to Technical and Further Education (FE) provision for pupils up to age 18 years, plans for County Colleges and an increase in adult education. A spread of authority and power across interested partners would ensure a more balanced

partnership with an increased role for Local Education Authorities and school governing bodies. Elected authorities, parents
(now obliged to see that their children are educated), teachers,
community interests, Churches and the (then) Ministry of
Education, were to act within a balanced system. There would
be one publicly-funded maintained system of schools which
would consist of county and voluntary schools. The Christian
faith was to be a compulsory element of the curriculum in all
schools; each day would begin with a collective act of worship.
Denominational teaching would be available in all Voluntary
Aided schools and for those children in Voluntary *Controlled*
schools whose parents asked for it.

It is interesting to read the first Agreed Syllabuses for
Religious Education. Their mood and intention is clear; the
reconstruction of post-war society must include a reassertion of
Christian faith which alone will sustain personal and social
growth and undergird the nation with common moral values.
These syllabuses, to quote the preface to one of them aim to
"make children Christian". They were evangelistic in the best
sense of that term.

The role of the Ministry of Education was part convenor of
discussions among the partners on national policies, part
founder of the system as a whole. It would delegate some
powers and authority, and a good deal of control to both Local
Education Authorities (LEA's) and individual institutions. It had
a slightly paternalistic role of 'Chairman' of a collaborative
enterprise. The extraordinary and unique characteristics of the
English system of partnership I did not fully appreciate until
distanced from it by twelve thousand miles and until experienc-
ing a highly centralized system of education. Whilst most
nation-states have disenfranchised denominational interests
from publicly-funded education, England and Wales acknowledge the historic share of the Churches in education in such a
way that the contribution is not isolated in the independent
sector. None of the major political parties has ever suggested in
its manifesto a total recasting of the maintained system, while
the continued presence of schools (and Colleges of Higher
Education) provided by the Churches suggests an endorsement
of an element of voluntarism in education and a healthy

eschewing of any notion of monolithic political control. Voluntarism suggests both a continuing of the philanthropic role of voluntary providing bodies through their institutions, and that degree of powersharing by democratically elected bodies which harness the goodwill and expertise of non-elected but interested parties.

10.3: The Nature of the Church-State Relationship in Educational Policy

There is a distinct difference between the activities of the Church of England in relation to educational policy, however, when compared with the Church's role in connection with social policy in general. Often the Church is commentator, sometimes critic, protagonist or pressure group in relation to the effect of policies on individuals or certain social groupings. In education, it may be called upon to be all these but it is more. The Church actually *implements* policy through its own involvement as a partner in the system. If this gives the officers of the Church access to many levels of discussion and debate, it also requires of them that they exhaust the potentialities of these many levels before, as it were, necessarily becoming publicly vocal on difficult issues. For example, exhaustive and exhausting discussions took place between senior Church officers and DES personnel on the best way to expedite the formation of new Instruments of Government for Voluntary Schools (each one of . which has a *separate* Instrument at present!). Under the new Education Act, 1980, both parents and teacher members were to be included; this required considerable logistic skill if the various majorities required were to be maintained. From time to time, cynical or acerbic letters or articles have appeared accusing the Church of 'dragging its feet' because, so it was suggested, it really did not want either teacher or parent governors. It is important in public relations to deal with such unjust criticism but the *main thrust* of the Board of Education's energies (or those of the National Society with which it works in tandem) must be within the collaborative and more realistic discussions with local and central government. Those who seem to demand from the Board a higher public profile might do well to ponder this point.

In what manner has the Church involved itself in the educational partnership; what is the style of its engagement with the other partners, particularly central and local government? In attempting to delineate some of the chief aspects of this dynamic, one must be careful not to give the impression that there exists a highly organized strategy consonant with some vision of engagement with the secular world. As in other organizations, patterns of working have evolved partly on idealistic grounds, mainly on the basis of sound pragmatism.

10.3.1: *The church's undistributed authority in a framework of secular power-sharing – the local level*

One of the results of the Education Act 1944 was the promotion of a service in which the various partners had positive roles (splendidly not over-defined) and power was shared along the ranges of partners. It remains curious, but understandable, that the Church of England allowed the focus of real authority and power to be left in the individual school and its governing body. Ownership would most likely be vested in local Trustees, often Vicar and Churchwardens, or a group of Trustees maintaining the traditions of worthy forebears. If the school were of Voluntary Aided status, the governing body would be able to appoint the staff, control the 'general direction' of the curriculum, have full control of Religious teaching, regulate the use of premises out of school hours and also frame an admissions policy. They would be responsible for 50% of the cost of extensive repairs and any capital costs (it was 50% in the 1944 Education Act; it is now 15%). They could request a change in the status of the school; a famous or, perhaps more accurately, infamous case concerned a change of Vicar whilst a new school was in building. The new Vicar, as Chairman of Managers, wrote to the Secretary of State asking that the Voluntary Aided status of the school be revoked, a request with which he was bound to comply. The Local Education Authority suddenly found itself faced with the cost of building a Voluntary Controlled school which had previously, as a Voluntary Aided school, been budgetted for through centrally held funds. Intervention by the Church at local or national level was through solely advisory committees or officers. Small wonder that a Chief Education Officer recently stated that he was far happier dealing with the Roman Catholic authorities. "You know where you are with them", he opined, presumably because of the degrees of authority and power which exist "up the line" of management. An administrator would appreciate that.

There is, then, a mismatch between the structured power-sharing of the education service as a whole, and the locally-loaded structure of the Church of England which has for too long tolerated an almost total autonomy of the individual school governing body.

What are the diocesan and national bodies and how are they, with totally advisory functions, able to relate to local and central government? A Measure of the Church Assembly (the national representative body of the Church of England before the development of Synodical government) of 1943, revised in 1955, obliged each diocese to set up a Diocesan Education Committee (DEC), the composition of which was laid down in the Schedule to the Measure. Variations from the composition can be authorized only by the Secretary of State. This is an interesting feature of the Church's educational structures in that changes to the given constitution can be made only with the permission of a secular official; another piece of the 'dual system' perhaps! The functions of the DEC relate particularly to Church schools though a wider remit is described at some points, for example, Religious Education in the diocese as a whole.

In a recent discussion paper,[1] I outlined how the *advisory* focus of the Diocesan Education Committee has shifted towards a more crucially *strategic* one:

'It is the *diocese* through its DEC that controls assets from closed schools under Section 86 of the 1944 Act and later Section 2 of the 1973 Act; it is the DEC representing the diocese that was likely to be consulted about development plans; it is with the diocesan authorities that LEAs are to consult in the re-planning proposed under the Department's Circular 2/81 on Falling Rolls.

[1] *A Future in Partnership*, a Green Paper for discussion published by the National Society (Church of England) for Promoting Religious Education, 1984, p. 92. Cited hereafter as *A Future in Partnership*.

It is with the DEC that individual governing bodies must consult before they negotiate any change of status, closure, alteration, amalgamation, restoration or rearrangement of their schools. Both the DES and the LEAs have had recourse to Diocesan Education Committees as bodies able to provide some overall strategy regarding the provision of Voluntary schools which can be set alongside the important but more narrowly focused viewpoints of individual schools. Yet the DEC remains, in fact, an advisory body and there is no *requirement* that any LEA must consult the DECs in its area. An unscrupulous LEA in developing its own plans for dealing with falling rolls could, therefore, insist on dealing only with individual Voluntary schools, disregard any advice from a DEC, and from its strong and authoritative position "pick off" Church schools one by one. It is in the interests of Church schools to support a more authoritative role for the DEC which would be able through its deliberations and consultations to provide, for both diocese and LEA, an overall strategy for the Church's involvement in the maintained sector.'

The strategic role of a DEC is reinforced by its increasing involvement in centralized patterns of finance in diocesan educational expenditure. As educational expansion gained momentum in the 'fifties, and more particularly during the unprecedented 8% growth in the 'sixties, local schools looked more and more to diocesan and national bodies for financial aid. For some decades, many dioceses had organized Barchester schemes (an unfortunate 'olde worlde' title for something quite up-to-date). Such schemes were essentially a form of central banking for educational purposes in a diocese. Capital was formed from realizable assets from old or closed schools, and loans or, more rarely, grants were given to governors often at extremely low rates of interest or even in some cases interest-free. Section 86 of the Education Act 1944, and later Section 2 of the 1973 Act, enabled the diocese to collect assets together and use them in a diocese for Aided school maintenance or capital works. Obviously, the centralization of capital assets provided an authority for the DEC which the Measure of 1955 did not envisage. One hard-pressed diocesan official was heard to say in reference to the schools in the diocese, "If they do not co-operate, they do not get money". It is highly questionable whether good policies can be hammered out by wielding financial considerations as a blunt instrument – though we are familiar enough with attempts to try in 1985!

The noticeable shift in the role of the DEC has, however, led to expectations on the part of Local Education Authorities and their officers. First, they tend to look to diocesan officers for some sort of overall strategy regarding Church schools in their Authority. Second, since it is often a diocesan Education Officer who sits on the LEA's Education Committee among the co-opted members, they sometimes assume that assent in that Committee to re-organization arrangements involves or includes the assent of any individual Church schools that might be part of the planned rearrangements. This, of course, is not necessarily the case, and LEA officers find it hard to accept that a diocesan official seems to have very little authority to act on behalf of the diocese, within the context of an agreed strategy, in a way that will actually oblige individual schools to co-operate. There have been cases where diocese and County have been agreed, after considerable consultations, on a particular development only to find that a maverick Governing Body of a Church school has appealed to the Secretary of State, won the day, and wrecked the plan.

Now, there are virtues in such a high degree of local autonomy. It prevents the sacrifice of historic, voluntary local arrangements to any smoothly engineered political plans for local education. To put it differently, it can act as a brake on political aspiration, however good and idealistic that may appear to be. A brake is useful in stopping one careering wildly about with the prospect that control may be lost. During the comprehensive reorganization, for example, there was a general willingness on the part of Church of England secondary schools to co-operate. The very cautious, critical way in which some governing bodies acted during the consultative procedures, however, appeared to some LEA's to be an obscurantism based on total self-interest. But governing bodies of Voluntary schools, particularly Aided schools, are well aware that any change which compromises, even a little, their local, Voluntary standing, may be one step nearer closure – and that is irreversible in most cases, due to the features of Trust Law which control the assets of closed schools.

There are also negative features surrounding the present high degree of autonomy, as was pointed out in the Allington Statement[2] from a group of headteachers working in London and neighbouring counties. They appealed for less autonomy *provided* that a sufficiently high standard of expertise was made available through the diocesan structures. What is difficult for individual schools to see is that retention of the present degree of autonomy, isolating individual schools from any overall diocesan strategy, may well allow an unscrupulous or irritated LEA to pick off Church schools one by one. In some areas that is already happening. Clergy (often elected as Chairmen of Governors in Church schools) have a proper and healthy mistrust of 'centrism' in the Church and *may*, therefore, be major protagonists in any battle to preserve local autonomy without change. There is an educational task for each diocese here in order to make sure that a greater sharing of authority will be generally beneficial.

I have tried, in the discussion paper to which I have already referred,[3] to outline a new Statutory Education Council for each diocese which would be a smaller body than the present DEC, intensely expert in statutory education and concerned not just with schools but the whole range of opportunities available to the Churches in the education of children and young people. But such a council needs more *authority* in relation to the LEA's than the present DEC.

10.3.2: The national level

It is important to have described the diocesan and LEA scene before embarking on a description of the question of the Church at a national level, in order to emphasize the degree of

---

[2] A Conference for Heads for Church of England Secondary Schools held in June 1981 and organized by the ILEA Religious Education Inspectorate at Allington Castle, Maidstone, Kent. After the conference, a statement was issued which received wide publicity. Another statement was issued in December 1982 called *Allington – One Year On*. See also, *A Future in Partnership*, pp. 54-56.

[3] *A Future in Partnership*, pp. 93ff.

power-sharing that exists in the education service, a degree not mirrored in the Church's own strategy. In addition, we must note at this point that one of the consequences of local autonomy and diocesan *advisory* structures can be an unfortunate dichotomy between vision and pragmatism. Those often described in popular terms as 'at the chalk face' immerse themselves in practicalities; they have little time to argue the fundamental Why? and How? of education, or so they say. They may turn to the diocese for a general support and inspiration only to find that diocesan officers attempt to hold together the inspirational and the practical and so will often challenge and disturb those at local level. For example, what happens when a school with a long waiting-list finds that an Appeals Committee (set up under the Education Act 1980 to hear parental grievances about admissions policies) allows thirty appeals? That, in fact, is an increase in the entry arrangements for that year by one whole class ('one form-entry'). The school appeals for a portable classroom or more teaching help – a very hollow laugh comes from the LEA office, grappling as it is with falling rolls in many County schools. The governors turn to the diocesan officers for help and discover a philosophy of the Church sharing diminishing resources and falling rolls with the LEA and strong criticism of any growth *at the expense* of LEA resources. The school faces the fact of 30 more children, the diocese want to challenge the school to operate on a wider view than its own local concerns. In that dilemma, I contend that a greater degree of power-sharing between diocese and school would provide a frame of reference based on thought-out principles within which the practical issues would be less haphazardly formulated and applied with less panic.

At a national level, the Church of England for many years operated through a Schools' Council (there was a corresponding Council for Church Colleges of Education) which was serviced by the National Society (Church of England) for Promoting Religious Education.[4] At length, under the old Church Assembly, a Board of Education was set up within which the work of

[4]Further information on the work of the National Society can be obtained from its offices in Church House, Westminster, London SW1P 3NZ.

the existing councils (Schools, Colleges, Adult, Youth, Children) was subsumed. The Schools' Committee of the Board was still serviced, however, by staff of the National Society. With the advent of synodical government, the Board of Education became an Advisory Board of that Synod. Its present functions are described as follows:

'The functions of the Board shall be:

(a) To advise the General Synod and the diocese on all matters relating to education.

(b) To take action in the field of education in the name of the Church of England and the General Synod on such occasions as is required.'[5]

It is these broad terms of reference which, I must say, lend a particular excitement to the post of General Secretary for it is within such breadth that a degree of creativity is possible.

In 1975, the National Society entered into a new arrangement with the Board of Education, moved into offices next to those of the Board in Church House, Westminster, and accepted a degree of collaboration which was largely reflected in a number of shared roles for certain officers. There was to be a joint Chairman and General Secretary. The Schools' Officer of the Board would be a staff member of the Society but service the Schools' work of both Board and National Society. Each body retains its own identity; it is a marriage rather than a merger.

The arrangement provides two channels by means of which educational work might be carried out. For example, the discussion paper, to which I have already referred, was published in March 1984 by the National Society. The Board will be able to assess the responses which are being made to that paper and at length make a contribution of its own and later prepare any policy changes that it thinks need putting before the General Synod.

Much of what has been said about the relationship between

[5]*Constitutions of Boards and Councils 1980-85* (GS 449), (London: CIO Publishing, 1980), p. 13.

diocesan Education Committees and local government structures applies to the General Synod Board of Education (and the
National Society). Its main function is advisory; the action it can
take in the field of statutory education is largely the result of a
relationship of trust and the hopefully high degree of credibility
it creates with dioceses, individual institutions and secular
bodies.

If the Board is the organ that takes *action on behalf of the Church
of England*, then national bodies, most notably the Department
of Education and Science will expect to relate to it, collaborate
with it and negotiate aspects of the education service with it. In
the sections that follow, I attempt to delineate some of the styles
involved in that relationship, collaboration and negotiation,
albeit in a 'broad-brush' manner.

In spite of reference to *action*, then, in the description of its
functions – action which it should be noted can be taken with far
more ease in the sphere of 'in-Church' education – when it
comes to statutory education, the Board's actual potential for
affecting action in its schools or colleges is not the result of any
clearly defined authority, for the weight of decision-making still
lies with the autonomous institution, but rather depends on a
careful cultivation of its own credibility. While this keeps the
Board and its staff on its toes, as it were, it is questionable
whether, at a time when the ideological and resourcing battles
still rage in the education service, the Church can continue to
load decision-making at one end of the system, namely the local.

I, therefore, suggested that General Synod should in the near
future define with more clarity the kinds of issues about which
its Board of Education needs more executive authority when
dealing with maintained schools. These are:

(a) Negotiations about proposals which aim at changing
existing educational law.
(b) Any discussions or negotiations which lead to the framing
of new regulations.
(c) Any negotiations concerning the overall distribution of
resources which are to be specifically applied to Voluntary
Aided schools, including capital building programmes and
sums for minor works.

(d) Any discussions concerning the interpretation of those parts of the Education Act, currently in force, which relate to school worship or the provision of Religious Education.

(e) Any discussions over re-organization plans in which the Secretary of State seeks a view of the Churches, including any review of curriculum provision.

(f) Any situation where the Secretary of State may require some mediating action in an area where a clash of interests between school or diocese and the LEA have become evident.

(g) Any formulation of policy in which generally acceptable good practice should become standard among all dioceses (as, for example, in the initiative taken by the Board and the National Society in attempting to simplify Instruments of Government under the Education Act 1980).[6]

I also pointed out 'that officers of the DES, indeed Ministers and the Secretary of State himself, do seem to recognize in the national body represented by the association of General Synod Board of Education and National Society, an organization which can provide overall views, a distinctive Anglican contribution to debate and advice on what it considers to be good practice in relation to maintained education'.[7]

The burden of this section is that while efforts are made within the education service as a whole to operate with models of shared authority and decision-making, the Church retains a rather old-fashioned view that local decision-making is the only way to avoid the trap of centralization. For a model of central control, no one in Board or National Society circles is lobbying at all; there is a need, however, to understand the importance and effectiveness of shared authority and to implement it in sufficient degree to re-inforce the value and place of *local, diocesan* and *national* tiers in the Church's involvement in the education service.

10.3.3: Elected members and appointed officers

Although it operates in a circular chamber, the General Synod when it is in session, appears to the casual observer to operate in

[6] *A Future in Partnership*, pp. 95-96.
[7] *A Future in Partnership*, p. 96.

very many respects with a parliamentary model of procedure. Its members are elected from the dioceses and certain other defined spheres (such as Universities and Religious communities) and some of its members are appointed to its Boards and Councils.[8] Thus, the Board of Education consists of a majority of elected members of Synod, the Chairman usually being a diocesan bishop. The range of policy issues that concern the Board, be they in statutory, voluntary or in-Church education, are remitted via a General Secretary to a staff of specialists who work full time as employees of the Central Board of Finance, the employing agent on behalf of the General Synod. As secular partners peer into the infrastructure of Synod and look particularly at the Board of Education, they see a body that seems analogous to an elected body in local government; interested but busy lay elected members and professionally qualified and experienced officers. Assumptions may, therefore, be made about the style of the Church's activity in education through its national Board.

First, drawing on the analogy with local government, it is all too easy to assume that some sort of line-management exists in the Church and that dealing with the national Board means contact with the 'head' of the line, the powerful end of it in fact. For example, in discussions with Board officers, those of the National Union of Teachers (NUT) seemed perplexed that the Board could not act with real executive authority in matters such as conditions of service of teachers or admissions policies in Voluntary Aided schools. We enjoy cordial relations with NUT officers and those of other professional organizations; I think they have appreciated the difficulties of working not with clearly defined executive authority, but with an achieved credibility.

Second, the assumption about the powerful end of the line may lead to expectation about the range of information that can be collected by the Board staff and which would clearly relate to its establishment of overall views. Most diocesan officers, for example, are scrupulous about the return of statistical or other questionnaires, but by no means all. The Board has no sanctions

[8]The general structure of the General Synod is further outlined in Chapter 5.

to use against the recalcitrant and the wholeness of its statistical
or other kinds of information is often lacking.

Third, and this is a warrantable assumption, drawing on the
analogy of the power-sharing in the education service, those
who deal with the Board have expectations regarding the degree
of consultation it undertakes with the dioceses. In this respect,
the Board enjoys extremely good relationships with diocesan
staff, all of whom relate in their specialities to a corresponding
specialist on the Board staff. For many years, diocesan Directors
of Education have benefited from two annual conferences
organized by the National Society. It was, in fact, from the
ranks of the Directors that the last two General Secretaries were
selected. A great deal of energy has to be channelled into the
consultative process for the time allowed by the DES for
responses by national bodies and LEA's is more and more
truncated.

There are those who feel, with some justification, that the
balance of the Board's agenda and activities seems to be
weighted towards statutory education and schools or Colleges
of Higher Education in particular. We can begin to see why, for
the effectiveness of the Board depends less on its operation
within a clearly defined set of executive parameters than on a
hard-won credibility which depends on more and more effective
engagement with both dioceses and secular bodies. Whenever a
bishop consults the Board staff, or a secular body invites a staff
member to speak at a conference or join a Working Party, there
is, hopefully, a growth in the Board's credibility. It is within
that context of credibility that the Board is able to bring matters
to the attention of the DES and ultimately of the Secretary of
State.

There is, then, positive advantage in the lack of too clearly
defined an authority for the Board. It must work at its
credibility. The striking disadvantage is the onus that is thrown
on the staff and its abilities, for a Board and its sub-Committees
which each meet only three or four times a year have neither the
time nor expertise to involve themselves in detail. Staff have to

be alert, selective, analytic, creative, and tend to turn to those areas where credibility matters most, and for those whose concerns are statutory education, that inevitably means within the education service.

Efforts to achieve a high-profile *there* have tended to lead to a lower profile for the Board in General Synod. The work of the Board surfaces in secular or ecumenical *educational* fields, its staff tend to turn outwards from Church House, from General Synod towards the frontier where Christian engagement with secular ideologies is such an urgent priority. General Synod might, therefore, bestow a certain *initial* credibility on the Board by defining with more clarity some of the areas in statutory education where it wished it to have a sufficient degree of executive authority which would enable it to act with more decisiveness, immediacy and boldness. Such a redefinition could not take place without facing the issue of the autonomy of the individual institution or the authority of diocesan structures and would also require some consultation with the Secretary of State.

10.3.4: The episcopal role

But the mistake he and others may well make in approaching the Church of England is to suppose that it is a democratic institution. It is an episcopal church, the bishop being chief shepherd, pastor, teacher in a diocese. Within an individual diocese, the Synodical structures help in the sharing of ministry, of mission, among the whole people of God. Ultimately, however, the true focus of mission and ministry is in the persona of the bishop. There is a current tension, between the potential for shared decision-making by Synods and the authority of the bishops.[9] Similarly, at national level, the fellowship and shared discussion and decision-making between the 43 dioceses that is possible with General Synod has to come to terms with the authority of the bishops who from time to time clearly exert oversight (episcope) by taking initiatives or curbing in some

[9] For an elaboration of this point, see Chapter 4 of this volume, especially Section 4.2.

way what they see as unwise movement within the Synod as a whole. The Church has found a useful tool in democratic participatory structures for sharing tasks and decision-making; its dilemma is not to wield it so clumsily that it whittles away the authority of the bishop.

It is often secular approaches to the Church on social policy matters that reveal a populist retention of the view that authoritative answers must be sought from the episcopacy rather than boards or committees. During 1981, the Education, Science and Arts Committee of the House of Commons set itself the task of discussing the secondary school curriculum for the 14–16 age range. In the course of its discussions, the Committee sought evidence from a wide range of sources. On matters connected with school worship and religious education, it asked the General Synod Board of Education to submit a memorandum. When, however, a public hearing of oral evidence was arranged, the Committee requested that any delegation should be led by the Archbishop of Canterbury. The attendance and participation of the Chairman of the Board of Education (at that time the Bishop of Bristol) and officers of the Board was welcomed, but clearly the Committee wished both to hear the Archbishop's views and extract from him policy statements on certain key issues if they could. No doubt the members of that Committee were well aware that Board officers would brief the Archbishop and tactfully suggest certain emphases in key areas, but what the Committee required and expected was 'the view of the Church of England'. To them an Archiepiscopal reply was more authoritative in that regard than any Board memorandum or Chairman's reply. In fact, the Archbishop was happy to have the Board's briefing, but his replies to questions in the public session had an inimitable sparkle and conviction which clearly gave them the authority the Committee sought.[10]

During that giving of evidence, the Archbishop, in reply to a question from a member of the Committee, provided what amounted to an assurance that the Church would co-operate in sharing, proportionally, the effects on schools of the falling birth-rate. It is worth pausing and pointing out that while the

[10]See Education, Science and Arts Committee: Session 1980/81. Minutes of Session held on 24 June 1881 (London: HMSO).

Select Committee might regard that assurance as having some considerable weight in view of its Archiepiscopal provenance,[11] in the long run if individual Church schools were determined to act with capricious disregard of such an assurance, they could do so, and thrive and grow at the expense of neighbouring County schools. Some, in fact, are doing just that. Now, if a chairman of a County Education Committee made a public statement saying that his Committee had agreed that all schools would bear, proportionally, the lack of resources due to 'rate-capping' legislation, he has the means to ensure that it takes place. Whatever authority the Archbishop's statements may have had, they were not immediately channelled into a line-management model to be translated into executive action. Thus, the tension between episcopal oversight and participatory democratic structures may exemplify the distancing of vision from *pragmatism* to which I have already referred.

10.4:   Style – Consultation, Negotiation and Confrontation

When I first took my seat as a co-opted member of a County Education Committee, I was reminded by the wise Director of Education not to see myself there to deal only with matters connected with Church schools. I would be expected to contribute to a wide range of issues, and implicit in what he was saying was a degree of expectation that I would inject a distinctively Christian, voluntary and perhaps apolitical contribution on many matters. Generally speaking, in local government, such expectation is evident, except perhaps where the political polarizations are most marked.

The intention and practice of the General Synod and its staff remain set within the widest possible context, and its style over the years testifies to its willingness and ability to relate as a partner within the education service to the Department of Education and Science and the Secretary of State on a wide range of matters. There are two inherent dangers in a policy of wide

[11]For a discussion of the Archbishop's ecclesiastical and political authority, see Chapter 4, Section 4.3.

political engagement. The first is the strain on resources, particularly manpower. The second is that engagement with other educationists on what for want of a better term I call the liberal secular, humanist frontier may compromise the theological and spiritual basis of the Church's educational work.

An illustration of the first danger is any meeting between Church of England officials and those of the DES. We are always heavily out-numbered; there will be a group of DES officers whose specialities bear in some way upon the issue under discussion, there will be a secretary to minute the discussions and likely as not someone from the private office of the Secretary of State and from the legal department. The Church will provide two officers, at most, who will have to cope with all the ramifications of the agenda. These extremely important and often fruitful meetings put considerable strain on the staff of the Board and National Society.

The second danger is harder to pin-point in an illustrative manner. Undergirding the Christian approach to education lies faith in the sovereignty of God, the redeeming work of Christ and the invigorating creative power of the Spirit. This faith informs the vision of human potential and the manner in which a human society might be created which begins to mirror in its life the Kingdom of God. There are officials in the DES and in local government and many teachers who share that faith and vision. Its precise relationship with what is vulgarly known as the 'nitty-gritty' of education is, however, extremely difficult to formulate. There are two particular difficulties in explicating the relationship, and they are closely related. The first is current pressure towards relativism, derived partly from the sociology of knowledge. Once all forms of knowledge are seen as human constructions, they are demystified, they become less powerful influences over society, they are accounted of equal value (i.e. they can be relativised). The often powerfully argued ideas from this kind of sociology appear to offer assistance to beleaguered officials faced with a cacophony of views from the pluralist marketplace; equal treatment becomes fair treatment. This affects the negotiating and consultative process in the political government of education as well as the development of curriculum. Do not, in fact, some modern Religious Education curricular materials, for example, seem to be based on a relativist viewpoint? The actual facts that the Judaeo-Christian tradition undergirds Western civilization, that post-Industrial Revolution Britain bred powerful secularizing forces which are eroding that foundation, contribute to an authentic *cultural bias* which relativism cannot eliminate. Perhaps one of the healthier aspects of the current sharp political polarization is that it represents a desire for integrity of view and distinctiveness of voice and action which together exemplify a vigorous opposition to the forces of relativism.

The second pressure that hinders the articulation of a distinctively Christian voice in education is, therefore, the consensus model that flows rather naturally from a relativist pressure. Accommodation of viewpoints becomes an easier option in the diverse partnership of the education service than the cultivation of a diversity which might dangerously teeter on the brink of divisiveness.

One of the consequences of the side-stepping of an awkward diversity of views is to concentrate on pragmatic issues and it has been all the easier to do that when economic recession wonderfully concentrated the minds of LEA and DES officials on what actually could or could not be done with available resources. But it is important not to see current pragmatism as stemming entirely from economic pressure. It could also have arisen as a direct result of the difficulties encountered in handling a very robust pluralism. By means of it, the 'How?' questions became the easier to deal with, while the 'Why?' questions remain so much more difficult to accommodate within a consensus model, that they are shrugged off. Vision and pragmatism may thus fly apart yet again.

So when the Board officers comment on a document concerned with science teaching or foreign languages in the curriculum, it is all too easy for them to construct their commentary within the benign, liberal, secular framework that many other commentators will be using. It makes it more acceptable, more reasonable to do so. But I wonder what would happen if, at a meeting round a table in Elizabeth House, a Church of England official said, "Look here, Jesus said, 'Blessed are the peacemakers' and also 'Except a grain of wheat fall into the earth and die, it cannot bear fruit', so we have been thinking out how Church schools might change, radically perhaps, so that Christians can exert a clearer reconciling peacemaking role in multi-racial areas", I wonder what the reaction would be? Certainly nervous shuffles at what might be dubbed 'preaching'! But is such a close correspondence of vision and practice any different from the eager politician who very properly appeals to his basic philosophy or the party manifesto?

Inherent, then, in the actual encounters between representatives of the central organs of the Church involved in education and Departmental or governmental officials, is the difficulty of explicating with sufficient clarity a characteristically Christian basis to a response, proposal or appeal, without being tediously polemical or arrogantly isolationist. With these preliminary considerations in mind, is it possible to analyse, succinctly, the style of the engagement between Church and government in educational policy and affairs? This I must now attempt, with a reminder that the personal nature of this chapter restricts the illustrations largely to school matters.

10.4.1: Consultation – by representation

The Church of England has a number of opportunities through regular or occasional membership of committees, working parties or 'quangos' set up by central government or other national bodies (such as CLEA or teachers' organizations) to engage in prolonged periods of consultation. I was, for example, a member of the Taylor Committee on school government. The present Deputy Secretary of the Board (at the time of writing; he is now General Secretary) is a member of the Committee which deals with the supply and education of teachers, and more recently has become one of the three Voluntary sector representatives on the National Advisory Board which deals with Higher Education outside the Universities. *Membership* of such groups, rather than mere observer status, enables participation on a representative basis – members are not delegates – and such participation can, therefore, be on the basis of personal contribution as well as attempts to be the mouthpiece of the Church.

My own experience of the Taylor Committee confirmed the

equality of membership that can exist in central committees – though this in no way implies an equality of contribution. There was a high degree of fellowship and respect and a conscious effort to close the gap between vision and pragmatism, essential if the recommendations were to be backed by cogency of argument and based on thoroughly explicated principles. The recommendations which followed the 'four-equal-shares' model for the school governing body, for example, seemed obvious enough consequences of a closely argued case to those of us on the Committee. To groups jockeying for power in the education service, the vision seemed so much 'pie-in-the-sky' that the recommendations were severely criticized.

Voluntary schools were not considered in detail by the Taylor Committee but a brief chapter was included on the possible effects of the Report's recommendations on the Voluntary schools. I and my Roman Catholic colleague were drawn in to help draft that particular section. Discussion and drafting over two years, involvement in the whole range of issues concerning school government, and the opportunity to consult with LEAs on a number of planned visits was, I believe, a valuable reinforcement, through my membership, of the partnership role of the Church of England, as well as being an enviable piece of in-service education on a more personal basis. Commitment by a diverse group to its Report and recommendations demonstrates the creative potential possible with this type of consultative process, while the return of the members to their own spheres of work (during and after the process) enables a subtle effective dispersal of the fruits of discussion in a manner quite different from a simple production of the printed Report.

The Church is wise, then, to engage in processes of committee-style consultation whenever it is invited to do so, whether on short-term committees or groups, or on longer-term more permanent bodies.

10.4.2: Consultation – by response

The most obvious exemplification of partnership on the part of national bodies concerned with the education service is in their simple requests for responses to proposals, documents or reports. There is a continuous flow of documents from the DES, and the mainstream voluntary bodies remain on the list of bodies who are asked to make responses. It is impossible in this brief chapter to quote more than a few examples but a list of some of the main responses made by the Church of England since 1976 is appended in a note. The nature of consultation may be simply *administrative* but whenever possible the Board and National Society have scrupulous regard to the request to respond; so often larger issues lurk in the seemingly innocent verbiage of an administrative document. The Board was asked (during 1983), for example, to comment on a form which it is intended to use in the 1984 Secondary School Staffing Survey.[12] Included in this draft form were questions about Religious and Moral Education which were treated *together* as though one area of study. As a result of our response, that particular section of the form was redrafted treating RE and Moral Education separately. This is important, since RE is statutorily required under the Education Act 1944 and Moral Education is not, and additionally, there are always those in the education service who would be more than willing to subsume religious education within moral education or some kind of overall humanities course.

Before the Taylor Committee met, the Board provided views about the government of schools, and after the Taylor Committee had published its Report, a response was made to its recommendations. This kind of broad response to wider issues assists in the *formation of policy*. For example, contrary to what articles and letters in the press have supposed, the Board actually requested that the Voluntary schools (excluded from the Taylor Committee's considerations) should not be left out of any legislative changes, particularly as regards the inclusion of parent and teacher members of governing bodies. The history of education in schools in Britain since the passing of the 1944 Education Act, demonstrates a degree of consultation between the partners unrivalled in any other country. It allows for the variable pattern of political control that exists in LEA's, it extends consultative processes to voluntary bodies and, up until the difficulties encountered in resourcing education during the present economic recession, eschewed a dominating 'centrist' role for the DES.

[12]1984 Secondary School Staffing Survey (ST26A/3/069), DES.

As far as the Church of England is concerned, the opportunity to respond is sometimes an occasion for taking an *initiative*. Clearly, one of the reasons for the exclusion of the Voluntary schools from the deliberations of the Taylor Committee was the extraordinary administrative and legal problem of reorganizing, in the case of the Church of England's schools, over six thousand *separate* Instruments of Government. The Board's suggestion of *grouping* instruments by diocese, though it met with procedural and legal objections along the way, has been accepted as a model for implementing the new-style governing bodies which are to be provided under the Education Act 1980.

10.4.3: Negative consultation

When issuing some statistics in 1982 relating to future initial teacher-training needs, the Department made a new and startling move. I described it in the discussion paper to which I have referred already:

'Even more serious was the proposal (by simply writing "NIL" against certain instructions) that at some colleges initial teacher-training should cease altogether. The colleges concerned would almost certainly have to close. Why? Were they failing to be cost-effective? Was their staff-student ratio too low? Were their results worse than other colleges? The simple device of writing "NIL" in a statistical table against a named institution provided no answers to such questions. To be fair, the Minister of State concerned with teacher-training (at that time the Hon. William Waldegrave MP) dealt justly and carefully with the detailed and rational objections that were presented to him, and some of the anomalies and threatened closures were avoided by his willingness to alter the figures.'[13]

Threatening an institution by an omission in statistics seemed a curious way to ask for consultation about its possible closure. The statistics as a whole provided, however, the context within which any justification for retention of that college would have to be made, for they were describing a pattern of cutback in initial teacher-training of which the institution's promoters

[13] *A Future in Partnership*, p. 74.

would need to take account in presenting their argument. Were the officials at the DES acting with more than their customary degree of cunning? What looked like a ham-fisted and unhelpful forecasting exercise (issued in August, to boot!) could, on reflection, have been a curiously planned threatening gesture to certain institutions which, at the same time, provided them with the general framework within which any justification for continuation would have to be made.

Perhaps the DES is increasingly forced to justify its expenditure for the Treasury within a framework of hard economic statistics and computer-based forecasting and is passing this process on to other partners in the education service. It is not surprising, therefore, to find that the bulk of the White Paper, 'Teaching Quality',[14] is based on a section called 'School Teachers-demand and supply'. While a market-place pragmatism rules educational planning, the Church, unusually hard-headed and realisitic though it has learned to be, may have the unenviable task of drawing to the attention of the DES and many LEAs, the fundamental visionary, idealistic basis to the function of education. The trouble with current pragmatism is its resistance to radical change. Its attitude to growth is based on *adaptation*, its resistance to radicalism is unfortunate in view of the present administration's genuine concern to understand and utilize the new technologies. We have become used to reading between the lines in Government documents on education. Now, we learn to look between the columns of statistics.

10.4.4: *Negotiation and confrontation*

That no political grouping, of those at present represented at Westminster, has ever stated its intention to abolish the Voluntary schools and so the 'dual system', cynics will observe may be due to fear of losing votes rather than any altruism regarding voluntary involvement in education. The lie to this is in the willingness of central government to meet Church leaders over issues where discussion and direct negotiation have become necessary. The best recent example of this is afforded by the

---

[14]*Teaching Quality* (Cmnd. 8836), HMSO.

discussions surrounding the Bill that became the Education Act 1980.

The Rt. Hon. Shirley Williams, whilst Secretary of State for Education and Science in the Labour Administration of 1975 to 1979, had published a Bill which, with regard to changes in school government, was very similar in scope to the later Bill published by her Conservative successor, the Rt. Hon. Mark Carlisle QC. Both Bills proposed changes in school government which would require central government and Church representatives to tread over some hard-won territory. The well-known two-thirds church governors, one-third other governors pattern for Voluntary Aided schools (and vice versa for Voluntary Controlled schools) was holy ground over which negotiations had hitherto not needed to tread. But to leave that pattern and allow for the inclusion of parent and teacher governors would so enlarge governing bodies that the situation for small schools would be quite ridiculous.

Both Mrs. Williams and, in the later Conservative administration, Baroness Young, Minister of State at the DES, met Church leaders at a series of discussions to which they both gave generously in time and seriously in commitment. A range of issues apart from logistics was discussed and negotiated. The two-thirds, one-third pattern was replaced in Voluntary Aided schools by a majority of two Foundation governors, three in bodies with more than eighteen members. There was some concern expressed at the possible omission of minor authority representatives and provision for them was replaced. There was discussion over the desirability of elections for parent governors who also represented the Foundation. The actual membership of the Head-teacher of a school on a governing body rather than the common 'seat, voice but no vote' pattern was left to individual Heads, but they must elect not to be governors. In other words, the discussions were detailed and the feel of both sets of meetings was that negotiation was welcomed and changes were, indeed, possible.

It is important at this stage, however, to describe the layers of discussion, as it were, that take place before senior representatives of Churches meet with Ministers or the Secretary of State. The Schools' Officer of the General Synod Board of Education and National Society and a legal adviser had a series of discussions with officers representing the Schools Branch at the DES. It is that sort of frequent engagement which enables both sides to sniff out the scents worth following up and to detect the false trails. The value of any brief given to the episcopal Chairman who will be meeting the Secretary of State depends almost entirely on the satisfactory conduct of preliminary discussions. Generally speaking, officers of Board and National Society meet officers at the DES (i.e. civil servants). It is the Chairman of the Board/National Society or in some cases sub-Committee Chairmen who meet with Ministers or the Secretary of State, though, of course, officers accompany them. At that level, the meeting will almost certainly be ecumenical (see Section 10.5 below).

It was during the discussions of the Bill to be presented to the House of Commons by Mr. Carlisle, that a proposed section on school transport came in for severe criticism by the Churches. The Section of the Bill (23) would allow Local Education Authorities to make charges for school transport and removed the right of the Secretary of State to *direct* LEAs to provide transport in special instances. This seemed to the Churches, particularly the Roman Catholic officials, an erosion of the position ensured by the Education Act 1944 which allowed free transport to pupils whose parents had opted for a particular school on religious grounds. Those of us who were negotiating on behalf of the Church of England were not happy with the Roman Catholic representatives' narrow view of free or subsidized transport. Widening the applicability of assistance to poorer families, those in special need (Welsh parents seeking a bilingual school, for example) or with particular ethnic cultural values which the system might need to accommodate (for example, Muslim parents seeking single-sex schools) seemed to us necessary, fair and proper.

Tactically, what was interesting about this particular confrontation was the misjudgement by Mr. Carlisle and his officials and by Baroness Young, who so admirably handled the whole Bill in the House of Lords, of the strength of feeling in the Roman Catholic Church. Their officials had sought advice of counsel and briefed Catholic peers to oppose Section 23 when it was dealt with at the Committee stage in the House of Lords. Cardinal Hume had corresponded with the Prime Minister.

In the marshalled list of Amendments to be dealt with in the Lords was one in the name of the Duke of Norfolk which sought to ensure that transport arrangements would be provided for children whose parents desired a particular religious instruction which was not available within walking distance.[15] At that time, the Chairman of the General Synod Board of Education (the Bishop of Bristol) was not a member of the Lords. But, of those bishops who were present during the Committee stage, two at least were from dioceses with large rural areas where the issue of free or subsidized transport was keenly felt. At the same time, as was properly pointed out to me, bishops are individual Lords spiritual who must be careful not to give the impression that they represent particular groups or bodies when they speak.

The House was packed for Clause 23; an impressive whip had been applied to Catholic peers. But the seal was set on the issue of transport by an eloquent speech from Lord Butler of Saffron Walden, architect of the 1944 settlement. He saw the issue of free transport as if not integral, at least a vital part of the settlement with the Churches, and part of that concordat was the reservation of power to the Secrerary of State, though it had been seldom used. He spoke of the enormous number of letters he had received on the issue. The Bishop of London (The Rt. Revd. and Rt. Hon. Graham Leonard) could not accept the clause either. It was, he said, 'a deep matter of conscience'[16] and he wanted to stand by the settlement made in 1944. The Bishop of Rochester (The Rt. Revd. David Say) voiced his concern over the issue 'as a community and society matter' rather than as a denominational issue.[17] In her closing speech, Baroness Young, rightly in my view, pointed to changes in the 1944 Settlement that had been made in the Churches' favour, notably the increase in grant-aid towards capital and maintenance costs of Voluntary Aided schools from 50% to 85%. The Churches had also allowed the provisions of the Bill before the House in 1980 to

[15]Marshalled list of Amendments (House of Lords) Education (No. 2) Bill, p. 4l.
[16]House of Lords – *Hansard*: Proceedings, 13 March 1980, Col. 1230.
[17]As in Note l6, Col. 1256.

change the 1944 Settlement regarding governing bodies. She, as it happened wrongly, accused Anglican education officials of not voicing opposition to Clause 23 at earlier meetings with her and DES officers. Our difficulty was that the clause on charges for transport was not in our opinion an issue on which we would choose to mount all our forces of opposition. The Roman Catholics chose to do so; now central and local government know how far the Catholic authorities can go in mounting such opposition and all the forces at their command have been exposed. There may be occasions when more fundamental and far-reaching proposals regarding education need formidable opposition from the Church of England; until then, no one has yet seen all the cards in the Anglican hand. When they are all played, it is my hope that they are used not to trump some self-interested, narrow, denominational interest but on behalf of the welfare of the whole education service.

10.5: The Ecumenical Dimension

The particular example of the 1980 Education Act draws attention to another interesting dynamic in the relationship of the Church of England to the political shapers and providers of education and that is the tension between *ecumenical resolve* and *denominational activity*.

What is known as the Lund principle, namely, that Churches should not do separately what they can do together has, since 1944, been increasingly applied to statutory education. There exists a Central Joint Education Policy Committee which consists of representatives and education officers of the major denominations. It is usually chaired by the Chairman of the Anglican Board of Education, at present the Bishop of London. He would certainly like this particular committee to have a higher profile, and to communicate more effectively with its constituent churches. Broadly speaking, the Committee deals with current issues and pressures in maintained schools and to some extent in Church Colleges of Higher Education (though the Association of Voluntary Colleges is a more prominent ecumenical base for Higher Education). It also acts as a planning group when the Churches wish to approach the Secretary of State or when he consults Churches. At the time of writing

(March 1984), for example, the Churches are preparing to meet the Secretary of State, Sir Keith Joseph, at his request, in order to discuss his speech made at the North of England conference earlier in the year, during the course of which he outlined plans for higher standards in secondary schooling. But the confrontation on school transport in 1980 exemplifies the tension between the genuine desire and need for the Churches to work together and their tendency, because of fundamental difference of theological understanding and educational outlook, to continue to operate as denominations.

The basic premise on which the Roman Catholic opposition to Clause 23 in the 1980 (No. 2) Bill was based was that Catholic children should be able to find a school with Catholic teachers and Catholic instruction and ethos both at primary and secondary level. On that premise, the total opposition of the Roman Catholics to charges for school transport is quite understandable. Anglicans live bifocally, and have tried in their schools to express two policies, Anglican education for those who seek it, and a general service to the nation's children through public education. When closing the ranks to negotiate with the Secretary of State, the Churches must not assume greater unity of purpose and action than in fact exists. If they do make such assumptions, they may well be pandering to that dangerous relativism to which I have already drawn attention.

10.6: Church and Education – Present and Future

This chapter has tried to delineate the style of the Church of England's involvement in the political and administrative shaping of publicly-funded education. It is necessary, finally, to draw attention, briefly, to those movements or pressures in Church or State which will affect the form or style of the Anglican contribution to the provision of schooling in this country.

First, partly due to relativist pressures and partly to attitudes of retrenchment within the Church itself, there is a pressure on Church schools and on Christians in education in general to reinforce identity and distinctiveness, by a retreat. Church schools for Anglicans only can become ghetto-like huddles, and there is a growing feeling amongst some Church people that what can be created by way of distinctive ethos in a school (or also in a Church College of Higher Education) will demand a setting-apart, and conscious efforts to gather those of faith together in a distinctive community. Stemming from this kind of emphasis is the language of two sectors, County and Voluntary, and a regrettable tendency among officials both centrally and locally to speak of denominational schools. There is *one* publicly-funded sector of school education; the Church must remember that. There are still those, however, who feel that advance can only be made by immersion in the whole educational world and that a distinctive contribution to that world is best made whilst committed to it and largely identified with it. The balance between these views will vitally affect the nature of the Anglican role as partner in the education service.

Second, the growth of 'centrist' views about the planning of education, and centralized efforts to force some kind of curricular consensus in the education service, are seriously disturbing the role of partners and increasingly putting at risk Voluntarist elements in the educational partnership. They are the elements most accused of waywardness and perhaps, therefore, treated as less controllable by the central organs of control. This may well require of the Church of England a higher public profile in educational debate and planning in order to exemplify the positive and creative role of voluntary elements in the service and also to act as an objective commentator on the increasing mutilation of the long-standing educational partnership between central and local government.

Third, the polarization of views about the education of children and young people has shifted its ground from the 11+ area, the transition from primary to secondary schooling, to the 16 year old and his future. Thus, what was largely an *educational* debate has become a debate about several overlapping areas of social policy. Most sixteen year olds are seeking work; the issues of employment and unemployment become enmeshed with questions of educational policy (the Department of Employment, through MSC and its Youth Training Scheme become an educational provider!). The vocational aims of education take the stage, the debatable and less tangible objectives of personal growth in education recede. Utilitarianism rules, OK? The 16 year old who seeks further education and is not destined for Higher Education, does not require a watered-down version of A-level courses but a mixture of school-based and FE College-based work combined with work experience.

At a time when the pace of change in the modern world would seem to dictate a wide base of experience for the 16 plus age-group (as in the good primary school), the focus of pupils is narrowed by early specialization or vocationally oriented courses for work which increasingly is not there. The relationship of the education of the 16-19 age group with the new information technologies is a field as yet virtually unexplored because prevailing pragmatism refuses to resource what appears to cautious planners as speculative.

The Church's institutional load is at the primary school end (2,000 plus Anglican primary Voluntary Aided schools over against 150 plus secondary Voluntary Aided schools). Shifting not only attitudes in the Church towards a fuller involvement across the education service and particularly to FE and tertiary styles, but also shifting resources so that they can be shared more equitably, will involve a huge collective act of will as well as a possible change in the law. Clinging to what is legally provided in institutions, may prevent the Church from vital ministries in more voluntary and informal situations in statutory education.

Fourth, and finally, perhaps the most challenging issues of educational policy arise from our efforts in the education service to make sense of a plural society. Particularly related to Church schools is the difficult choice between open or closed admissions policies. There is the challenge of building a Religious Education curriculum which has a thorough Christian base but which does not ignore the need for growing sensitivity to the claims of other faiths. There is, in general, a need to be aware of cultural bias, essential if education is to initiate children into what is publicly validated as worthwhile; but how do we handle such bias so that ethnic groups do not feel discriminated against? How can diversity, to put it differently, be prevented from being a force for divisiveness?

The Church of England faces, as a partner in the education service, the challenge of producing a distinctive style of engagement based on theological and educational understanding, a distinctiveness that is seen to contribute to the richness of the service as a whole rather than enabling a self-interested isolation.

APPENDED NOTE

In a paper prepared for a committee in Church House, Westminster, the Board of Education, in 1981, drew attention to responses to the DES, made since 1977. This list illustrates the heavy involvement of Board officers in responses to central government.

1976 The Taylor Report on Government of Schools
1977 The Holland Report (on Youth Unemployment)
*1978 The Oakes Report on Higher Education
*1978 The Warnock Report on Special Education
*1978 Higher Education into the 1990s
1979 The Waddell Report (on 16+ Examinations)
1979/80 The Keohane Report (ditto)
1980 McFarlane Report on Education for the 16-19s
1981 Green Paper on Management of Higher Education

Documents in 'The Great Debate' initiated by Mr. Callaghan in October 1976:

1977 Education and Schools (Green Paper)
1977 Ten Good Schools (HMI)
*1977 Curriculum 11-16 (HMI)
1978 Mixed Ability Teaching in Comprehensive Schools (HMI)
1978 Primary Education in England (HIM Survey)
1979 Aspects of Secondary Education (HMI)
1980 A View of the Curriculum (HMI)
1981 The School Curriculum (DES)

Major legislation

*1978 Education Bill No. 1 (Labour Government)
*1980 Education Bill No. 2 (present Government)
*1980/81 Passage of Bill as Education Act 1980

Select Committee on Education and Science

1981 Evidence on Higher Education
1981 Evidence on Religious Education (Officers accompanied the Archbishop to give oral evidence on RE)
1981–82 Manpower Services Commission paper on new Youth Training Scheme
1981 Evidence to Committee preparing Report on the Youth Service in England (submitted via NCVYS)

Those documents marked * required *two* submissions, (a) evidence *before* the Report was compiled, and (b) comment subsequent to its publication.

Chapter 11

THE CHURCH AND ECONOMIC POLICY
John Sleeman

11.1: Introduction – In What Sense Can One Talk of an Anglican Economic Policy?

The Church of England is, of course, only part of the Anglican Communion. Even within Britain, the Church in Wales, the Scottish Episcopal Church and the Church of Ireland, must also be considered. Though these are minority Churches, they often have an influence on economic and social thinking in their countries out of proportion to their size. Yet the size and the establishment of the Church of England give it a leading role, if only because it can muster a much larger force of theologians and social thinkers in the universities and in its own organs such as the Board of Social Responsibility, and because it is nearer to the centres of power.

Anglicanism, however, in its very nature, is extremely diverse and non-authoritarian. In the Roman Catholic Church, for instance, the Pope's encyclicals, such as the recent 'Laborem Exercens' on labour and industrial relations,[1] have an authority over the faithful deriving from the magisterium. The pronouncements of Church of England synods, committees and commissions, still less those of archbishops and bishops, can have no similar authority over or against the diverse and often contradictory opinions of different groups among the Church's members. Moreover, opinions on economic and social issues held by Anglicans are not easily distinguishable from those of members of other Churches, in particular the Methodists, the Church of Scotland, the United Reformed Church and indeed many Roman Catholics. All share in the social and intellectual

[1] *Laborem Exercens*, Papal Encyclical (London: Catholic Truth Society, 1981).

256

climate of their country and time, and in so far as they differ in their social philosophies, these differences tend to cut across denominations rather than coinciding with them.

Hence, in many cases, the views held by churchpeople do not differ greatly from those of large numbers of men and women of goodwill who would not claim a close relationship to any Church. In particular, there is a basic Left-Right dichotomy which runs right through social and political thinking, reflecting to some extent economic position and interests and to some extent temperament and cast of mind. Some are natural conservatives and some natural liberals or radicals. One would like to think that Christians, trained to be self-critical and aware of their own biases, should be better able to transcend such considerations in the light of the Gospel. This is often true, yet the disagreements between Christians still remain, as do the agreements on political policies between Christians and non-Christians.

Yet, though we cannot claim that there is 'an' official Church of England, or Anglican, economic doctrine, this does not mean that there are not distinguishable predominant economic philosophies which can be regarded as characteristic of the most influential Anglican circles. The most distinctive of these in recent decades is what we call for convenience, the 'Social-Catholic Tradition' and on this we will concentrate, though we must look later at an opposed, more conservative tradition, which we will call the 'Liberal-Evangelical'.

11.2: The Social-Catholic Tradition

The social-catholic tradition, as its name implies, is associated with the Anglo-Catholic strain of Anglican thinking, rather than Evangelical, but it is much wider, embracing a great number of those who see a concern for social justice and the welfare of the community as an integral part of the Gospel. In this sense, it reflects Catholic incarnational theology, in which the Incarnation involves a concern for the whole world which Christ came to save and of which he became a part. Individual salvation, men's personal relationship with God, cannot be separated from their membership of community. What they are and how they relate to God and their fellows is affected by the society to which they belong, which profoundly influences and moulds them. Hence, a concern for social, economic and political justice is inseparable from the proclamation of the Gospel.

This tradition goes through Anglican thinking from the Oxford Movement onwards, through Maurice and Kingsley and the Christian Socialists, Tawney and his analysis of the relationship between capitalism and religion, Gore and Temple and the COPEC movement of the 1920s, the Christendom Group of the 1930s, in spite of their aberrant interest in Social Credit, more recently through Temple's *Christianity and the Social Order*,[2] and more recently still, the writings of Professor Ronald Preston of Manchester. It is by no means confined to Anglicans. It is strong in the Iona Community in the Church of Scotland, in Methodism with its long social tradition, and indeed a great deal of the work of the British Council of Churches and the World Council of Churches.

Because of its acceptance of the influence of social and economic factors on the beliefs and opinions of people in different positions in society, the tradition accepts the relativity of economic and political views. It does not believe in the possibility of 'a' Christian political or social philosophy, though accepting that Christian belief and commitment must always act as a critique of all economic or political positions. We must always be prepared to hold our views under the judgement of God's truth as revealed in Christ and to recognise the extent to which our sincerely held beliefs may be influenced by our individual or group interests and our differences in background and temperament. The truth is much greater than any individual and it is not to be accepted that Christians, any more than anyone else, will arrive at the same opinions.

Hence, it is not surprising or shocking, for instance, that businessmen take a different view of the role of private enterprise and profit as against that of the Government, than do industrial employees, or, say, teachers, social workers or those working in the National Health Service.

[2]W. Temple, *Christianity and Social Order* (London: Penguin, 1942), reissued by SPCK and Seabury Press, 1976.

For the same reason, those in this tradition would deny that it is possible directly to derive principles for the organisation of government and the econony by taking texts from the Bible. In part, this arises from a Catholic understanding of the Bible, which sees it as only one of the means through which God speaks to men, along with the tradition of the Church and the guidance of the Spirit to the individual conscience. It also arises from a less mechanical understanding of the ways in which God speaks to men, which sees him as acting through their minds and experience as they seek His Will in the situation in which they find themselves. This applies as much to the tradition of the Church and to the individual conscience as it does to the Bible. Whether it be the Deuteronomic writings or the words of the prophets in the Old Testament, those who recorded Christ's words and deeds in the Gospels, the letters of Paul and the other epistle writers, or the teachings of the Fathers and the Councils of the Church, the writings of the Reformers or the thoughts and actions of Christians today, each has to be taken in the context of the situation in which it was being spoken or written.

In this connection, a good deal of prominence has been given to the concept of middle axioms, which was first put forward in a book prepared for the Oxford Conference on Church, State and Community in 1937.[3] These are 'middle' in the sense that they lie between the general principles of the Christian Faith, on which all, or most, Christians would agree, on the one hand, and detailed statements on particular policy issues on the other hand, on which Christians, like other people of goodwill, would probably disagree because of differences of background and temperament and variations in level of technical competence.

Middle axioms thus embody fairly broad statements of agreed consensus in particular areas of practical policy, on which Christians with the requisite knowledge and experience can come to agreement and which they can commend as a basis from which to approach more detailed practical issues. Often the consensus will be shared by many with a broad humanist background who would not call themselves Christians. Two examples from the economic field were given by John Bennett

[3]J.H. Oldham and W.A. Visser t'Hooft (eds.), *The Church and its Function in Society* (London: George Allen and Unwin, 1937).

in 1946 [4] and are quoted by Ronald Preston:[5] (i) the government has the responsibility of maintaining full employment and (ii) private centres of economic power should not be stronger than the government.

As these examples make clear, such axioms are always provisional and temporary. The first of them was not accepted before the days of Keynes and the Keynesians and has already been seriously questioned by the monetarists. The second is perhaps on firmer ground, though some extreme economic liberals would probably query it. Both would, however, find general acceptance among those in the Social-Catholic tradition. The great advantage of this approach, however, is that it avoids the opposite dangers of, on the one hand, taking refuge in generalisations so wide and innocuous as to be platitudinous, coupled often with a retreat into pietism, or on the other hand, claiming the authority of God for particular policy positions which many Christians on grounds of conviction find themselves unable to accept.

It follows that those who adopt such an approach are reluctant to commit themselves to the position that support for one political party or economic system comes nearer to being 'Christian' than another. We all know that there are very many sincere Christians who are committed to the Conservative, Labour, Liberal, Social Democrat and other 'mainline' parties, such as the Scottish and Welsh Nationalists. There are many who are convinced Socialists and others who are firm supporters of private enteprise.

Nevertheless, it is fair to say that the proponents of the Social-Catholic tradition broadly favour what may be called a social democratic approach to political and economic problems, though with a small 's' and 'd' and not to be identified with support for the Social Democrat Party. Such an approach implies the acceptance of a mixed economy, with an active role for private enterprise and the free market, but also an active and positive role for the Government, in macroeconomic policy to

[4]J. Bennett, *Christian Social Action* (London: Lutterworth Press, 1954).
    [5]R.H. Preston, *Explorations in Theology – 9* (London: SCM, 1981), p. 39. Reproduced from *Crucible*, January-February, (1971), pp. 9-15.

hold the balance of the economy, in economic planning and the guidance of investment and above all, perhaps, in the maintenance and improvement of the Welfare State and in concern to reduce poverty and inequality.

Their attitude both to capitalism and to socialism has been ambivalent. They have tended to have a strong sympathy for the ideals of socialism, as embodying a concern for a juster and more equitable society, based on service of others rather than self-seeking. They have also had a distaste for capitalism, because of its emphasis on profit-making and personal gain and its tendencies, if uncontrolled, to lead to inequalities of wealth and power, to exploitation of the weak and an emphasis on money rather than service. This can be clearly seen in the writers mentioned above, from Maurice through Gore and Temple, from Tawney's *Religion and the Rise of Capitalism* to Demant's *Religion and the Decline of Capitalism*.[6]

Yet they have been influenced also by the other side of the coin. Experience of the only historical models of socialism which we have, the economies of Eastern Europe, China and Cuba, for instance, have made it clear how difficult it is to combine State ownership and control with economic efficiency, particularly if centralised planning is attempted. Such an overall control fails to provide the goods and services which consumers want and gives the producers no incentives to use resources efficiently, while the complexity of the decisions which have to be made by the planners is such that, even with computers, they cannot conceivably undertake them all themselves. The concentration of economic and political powers into the same hands also leads to a denial of intellectual and political freedom and all the evils of totalitarianism.

On the other hand, the free market system and the pursuit of profit undoubtedly provide a stimulus to efficiency in meeting consumers' wants, by encouraging enterprise and penalising inefficiency and providing a feedback through the price system from consumers to producers. This is the more true if the market can be kept reasonably free by curbs on monopoly

---

[6]R.H. Tawney, *Religion and the Rise of Capitalism* (London: Penguin, 1938); V.A. Demant, *Religion and the Decline of Capitalism* (London: Faber and Faber, 1952).

power and by intervention by the Government to provide publicly those services which the market and the profit motive cannot provide adequately, since public benefits and costs do not reflect private benefits and costs.

Thus, in 1977, Professor Preston gave his Maurice Lectures the title of 'Religion and the Persistence of Capitalism',[7] pointing out that capitalism, for all its contradictions, had persisted with a vigour which earlier socialist critics might find surprising, largely for the reasons just mentioned.

The tradition is also essentially outward-looking in concern for the whole world, though this aspect has become more prominent in the post-1945 period, reflecting the general movement of opinion. The social and economic problems of Britain today can only be understood in the light of our wider involvements. Hence, there is concern for our relationships with Europe, including a generally favourable, though far from uncritical, attitude to our membership of the European Economic Community. There is a strong emphasis on the responsibility of the rich North in the world towards the poor South, reflected in active support for voluntary agencies such as Christian Aid and Oxfam, but also for the principles of the Pearson and Brandt Reports.[8] There is a concern also for West-East relations and a desire to find a more constructive and less confrontational approach. Similarly, on defence issues, though Christians are deeply divided over unilateral or multilateral approaches to nuclear disarmament, there is an emphasis on avoiding a retreat into sterile confrontation and on seeking ways towards genuine understanding.

11.3: The Individualist-Evangelical Tradition

Alongside this dominant tradition, there is another one which has equally deep roots which we can call the 'Individualist-

[7]R.H. Preston, *Religion and the Persistence of Capitalism* (London: SCM, 1979).

[8]*Partners in Development: Report of the Commission on International Development* (Pearson Report), (London: Pall Mall Press, 1969); *North-South: A Programme for Survival* (Brandt Report), (London: Pan, 1980).

Evangelical'. Evangelicals have rightly always placed a great stress on the individual experience of salvation, accepting the call of God and the new life which he offers in Christ and the individual responsibility to work out what this means in terms of personal life, work and business experience and life in the community. Frequently, though not always, this has tended to lead to a less active concern for the community itself and its influence on the lives of its members. Stress has been laid on the individual's obligation to serve his neighbours through personal service and support for charities as well as public social services, but not so much on the responsiblity for working out the meaning of the Kingdom in terms of how the community as a whole orders its political and economic life.

Because of this individualistic approach, the emphasis comes to be placed more on economic freedom, on business success as the fruits of working out a vocation, on the working of the market as a means to personal fulfillment and the good life, and on the responsibility of each person to give conscientious service in his or her work.

In another sense, however, this tradition is more authoritarian than the social-catholic one, as that is found in Anglicanism. This is because it starts from a strong sense of the authority of Scripture and of God's law as embodied in it. Hence, it believes that in the Bible can be found an authoritative guide to all aspects of Christian ethics, both personal and collective.

Interestingly, there are two streams of thought which arise from this tradition. One, the more individualistic, is roughly what is outlined above, namely that the Christian's duty is to follow his call, keep God's law in his personal conduct and be active in good works and charities on behalf of others, to the extent that he is blessed with material riches. But there is also a more collectivist strain, which sees a possible blueprint from which an ideal community could be built in the social teaching about the life of Israel, especially as found in the Deuteronomic tradition in the Old Testament. Those who follow this line place great emphasis on what can be learned, for instance, from the teachings about the redistribution of property under the Law of Jubilee, the freeing of debtors after seven years and the prohibition of usury.

An important example of this is the development of a theology of social change from an evangelical and biblical point of view by the Unit on Ethics and Society of the Theological Commission of the World Evangelical Fellowship, concerned particularly with justice between the rich North and the poor South of the world. It is well expounded in a recent work edited by Ronald Sider entitled *Evangelicals and Development: Towards a Theology of Social Change*.[9] Nearer home, we may mention the work of Donald Hay of Oxford and Anthony Cramp of Cambridge.

Nor should we forget the very important part played by Evangelicals in campaigning for and carrying out practical measures to combat social injustices, from the days of Wilberforce and Shaftesbury onwards.

11.4: The Conservative Reaction

There has also been a conservative reaction against the social-catholic tradition which has been associated with traditional central churchmanship rather than the Evangelical position. This has been articulated most explicitly by Dr. Edward Norman of Peterhouse, Cambridge, but it has clearly found widespread rank and file support. It has even been expounded *ex cathedra* in leading articles in *The Times*.[10]

The criticism which these conservatives make is that the dominant social, economic and political thinking of the Church has confused the Gospel with left-wing theories and policies, rather than attempting to work out a specifically Christian economic and political philosophy. They would quote, for instance, the support for an active role for the Government in the economy, the concern to support the Third World countries both politically and economically with an alleged disregard for their internal weaknesses and injustices, and a hostile attitude to South Africa which is not matched by equal hostility to the

---

[9]R. Sider (ed.), *Evangelicals and Development: Towards a Theology of Social Change* (Exeter: Paternoster Press, 1981).
[10]Cf., *The Times*, November 21st 1983, on the Archbishop of York's Enthronement Sermon.

misdeeds of the communist regimes. Some of them would go further and maintain that the Church is mistaken in giving importance to the pursuit of social and political justice and should be concentrating rather on proclaiming the good news of individual salvation and upholding moral standards.

It is not surprising that the 'eighties have seen a reaction from exaggerated hopes of what could be achieved by the Government through macroeconomic policy, the Welfare State and the search for a juster international order. In the harsh climate of today, with world recession, high unemployment along with inflation and the growing calls on the public purse if we are to stay where we are in the social services, together with the threatening international situation, people are tempted to withdraw into concern for themselves and their families and an emphasis on self-help and individual effort. The monetarist economic theories of Friedman and his followers have provided the necessary intellectual base for a renewed emphasis on the primacy of the market, while the Keynesianism which underlay so much of the policies of the 'fifties, 'sixties and early 'seventies is widely held to be discredited.

The social-catholic tradition is thus under attack, but it seems to me that its supporters have a good case for meeting the attacks head on. It must be accepted that none of us is completely unbiased and disinterested. We are all influenced in our thinking by our family background and our economic and social position as well as by our natural cast of temperament. There are natural 'leftists' and natural 'rightists', as well as some who move from the one to the other. This has been true of the holders of all social philosophies throughout history. Hence one cannot arrive at a wholly Christian social philosophy based solely on pure theology, since the way we look at God and his purposes is influenced by all these background factors.

If, then, the social-catholics have a predilection for the Left in their thinking, it is fair to say that the neo-conservatives have a predilection for the Right, for the values built into traditional 'Christendom' as it has developed in the West, for the ordered, somewhat hierarchical society which reflects our national historical experience. One is reminded of the local newspaper in the 'thirties which reported that, with the defeat of the last

Labour member on the County Council, the Council had
become completely non-political.

What must be maintained by true Catholics and true
Evangelicals alike is that a purely private Christianity, which
seeks to confine itself to an individual's relationship to God
without taking any responsibility for the society which moulds
individuals and is moulded by them, is an absurdity which bears
no relationship to orthodox Christianity. Personal salvation and
the coming of the Kingdom of God cannot be separated, and,
though the relative emphasis on each may vary, they are each
part of one Gospel.

11.5:   What Influence Can the Church Have on Economic Policy

In view of the nature of Anglican authority and the diversity of
views among Church members on most economic and political
issues, direct official Church influence on policy is inevitably
limited. Archbishops and bishops can express opinions, the
General Synod can pass resolutions, and official and semi-official
committees can produce reports, but while these can be valuable
and effective in helping to form and express Christian opinion,
they cannot have binding authority.

In the Church of England, the Board for Social Responsibility
has a special role to play in this process.[11] It sees its function in
just this way, namely to collect information and think through
problems and formulate the results so as to provide background
material for the General Synod's debates, the decisions and
statements that Church leaders have to make, and the guidance
of both the Christian public and wider public opinion. This
work it carries out through its standing committees and through
special working parties. The publications it produces vary from
short briefings and working papers up to full-scale booklets of
seventy pages or so.

Among outstanding reports in the economic field in recent
years may be mentioned that on 'Work and the Future',
published in 1979, the study of industrial conflict entitled

[11]As is more fully argued in Chapter 5 of this volume.

'Winters of Discontent', which came out in 1981 and the more recent work on 'Transnational Corporations'. In the more political field, the one which achieved most prominence was that on Nuclear Disarmament by the Committee chaired by the Bishop of Salisbury, published in 1982.[12] Indeed, the debate on this subject in the General Synod in February 1983, is perhaps one of the best examples of both the strengths and the limitations of what the Church can do, admittedly in a field where concern runs very deeply, but opinion is strongly divided. The debate was generally admired as a model of seriousness and charity, but the upshot was that, although the Committee had come down in favour of a unilaterialist approach, the final vote was decisively on the side of multi-lateralism.

Yet there are very few specific economic, or indeed political, issues on which the Government's action has been changed as a direct result of representations by Church leaders or resolutions of Church governing bodies. This does not mean, however, that the prevailing social, economic and political ethos of the Church has not had a remarkably pervasive effect.

The indirect effect of the social–catholic tradition was indeed very strong, especially in the thirty years after 1945. It may be said to have underlain the central ethos of both Labour and Conservative Governments in the era of Attlee, Gaitskell, Macmillan, Wilson and Heath. What came to be called 'Butskellism' was generally embraced by all but the extreme fringes of left and right in British politics. This included an historical acceptance of the mixed economy. This entailed a basically free market but coupled with a framework of government responsibility to maintain a high level of economic activity, government influence over the location of industry and the general lines of investment, public ownership of utilities and

---

[12]*Work and the Future: A Report from the Industrial Committee of the General Synod Board of Social Responsibility* (London: CIO Publishing, 1983); *Winters of Discontent: Industrial Conflict: A Christian Perspective* (London: CIO Publishing, 1981); *The Church and the Bomb: Nuclear Weapons and the Christian Conscience* (London: Hodder and Stoughton, 1982), for a detailed review of which see Chapter 8; *Transnational Corporations: Confronting the Issues* (London: CIO Publishing, 1983).

certain key industries, active building up of the Welfare State and a generally outward-looking commitment to world trade and development.

There was considerable difference between Conservatives and Labour as to what this implied in detail. Labour was in favour of a more active role for government, for instance, in steel nationalisation, investment planning and local authority house building, while the Conservatives regarded private enterprise more favourably and encouraged council house sales. It must be remembered, however, that the Heath Government was responsible for a considerable extension of government influence over industrial investment in the Industry Act of 1972, as well as for the most active attempt to use fiscal policy to force faster growth under Mr. Barber's chancellorship at that same period. Labour, on the other hand, introduced the first large-scale cuts in public spending in 1976 under pressure from the International Monetary Fund. But the basic assumptions of the mixed economy and the Welfare State were hardly questioned.

Of course, it is hard to say how far this reflected an influence of Christian social thinking on the political and economic climate and how far it reflected rather the effect of the prevailing 'social democratic' political ethos on Christian thinking. Many politicians in all the main parties were active and committed Christians, and others who would have called themselves humanists had grown up in the British human radical tradition which owed more to Church and Chapel than it did to Marxism or other secular ideologies. All had been influenced by Tawney, the Webbs and Temple, or by the organic and paternalistic tradition within Toryism which stems from Burke and Disraeli. All of them had reacted sharply from the waste and suffering of the depression of the 'thirties, as well as from the horrors of the totalitarianism of both Fascists and Communists. All had been inspired by the successes of British wartime planning, which had succeeded in laying the foundations of the Welfare State and maintaining fair shares, while successfully mobilising the nation's resources for war. They were determined that a juster and fairer social order could be built within the democratic and pragmatic traditions of British society.

In fact, this consensus is a good example of the conception of

Christian economic and social thinking described above as underlying the social-catholic tradition. The insights of the Faith about the nature of man and society and God's purpose for them are held in tension with the actual economic, political and social situation, and with the attitudes and policies which arise from it. The Christian is seen as trying to discover and express what God is saying to his people where they are, in the society in which they live, and hence what He would have done in such a situation. It is not surprising, therefore, that we found a consensus based on a mutual interaction of analysis and prescription by Christians and humanists together. Nor is it surprising that this general approach cut across differences of denomination and was shared by Anglicans, Roman Catholics, Presbyterians, Methodists, members of the United Reformed Church and of the Society of Friends – indeed by all who held what could be called in the broadest terms a catholic theological approach and by many Evangelicals too.

In the harsher economic climate of the 'eighties, this consensus has tended to break down and there has been a polarisation both to the Right and the Left. The new conservatism of the Thatcher era is much more individualistic than the traditional conservatism of Disraeli, Baldwin and Macmillan. Its economic ethos is more that of Continental liberalism or of American conservatism. It is based much more squarely on individual enterprise in pursuit of profit; hence it glorifies private enterprise and seeks to minimise the role of the State. It puts more emphasis on the family which cares for its own needs for education, health services, pensions and the like and has less concern for the ideals of community responsibility embodied in the Welfare State. In this, it is in sympathy with the new Christian conservatism discussed above.

The new Left in the Labour Party which came to the fore in the years leading up to the 1983 General Election is also alien to the tradition. It is based more on a Marxist analysis than a Christian one and it finds its political base in the activists and militants in local constituency parties and trade union branches, rather than in the Parliamentary party and the electors.

Nevertheless, the British radical tradition, rooted in Christianity, liberal humanism and Parliamentary democracy is still very strong. It was perhaps most clearly seen in the rise of the Liberal–Social Democratic Alliance, which brought together its more varied, diffuse, populist and sometimes eccentric manifestations as found among the Liberals, with its more technocratic and professionalist expression among the Social Democrats. Since the election of June, 1983, however, it has become clear that it is by no means dead among the two larger parties also.

Among the Tories, the election success meant that Thatcherite ideas of market-based efficiency were reinforced, but the older, more liberal (in the British sense), even at times paternalistic, Toryism is still strong among many of the rank and file MPs, for instance. It has been seen very clearly in the strong reaction to any apparent attacks on the central principles of the Welfare State, such as the maintenance of a publicly financed National Health Service and the need to provide adequately for the unemployed. In the Labour Party, the rethinking forced by defeat seems to be enforcing a swing back to a more central position both in the party machine and in the unions, one which reflects the broader, less well defined ideals of socialism as concerned with the welfare of those ordinary men and women whose electoral support is vital.

In 1983 there were rightward swings in both party and union elections and a change of emphasis on policies which had proved unpopular with the electorate. The Miners' Strike of 1984–5 put the leadership under strain and caused left-wing revivals and it remains to be seen what will happen after the Strike is ended.

In view of these trends and of the revival of 'conservative' thinking within the Church, it is not surprising that some rank and file church people, as well as some politicians, have expressed concern that the Church is getting involved in politics, instead of concentrating on spiritual issues. Church leaders have, however, been robust in maintaining the inseparability of concern for the whole community, and hence for political and economic issues, from concern for personal salvation. They show no sign of being willing to abandon what they regard as a clear responsibility for proclaiming what they believe God is saying to his people, while, of course, accepting that on the technical issues involved, their judgement can be no better than that of other concerned citizens.

11.6: The Economic Impact of the Church

So far we have been considering the influence on events and policies of the social and economic philosophies predominating in the Church of England. But, of course, the Church also has a considerable direct economic impact as a large corporate institution, through the people who work for it, the property it owns and the investments it makes.

The total number of diocesan clergy amounted in 1982-3 to 10,815.[13] Since they are widely dispersed, they are unlikely these days to have much impact on the labour market, whatever may have been the case in the days of Barchester Towers. Their political and social views are likely to vary considerably, so that the effect of how they spend their own modest incomes is also unlikely to have much effect on the level and direction of consumers' demands or savings. The scale of the matter is different if we consider the whole number of those who regard themselves as active lay members of the Church such as the 1.7 million Easter communicants, or the 1.8 million on the electoral rolls.[14] But these are even more diverse in their tastes and opinions and most unlikely to be susceptible of organisation so as to affect consumer demand, though campaigns such as that for the boycott of South African goods show that there is some scope for organised action by smaller groups with strong convictions on particular issues.

More important is the impact of the Church through property ownership and investment. The Church Commissioners, in whom most of its property is vested, had total assets in 1982 of £1,400 million, including £866 million in land and buildings and £477 million in Stock Exchange assets. Their net income from holdings of capital assets for the year amounted to £66 million.[15] This makes them comparable in potential

[13]*Church of England Yearbook*, 1983, pp. 385-6 (London: CIO Publishing, annual).
[14]*Ibid.*.
[15]Church Commissioners, *Report and Accounts*, 1982, pp. 8-14.

economic impact with a large property company or a pension fund.

Perhaps the strongest influence on the Church's economic policy, however, has been the negative one of inflation. The continued rise in prices over the decades has largely eliminated the gross and arbitrary inequalities of income among the clergy which resulted in the past from the dependence of their stipends on the varying endowments attached to particular incumbencies and offices. In the 'thirties, stipends of parochial clergy might vary from as little as £200 a year to as much as £2,000 or over and the variations bore no relationship to respective burdens of duty or living conditions. Bishops and deans got incomes of £5,000 or more. In 1983–84, most incumbents were on the recommended minimum stipend of £6,080–£6,450, suffragan bishops, deans and provosts got £9,905 and diocesan bishops, all but the five most senior, got £12,165.[16] The expenses of office and staff of bishops are now paid separately by the Commissioners and do not have to be met out of the revenues of the see. They also take the responsibility for assisting in the provision of suitable housing.

In order to reach this position, there has had to be a drastic reorganisation of funds. Parochial and other endowments have been pooled and the proceeds shared out more equally. Rising prices have also meant that congregations have to find much more of the revenue necessary to meet stipends, over 40 per cent in 1982–3 as compared with only 25 per cent in 1978–79.[17] The Church of England is still fortunate in that over half the cost of paying its clergy is met out of the generosity of past generations, but it is moving steadily nearer to the position of other Churches, where present congregations have to shoulder the great bulk of this obligation.

There has been much heart-searching in recent years about the ways in which the Church uses its resources. The extent to which manpower and money are tied up in the struggle to keep falling congregations going and keep the roof on obsolete buildings, instead of being available for redeployment to carry out effective mission, has been much criticised. Inflation has

[16]Church Commissioners, *Report and Accounts*, 1982, p. 16.
[17]Church Commissioners, *Report and Accounts*, 1982, p. 15 (diagram).

itself forced much reorganisation such as the merging of parishes especially in rural areas, and the abandonment of churches in areas from which people have largely fled. In spite of many brave experiments, no one would maintain that the Church has successfully reorganised itself for mission, but at the same time, no one can claim to be certain what sort of structure would in fact be appropriate for the uncertain tasks of the late twentieth century.

It is perhaps fortunate, therefore, that the Church of England has the control of its main resources entrusted to a body like the Church Commissioners which is somewhat isolated from the fashions and the pressures of ecclesiastical politics as they find expression in the General Synod and elsewhere. This is not to say that the Commissioners do not try to be alert to the movements of social conviction in the Church, as they seek to exercise a responsible stewardship. They have been active in furthering the process of pastoral reorganisation in the dioceses. In their investment policy, they avoid direct investment in companies whose business might cause controversy or give offence to large numbers of Christians. Notably, they avoid companies operating wholly or mainly in armaments, gambling, breweries and distilleries, tobacco, newspapers, publishing and broadcasting, theatre and film, or Southern Africa. They seek to avoid investing in companies whose management raises doubts whether social and ethical considerations will be given due weight, and to invest in those whose managements show that they accept a responsibility wider than that solely of maximising profits. They accept that they must concern themselves with the ways in which those companies in which they invest run their business.[18]

In the management of their real property also they seek to pursue social aims as well as purely financial ones. They have developed many of their estates so as to provide good housing for those of moderate means, for instance through their programme of sales of freehold to sitting tenants on their Maida Vale estate in West London. They recently invested half a

[18]Church Commissioners, *Report and Accounts*, 1981, pp. 8-9.

million pounds in a collaborative venture to set up an industrial estate in Plymouth.[19]

Nevertheless, the Commissioners inevitably see themselves primarily as trustees for the use of the historic resources of the Church, to make possible the payment of its ministers during work and in retirement, and the maintenance of its property. Their aim has, therefore, been to provide a steadily growing income year by year to meet their present and future obligations. This means holding a balance between maximising present income and securing regular increases of income in the future.[20] Any departure from this, involving, for instance, a large-scale redeployment of their resources to pursue particular economic and social policies, they would regard as being morally a breach of trust. Indeed, it would undoubtedly be so regarded legally also.

We cannot realistically expect, therefore, to see the Commissioners selling off the Church's investments in order to use the funds for development programmes in the Third World, nor taking the initiative in getting rid of buildings and paying off the full-time clergy in order to sponsor a system of house churches.

11.7: Conclusions

What can one say in conclusion about the economic witness of the Church of England in the last decades of the twentieth century, both through how it is organised and structured and through what it says and does?

So far as structures are concerned, there is, of course, no room for complacency and it is all too easy to point to weaknesses and anomalies. Yet it must be said that in the way in which it controls and makes use of its resources and in its organisation centrally and in the dioceses, it is certainly more efficient, honest and equitable than it has ever been in its long history. While the formal Establishment has been maintained, the connection has been loosened enough to enable the Church

---

[19]Church Commissioners, *Report and Accounts*, 1981, p. 8.
[20]Church Commissioners, *Report and Accounts*, 1981, p. 9.

to develop an efficient administration and a workable system of internal representation.

Similarly, the loosening of the connection with the 'establishment' in the less formal sense, has enabled the Church to witness more effectively on economic and political issues. In an increasingly secularised society, it is no longer closely linked with the holders of wealth, power and privilege and this has left the way clear for the development of an effective prophetic witness within it, by those who are prepared to bring together theological insights with practical experience of the working of the economic and political order. Since this is Anglicanism, there is not one official Church party line, rather a whole spectrum of views, though we can distinguish certain schools within it, such as the social-catholic, the individualist-evangelical and the new conservative, which we have discussed above. This has both helped Church members to understand more clearly the economic situation in which they have to live their lives and has also been a prophetic witness to the wider community of the kind of moral and ideological issues which are raised by the economic problems of our day.

Again, there is no room for complacency. Most people probably still have had little chance to question the view of the world which arises from their immediate personal, family and class interests. But, at the same time, it is also true that never before has there been such a high level of theological awareness in the Church, in the wider sense of the word 'theological' as distinct from the narrowly doctrinal ones. The Church is alive and thinking, and though most of the nation is no longer to be counted among its active members, the voice of its spokesmen is heard and respected, even if not always agreed with.

Part Three

**REFLECTIONS ON CHURCH, STATE
AND POLITICS**

INTRODUCTION

Throughout this volume analysis of the Church of England's political role has repeatedly touched upon its established status. For it is this status that has conditioned the fundamental nature and quality of its relationship with the secular state and with the society it seeks to serve. Equally, it has helped both to shape the influence the Church can have on public policy and to support a set of cultural assumptions that has constrained the sort of advice it has offered to government. It is entirely appropriate, therefore, that in this final section this leit-motif should form the principal focus of a theological and philosophical reflection.

In the first of the two papers, Anthony Dyson's basic aim is to subject the four main reports on the Church-State relationship in the twentieth century to close and critical scrutiny. He finds faults to varying degrees with all of them. For example, the 1952 contribution he argues was theologically weak and pretentious; it ignored important social and political trends, was too deferential to the State and altogether over-cautious. Its successor in 1970 is also found somewhat lacking in theology, too gradualist in its view of change, dismissive of minority views and, again, made 'no real attempt to grapple with the nature and effect of changes in society, politics and religion'.

He then goes on to consider what the Reports reveal of the typical Anglican style, the Church's understanding of itself and its perceptions of the political realm. He finds, in brief, a surprisingly pervasive continued acceptance of the Reformation Settlement within the Church, a settlement which in turn provides it with a normative framework for the evaluation of other major issues. This he finds very unsatisfactory, not least because the arrangements Henry VIII laid down were both 'quirky' and historically 'contingent'. It then surfaces even today not only in the Church of England's rather grudging acceptance of other Churches and its half-hearted embrace of ecumenism, but also in a basic self-denying ordinance about the manner of its political engagement. In other words, the legacy of the

279

Reformation, which subordinated Church to State, is still to be found reflected in its general unwillingness to adopt a corporate prophetic role that might radically challenge the socio-political consensus rather than support or only marginally modify it. It is, in short, 'hypnotised by history', largely reactive rather than creative and too prone to the view that it can somehow exist outside of, or apart from, England's domestic political life. This assumption, he feels, is now totally outmoded. Religion must inevitably be political but the Church alone should decide and define how that imperative is to be worked out in practice.

It is at this point that the final contribution by Raymond Plant becomes so crucially relevant. For if the Church is to reflect anew and in an historically unihibited way on its political engagement then the analyses provided in Chapter 13 concerning the four basic relationships it could conceivably adopt would be very pertinent. These are, respectively, the Christendom, pluralistic, secularist and conservative perspectives. The first entails a very close involvement in the state, an involvement butressed by a corporate political theology that provides it with a unique and established status. But it seems clear to the author that such a theology would be difficult to develop insofar as it would have to be sufficiently specific to provide a framework for policy decisions yet general enough to command a consensus amongst the faithful. The idea of middle axioms, referred to earlier in the book, is one (not always successful) attempt to try to resolve this central dilemma.

The pluralistic view Raymond Plant finds equally difficult to accept. Not least is this true when the plurality of modern society begins to threaten Christian values about human life and individual rights. In these situations, there is need for a communal or corporate definition of 'the good' but that in turn begins to undermine strict pluralistic assumptions. The 'secularist' position the author thinks is 'characteristic of a good deal of the modern social and political stances of the Church'. But as it entails the endorsement of those policy positions derived from purely secular analyses which are also found to be most consistent with perceived Christian thinking, it tends to relegate the Church's role to that of supporter rather than prime mover. It is, furthermore, an admission of the failure of the Church to think through thoroughly enough its own distinctive contribution to the relevant debates. Yet this is precisely Raymond Plant's experience (so he records) when he chaired a British Council of Churches' working party on poverty – he found no political theology on the issue, only 'vague formulations'. Inevitably he and his committee were left 'making rather ad hoc adjustments to prevailing secular theories in this field'.

It is precisely situations like these, of course, that invite criticism from some quarters that the Church, by backing secular ideologies, is selling out to contestible, relativistic and usually liberal-bourgeois ideas. This is part of the claim of the conservative vision which is also explored in the chapter. From this point of view, the Church should concern itself principally (and for some exclusively) with the individual spiritual condition. Any attempt to articulate a political platform entails, they argue, a compromise with principles that lack the eternal authority of the Church either in defined 'religious' matters or in issues of personal morality. But this criticism, he says, also lacks credibility for personal morality connects with social and political morality. Furthermore, without a vision God as 'the Lord of History', judging men by standards that men may only imperfectly understand but which nevertheless do exist, then the meaning of being a Christian becomes very vague and insubstantial indeed.

He concludes, therefore, and as many have in this book, that an ecclesiastical involvement in public and political life is inevitable. That being the case, the Church should take its political involvement much more seriously. It should also seek to articulate a distinctive Christian theology on which to base that involvement and then, in turn, it will be taken more seriously by society and by politicians, even if their lives may become more uncomfortable as a result. Is this part of the answer to defining a relevant role for the Church in modern secularized England?

Chapter 12

"LITTLE ELSE BUT THE NAME"
– REFLECTIONS ON FOUR CHURCH AND STATE REPORTS

Anthony Dyson

12.1: Introduction

In 1755, when the English colonies in America were at war with
the French, a number of senior members of the Religious
Society of Friends (Quakers), who were members of state
legislatures, found themselves in a dilemma. For these legislatures, by policy-making and by levying of special taxes, were
supporting the waging of the war. John Woolman, noted for his
leadership in the struggle against slave-owning and slave-trading
among Quakers, and for his consistent advocacy of the Quaker
peace-witness, commented as follows:

'Such being in doubt whether to act or crave to be excused from
their office, seeing their brethren united in the payment of a tax
to carry on the said wars, might think their case not much
different and so quench the tender movings of the Holy Spirit in
their minds. And thus by small degrees, there might be an
approach toward that of fighting, till we came so near it as that
the distinction would be little else but the name of a peaceable
people.'[1]

Woolman's reasoning is crisp and plain. It is tempting for these
Quaker members of legislatures, faced by unanimity among
their colleagues about pursuing the war and about levying taxes,

[1]Ed., Phillips P. Moulton, *The Journal and Major Essays of John
Woolman* (New York: Oxford University Press, 1971), p. 84. For
background, see Arthur J. Worrall, *Quakers in the Colonial North East*
(Hanover, New Hampshire: University Press of New England, 1980).

to feel that they should step into line. But that would be to resist the peace-making promptings of the Holy Spirit. Once that kind of accommodation was begun, it was only a short way, by small degrees, to the practical obliteration of the Quaker peace-witness with the result that the commitment to pacifism would exist now only in the *name* 'Quaker' but not in deed or reality. The only thing that would distinguish these Quakers from their colleagues would be a *nominal* witness to peace.

Woolman's moving and uncompromising analysis of this moral choice and its consequences serves as an apt preface to this brief essay on the four Church and State Reports which have issued from the Church of England in course of this century.[2] I do not set out to deal with the wider history of Church-State relations in this period – a task undertaken by another contributor[3] but rather from an exploration of these four texts to see what might be implied about the temper of the Church of England as an established church. My interest is in the last analysis theological. How far do these texts witness to a primary concern for the clarification, proclamation and application of the Christian gospel? Or is that concern compromised by establishment and if so, in what way and to what extent? I shall deal briefly with each Report in turn and then attempt some general observations.

[2] *The Archbishops' Committee on Church and State: Report, with Appendices* (London: SPCK, 1917), cited hereafter as *Selborne 1917*; *Church Assembly, Church and State: Report of the Archbishops' Commission on the Relations Between Church and State*, Vol. I, Report and Appendices, Vol. II, Evidence of Witnesses, Etc. (London: Press and Publications Board of the Church Assembly, 1935), cited hereafter as *Cecil 1935*; *Church and State: Being the Report of a Commission Appointed by the Church Assembly in June 1949* (London: Church Information Board of the Church Assembly, 1952), (CA 1023), cited hereafter as *Moberley 1952*; *Church and State: Report of the Archbishops' Commission* (London: Church Information Office, 1970), cited hereafter as *Chadwick 1970*. In the essay 'Church' will normally refer to the Church of England, 'church' to the church in a more general sense, and 'the churches' to the several churches or denominations.

[3] See above, Chapter 2.

12.2:   The Four Church and State Reports

12.2.1:   The Selborne Report, 1917

Selborne 1917 was produced by a Committee set up by the Archbishops in 1913. Its terms of reference were: 'that there is in principle no inconsistency between a national recognition of religion and the spiritual independence of the Church, and this Council requests the Archbishops of Canterbury and York to consider the advisability of appointing a Committee to inquire what changes are advisable in order to secure in the relations of Church and State a fuller expression of the spiritual independence of the Church as well as of the national recognition of religion'.[4] The historical context lies in the frustration increasingly felt at the difficulty of persuading Parliament to give time and attention for the enacting of reforms desired by the Church of England, no other form of legislation being available. For example, statistics reveal that, between 1880 and 1913, out of 217 church bills introduced into the House of Commons, only 33 were passed, whereas 183 were dropped.[5]

In 1904, the Representative Church Council had been set up, composed of the Upper and Lower Houses of the Convocations of Canterbury and York, and the new Houses of Laymen of the two provinces. It was hoped that the Council would engage in preparing legislation, so saving to some extent the time and energies of Parliament. But the Council had no legal status. It was this same Council which, in 1913, passed the above-quoted resolution which later served as the terms of reference for the new Archbishop's Committee. Whatever broader scope of enquiry these terms of reference may suggest, it is clear that the Committee interpreted the Council and the Archbishops as wanting the Committee to devise plans and legislation for an official Church body which could promote legal and effective action, on behalf of the Church of England, in Parliament.

The composition of the Committee reflected this restricted

[4]Selborne 1917, p. 1.
[5]Selborne 1917, p. 29.

task. It included 9 current or former MPs,[6] 3 bishops,[7] 3 persons concerned with law and constitution,[8] and a canonist-historian.[9] It was, in effective majority, a Committee of historical-legal-constitutional[10] inclination, well-suited to the delicate diplomatic and political task of preparing material acceptable in tone and content to the two Houses of Parliament. The Committee reached unanimous agreement on a scheme for the creation of what was later called the Church Assembly and of church councils at other levels (all, except Parochial Church Councils, to exclude women), as well as of an Ecclesiastical Committee of Parliament and a new procedure of more automatic legislation, but with appropriate vetoes. In no respect did the proposed scheme weaken the control of Parliament; the "one-sided reciprocity"[11] was not challenged. But it would facilitate legislation for the Church and it would aspire to rebut the claim that the only truly representative assembly of the laity of the Church of England was the House of Commons.

Of the four Reports, *Selborne 1917* is the most comprehensive, well-researched and polished. It set a style and a method which the subsequent three Commissions broadly followed. It included a survey of Church-State relations in England by Sir Lewis Dibdin and A.L. Smith,[12] with a related longer memoran-

---

[6]Earl of Selborne, Sir William Anson, A.J. Balfour, Lord Hugh Cecil, The Duke of Devonshire, Lord Parmoor, Col. Sir Robert Williams, Viscount Wolmer, Hon. Major Edward Wood.

[7]The Bishop of Liverpool (F.J. Chevasse), The Bishop of Oxford (Charles Gore) and the Bishop of Bristol to 1914 (G.F. Browne).

[8]Especially note Sir Lewis Dibdin, Dean of Arches 1903-34. Advised Randall Davidson almost daily on all except patronage (DNB: 1931-40, p. 225). Ecclestiastical Commission, 1905-30; Vice-Chairman, House of Laymen, Convocation of Canterbury. See his *Establishment in England*, 1932.

[9]Rev. W.H. Frere.

[10]In addition to those already named were Rev. H. Gee, Professor of Church History at Durham (1910-18) and Canon J.H.B. Masterman, Professor of History at Birmingham (1901-9).

[11]Peter Hinchliff, *The One-Sided Reciprocity* (London: Darton, Longman and Todd, 1966).

[12]Fellow, later Master, of Balliol. 'Rugged, forceful and original', J.G. Lockhart, *Cosmo Gordon Lang* (London: Hodder and Stoughton, 1949), p. 37.

dum by Bishop G.F. Browne; detailed draft proposals for the new arrangements; and an extensive survey of the constitutions of the churches of the Anglican Communion. The central theological principle of the Report, namely the "principle of spiritual independence", briefly expounded in Chapter Four, drew upon the longer memorandum by Bishop Gore.[13]

This principle, which is repeatedly invoked in the later Reports, refers in Gore to the conception of the Church as a self-governing society, ready and able to cooperate with the civil power but maintaining its independent existence. Thus, the Church seeks a method by which, without encroaching either on the supremacy of the Crown or on the rights of Parliament, it is able to regulate its own affairs. Chapter Four of the Report did not speculate upon what degree of self-regulation might really be involved in self-governance. Bishop Gore, already a supporter of Welsh Disestablishment, did. According to his memorandum in Appendix VIII, it might include the liberty to establish new bishoprics and provinces, to reform systems of representation, to elect bishops or at least to be able to refuse bishops nominated by the Crown, to revise doctrinal standards, standards of discipline, rites and ceremonies, and to exercise discipline. The State would of course, retain the right to reverse any of these decisions. But if the Church, in the last resort, could not accept their revisions, then disestablishment might be the only recourse. When, however, the Report as a whole is viewed, it is clear that its outcome was not one whit to reduce parliamentary control. Certainly it did not at all go as far as Gore's doctrine of spiritual independence might seem to imply, namely, cooperating with the civil power but with the Church maintaining its independent existence. Such a state of affairs was *not* the consequence of the English Reformation settlement, nor was it, in truth, the intention or result of *Selborne 1917*.

For the most part, the Report moves with sound common sense in the realms of history, law and administrative machinery. It is cautiously firm and firmly courteous in tone showing no disposition to overstate any of its cases. It takes its stand on what it judges all reasonable people will see to be prudential, just

[13] *Selborne 1917*, pp. 243ff.

and reasonable. It disturbs only that which must be disturbed. In this 'high table' company, there is apparently little sense of those momentous changes in the wider society in the later 19th century and in the First World War which created social and political conditions quite different from those in which the Anglican settlement was fashioned. At only two points, buried deep in the Appendices, does a more earthy and realistic view emerge. One occurs in Bishop Gore's memorandum already mentioned. 'We are familiar also with the fact that now for a long time the old conception of establishment. . .has completely broken down.' 'It is only in a very restricted sense that the Established Church can be truly spoken of as still the organ of the State for religious and moral purposes.' '[The Church] stands only as one of various religions making a moral claim upon the voluntary allegiance of men.'[14] The other, even more interesting, point is found in Appendix IX by A.L. Smith and H.E. Kemp and approved by Albert Mansbridge,[15] with its sections on "Church and State", "The Points of View of Workmen towards the Church", "Methods by which the Working Classes may be represented in the Councils of the Church", "The Representation of Teachers and Students", and "The Relation of the Student Christian Movement to the Church". The writers challenge the narrow interpretation by the Committee of its terms of reference:

'Certainly a "consideration of the relations between Church and State" would to the ordinary layman mean, among other things, this especially, viz., a consideration of the place which religion actually holds in practical life at this moment; and, further, a consideration of the means by which it might be made to take a larger place, that is, to cover a wider area of social activities, to

[14] *Selborne 1917*, p. 247.

[15] Mansbridge, the moving spirit of the W.E.A. was closely linked with other members of the Committee, namely William Temple (first President of the W.E.A. in 1906), A.L. Smith who took up the W.E.A. cause 1907-8, Bishop Gore (a friend of Mansbridge for many years), and the Dean of Christ Church (Dr. Strong), Chairman of the Oxford University Extension Delegacy. Mansbridge signed the Life and Liberty letter to *The Times* in June 1917. See Albert Mansbridge CH, *The Trodden Road* (London: J.M. Dent, 1940).

enter into them more boldly and more habitually, and to penetrate them more deeply; in other words, how can religion from a force acting on individuals as it were privately become more of a force acting on them in their social relations also?. . . Then we may ask whether anything can be done by us to prepare the way for Christianity to recapture the world of labour, the student world, and even the world of business.'[16]

Clearly the Committee as a whole was not prepared to set forth upon choppy waters such as these.[17] As a consolation prize to A.L. Smith *et al.*, the Committee's recommendations included a provision for the House of Laymen electors on the Diocesan Conference to contain 'wage-earners selected by the Diocesan Conference to a number not less than 5%' and 'students. . .to represent the churchmen and churchwomen of Universities, University and Training Colleges, and School Staffs in the Dioceses'.[18] In contrast to Appendix IX, the concluding paragraphs of the Report dissolve into paroxyms of sycophantic deference:

'Some churchmen....may feel anxious lest the more facile and expeditious process of law-making which we propose may usher in dangerous and revolutionary changes. But we are confident that such fears are unfounded.' 'No one. . .will be troubled by anticipations of reckless or violent change.' 'In all three Houses [of the proposed Church Assembly] the dominant temperament will be one of prudent conservatism.' 'We cannot help it if the voices of those who must be heard in respect to changes in an Established Church are voices rather cautious than sanguine; more prone to answer in the negative than in the affirmative.' 'Our plan removes this great and scandalous evil. . .and if those changes [which are made in consequence of it] are not likely to be such as to alarm even the most timid, that is because the proper authorities of Church and State have little taste for violent or revolutionary developments.'[19]

[16]*Selborne 1917*, p. 250.
[17]See Dibdin in *Selborne 1917*, p. 68.
[18]*Selborne 1917*, p. 86.
[19]*Selborne 1917*, pp. 64ff.

Hensley Henson dubbed the Report 'highly controversial'![20]

What are the main features of *Selborne 1917*? 1. The primary appeal is retrospective, i.e. to history. 2. The appeal to theology is scant and imprecise. I shall argue later that the principle of spiritual independence implies an unhealthy dualism, an expression of which occurred early in the life of the Church Assembly to which Randall Davidson steered nuts-and-bolts business, but referred 'spiritual' matters to the Convocations. 3. The Report effectively equates 'Church and State' with 'links with Crown and Parliament'. 4. There is little contemporary historical or sociological awareness. 5. The Report adopts a highly submissive attitude towards the powers-that-be. 6. There is virtually no ecumenical consciousness.

Selborne 1917 led ultimately to the Enabling Act, the Church Assembly, and legislation by Measures ultimately receiving Royal Assent. If Iremonger is correct, in the Church Assembly, the 'legalists' (e.g. Sir Lewis Dibdin, a chief architect, as we have seen, of *Selborne 1917*) soon came to dominate the 'moralists' (e.g. Life and Liberty Supporters).[21] Be that as it may, one item which did not get to the point of Royal Assent was, of course, the Prayer Book Measure which foundered in the House of Commons. This defeat served as the impulse to the second Church and State Report, *Cecil 1935*.

12.2.2: The Cecil Report, 1935

Pages 30ff. in the historical introduction to *Cecil 1935* provide a useful retrospect on the years 1906-1928. It is confirmed that the Enabling Act, despite possible appearances, had not marked a new concordat between Church and State. In the next section, the Report interprets the Prayer Book Measures of 1928-29 as a development in the spiritual life and activity of the Church, and thus their defeat as a sign that 'in the legislative sphere at any rate, the Church had not attained to spiritual freedom'.[22] Moreover, the defeat revealed 'the subordination of the Church to a Parliament which might consist largely of non-Christians,

[20]F.A. Iremonger, *William Temple* (Oxford: Oxford University Press, 1948), p. 229.

[21]Iremonger, p. 28l.

[22]*Cecil 1935*, p. 41.

and does consist largely of persons who are not members of the Church of England'.[23]

The new Commission was appointed by the Archbishops in 1930 following a Church Assembly resolution: 'It is desirable that a Commission should be appointed to enquire into the present relations of Church and State, and particularly how far the principle, stated above,[24] is able to receive effective application in present circumstances in the Church of England, and what legal and constitutional changes, if any, are needed in order to maintain or to secure its effective application; and that the Archbishops be requested to appoint a Commission for this purpose'. A group of only sixteen (compared with *Selborne 1917*'s twenty-six) included four current and erstwhile MPs,[25] one archbishop (Temple) and two bishops,[26] three legal persons (among whom was Dibdin from 1917)[27] and one woman.[28] *Cecil 1935* took and published evidence from twenty-seven persons or organisations. Notable among the witnesses was Professor Norman Sykes who was to reappear as a member of *Moberley 1952*. His conclusion was that 'the present constitutional relations between Church and State offer no violence to the spiritual independence of the Church. The *onus probandi* in this regard lies upon the advocates of change'.[29] The main Report makes proposals about: new enabling legislation; the ecclesias-

---

[23]*Cecil 1935*, p. 41.

[24] 'It is a fundamental principle that the Church, that is, the Bishops, together with the Clergy and Laity, must in the last resort, when its mind has been fully ascertained, retain its inalienable right, in loyalty to our Lord and Saviour Jesus Christ, to formulate its faith in Him and to arrange the expression of that Holy Faith in its form of worship.' Archbishop Davidson to the Church Assembly, 2nd July 1928.

[25]Sir Ernest Bennett, who joined the Labour Party in 1916 and Lord Balniel. Cecil and Selborne were erstwhile MPs.

[26]Williams of Carlisle and Bell of Chichester. The latter became one of the most enthusiastic members of the Commission.

[27]Sir Philip Baker-Wilbraham, First Church Estates Commissioner, Dean of Arches, and Mr. H.B. Vaisey, Vicar-General in the Province of York 1934-44. Canon E.W.J. Hellins may be added. He had been Director of Law Studies at St. Catherine's, Cambridge, 1902-8.

[28]Viscountess Caroline Bridgeman.

[29]*Cecil 1935*, p. 304. Historians on the Commission included Sir Charles Grant Robertson and Professor E.F. Jacob.

tical courts; the pastoral authority of, and arraignment of, bishops; clerical assent; the appointment of bishops; the law of marriage; and canon law. By comparison with the brisk urbanity of *Selborne 1917*, the mood of *Cecil 1935* is bruised, wistful, but rather more direct. The effects of 1928–1929 still made themselves keenly felt.

The theme of 'spiritual freedom' recurs. The option of disestablishment is treated somewhat more seriously than in *Selborne 1917*. But it is 'not to be desired' if other means can be devised of securing for the Church 'freedom of action in things spiritual'.[30] For non-spiritual legislation, the Measures promoted under the Enabling Act are satisfactory. But for spiritual Measures, i.e. Measures touching doctrine and worship, a mode of legislation free of Parliamentary control is needed. To this end, the Report proposes that the Archbishops, the Lord Chancellor and the Speaker of the House would have to certify that a proposed Measure was, in fact, 'spiritual'. Granted that there was also an obligation to establish consent by the Church's laity, a spiritual Measure should not require the approval of Parliament but should forthwith be presented to the Crown for Royal Assent.

Cecil 1935 was much less optimistic than *Selborne 1917* that its recommendations could be realised. For its whole approach depended upon the Church being able to demonstrate its spiritual unity of conviction and purpose as a precondition of seeking revision of doctrine or worship, and 1928–1929 had shown that such unity was absent. The Commission was, therefore, clear that the Church could not go to Parliament with new demands for legislative powers unless there was plain evidence of unified desires. So its first proposal laid upon the Archbishops the forlorn task of summoning a Round Table Conference[31] to try and secure agreement between the different schools of thought on deviations from the 1662 Order of Holy Communion and on reservation.

The main features of *Cecil 1935* include: l. The primary appeal to history for a clarification of the Church–State relationship. 2.

[30]*Cecil 1935*, p. 51.
[31]This exercise is fully described in Ronald C.D. Jasper, *George Bell* (London: Oxford University Press, 1967), pp. 179ff.

A minimal appeal to theological considerations. 3. A continuation of the equation of 'Church and State' with 'formal links
with Crown and Parliament', thus excluding any allusion to the
painful upheavals of the inter-war years as a new context for
Church and State. 4. The attitude to Parliament is slightly less
deferential than in 1917, but there are few signs of boldness. It is
not surprising that critics of Archbishop Lang regarded these
in-between years as colourless and inert. 5. The published
evidence varies greatly in quality. Much of it is historical
analysis and justification, with little evidence of contemporary
insight. There is a solid body of support for disestablishment as
well as for establishment. 6. The ecumenical dimension receives
little attention. One Free Church witness registers a 'don't
know' to disestablishment; another advocates it.

J.R.H. Moorman is guilty of exaggeration when he describes
Cecil 1935 as 'a notable report'.[32] Where it is similar to *Selborne
1917*, it is dependent upon it. Where it breaks new ground, it
carries scant conviction. What was its outcome? The Round
Table Conference was duly assembled by the Archbishops in
1938. It limped on unpromisingly to October 1939 when it was
suspended never to reconvene. *Cecil 1935* was full of good
intentions, but, in the circumstances, sent out an almost pathetic
plea for unity. It came at an unpropitious moment. Hearts were
not to be softened. The clouds of war were bunching on the
horizon.

12.2.3: The Moberley Report, 1952

Moberley 1952 was the work, again, of a Commission set up in
response to a Church Assembly resolution: 'That the Assembly,
while valuing the "Establishment" of the Church of England as
an expression of the nation's recognition of religion, nevertheless is of the opinion that the present form of it impedes the
fulfilment of the responsibilities of the Church as a spiritual
society, and therefore instructs the Standing Committee to
appoint a small commission to draw up resolutions on changes
desirable in the present relationship between Church and State
and to present them to the Assembly for consideration at an

[32]J.R.H. Moorman, *A History of the Church of England*, 2nd. ed.
(London: A. & C. Black), p. 418.

early date'.[33] This was the smallest of the four groups – ten members including two bishops,[34] two MPs,[35] two persons with legal expertise[36] and a leading ecclesiastical historian.[37] The immediate impression created by the membership is one of powerful conservatism, *viz.*, Bishop R.C. Mortimer, and Professor Norman Sykes whose views were already well-known from his submission of evidence to *Cecil 1935*. Apart possibly from Dean Selwyn, there was no systematic or doctrinal theologian on the Commission, no woman, and no-one with sociological interests. The tone of the Report is set by a testy remark in the Preliminary to the effect that 'we have interpreted the expression of opinion which [the resolution] contains as giving us a thesis for examination and not a governing assumption; indeed, not all of us would have agreed to serve on any other basis'.[38] This cavil presumably refers to the phrase 'impedes the fulfilment' in the resolution quoted above. *Moberley 1952* is the shortest of the four reports, it being thought unnecessary to traverse again the ground covered by the 'exhaustive studies' of 1917 and 1935.

Both *Selborne 1917* and *Cecil 1935*, to a lesser and greater extent respectively, tended first to paint a gloomy picture, which might imply the need for radical change, and then by rather insubstantial argument, paint a happier picture which showed that after all Establishment was a good thing. For example, in 1935: 'It is impossible to estimate the precise amount of value which should be attributed to the national recognition of Christianity. . .But we are persuaded that its value is great....We are convinced that even in those parts of the Empire where the Church is not established, they value the Establishment in England as a recognition for the British peoples as a whole of the connection between Christianity and the Empire'.[39]

[33] *Moberley 1952*, p. 1.
[34] Mortimer of Exeter and Chase of Ripon.
[35] Eric Fletcher and L.W. Joynson-Hicks.
[36] Mr. Justice Vaisey (on *Cecil 1935*) and Fletcher.
[37] Norman Sykes.
[38] *Moberley 1952*, p. 1.
[39] *Cecil 1935*, p. 50.

Moberley 1952 begins soundly with a statement of the Church's position in the world today amid avid nationalism, hostility and indifference. 'Our world is in many respects a "post-Christian" world.'[40] There follows the claim, however, that in Britain, secularisation has been less complete than in most countries. The only evidence cited is that it is thus that 'foreign visitors often remark'. But the Report then goes on to argue how and why the traditional relationship between Church and State might have to be viewed in a new perspective, given a predominantly urban society with new social habits and a welfare state. Are, therefore, Christian or pagan meanings to inspire our conceptions of life? In this situation, the task of the Church of England is 'a forward move, missionary and militant. . .'.[41] There follows a satisfactory account of the meaning of 'establishment'. But in going on to speak of establishment's value, the Report claims that its outward features *'symbolise the nation's confession* that national policy at home and abroad, the relation of this nation to others, the ordering of society and the distribution of wealth are all ultimately subject to the will and judgement of God'.[42] The disestablishment of the Church would be taken as the 'British People's deliberate repudiation of a continuous Christian tradition'.[43] Establishment also furthers the spiritual work of the Church. 'In many of our great towns today, the influence of the parish church in the life of the community is very strong. The parish church stands for Christianity as a whole; it is not merely the meeting place of a particular Christian sect.'[44] (Which Churches does the Report intend by such 'sects' – Baptist, Methodist, Roman Catholic?)

The Report then records some grounds for disquiet which are felt 'despite these considerations'. Does not establishment threaten unconditional loyalty to Christ, does it not induce a subtle worldliness, does it not reflect vanished political conditions, does it not alienate Free Churchmen? The Report's

[40] *Moberley 1952*, p. 3.
[41] P. 6.
[42] P. 10 (my italics).
[43] P. 10.
[44] P. 12.

response to these questions is remarkable. It is couched in terms of a claim that the Church of England is through and through a pure example of, in Troeltsch's categorisation, 'the church-type'. The church-type 'aims at including whole peoples and not only a select few. Its procedure is gradually to permeate rather than to challenge and to condemn. It is receptive of the secular culture and civilisation amid which it is placed. It is tolerant of anomalies in logic and of compromise in practice. . .Its distinctive text is "he that is not against us is for us".'[45] *Moberley 1952*, heartened by these sentiments, is bold then to claim that in fact 'in some respects the nation is more rather than less Christian that it was', that the Church's 'prophetic message is less obscured', of which the Archbishops' and Bishops' actions in the House of Lords is one symptom, and that tension with Free Churchmen over establishment 'seems to be less than it was'.[46] So, by a process of noting, and then of leaving behind, weighty objections, the Report comes to affirm that the establishment "is of great benefit to the nation and affords great opportunities to the Church".[47]

There follows a section on the control of worship by Parliament in which a careful analysis of the 1928–1929 debacle is offered, rationalising that on this issue Parliament was delaying change until the Church's mind was made up. The Report looks at various possibilities for the Church to claim spiritual freedom in worship and comes up with a proposal that Parliament should give the Church authority to allow experimental deviations for an interim period with a view to putting forward statutory amendments to the Prayer Book at a later stage. Thus, the Report issues in a proposal which again leaves Parliament's role largely undisturbed. In the next section on the appointment of bishops, after considering a variety of options, it lamely concludes that 'if the Archbishops think it desirable, a small consultative body should be set up to consult with and advise the Archbishops'[48] about appointments to vacant sees. The Report

[45] Pp. 15ff.
[46] P. 16.
[47] P. 17.
[48] P. 46.

deals sensibly with the matter of Church courts, especially regarding the composition of a Final Court.

Moberley 1952 opened on a note of high drama about the life of nations. It moved on to hypothesise criticisms of establishment. It put these in their place and finished up with some highly tentative proposals about the control of worship, bishops and the Church courts which were no more adventurous in spirit than those of *Selborne 1917*. In the "Concluding Note", the Commission considers its stewardship. It prepares its defence by saying that its task, as allotted, was to diagnose immediate practical complaints and to suggest immediate practical remedies. In fact, as the terms of reference noted above reveal, this is an excessively pragmatic interpretation of its brief. On the other hand, the Commission does claim that its proposals 'are immediately concerned with machinery but they are made solely in order to remove some of the obstacles which now hinder the Church from leading a crusade'.[49] But the tone of the closing paragraphs is characteristic. The mutual confidence between Church and State flourishes most when not too closely defined. 'This accords with the English tradition, which has neither the clear-cut logic of the Latin nor the systematic comprehensiveness of the Teutonic mind, but rests on our inveterate national habit of spontaneous conformity'.[50]

What may be said of *Moberley 1952*? 1. It is a somewhat pretentious piece of work, describing many flourishes but yielding distinctly meagre returns. It is not so much an exploration as an arrival at conclusions largely defined in advance. It is full of unsupported generalisations and special pleading. 2. It is theologically weak. Wedded to the 'church-type' understanding of the Church of England, in the end it offers no theological articulation of the Gospel, no sense of its challenge. 3. The Report has nothing of significance to say about ecumenical relations; what it does say is patronising. 4. The Report again sees Church-State relationships almost exclusively in terms of Parliamentary and coronocentric links. 5. The Report is notably deferential towards the State. 6. When it comes to the point of decision, all references to the social,

[49] P. 67.
[50] P. 68.

political and economic changes in English society are forgotten. The Church's adaptation to the new society will be significantly forwarded through cautious, piecemeal, inoffensive constitutional change. No hint emerges that ethos and outlook at large might be very different compared with 1917 and 1935.

As an elaborate dressing-up of a tactical manoeuvre on the part of the Church to move by stealthy stages towards fuller control of its worship, the Report may be hailed a success. It may be said to have prepared the way for the Alternative and Other Services Measure of 1965, allowing the Convocations and the House of Laity to sanction new forms of service for an experimental period, and thus for the eventual appearance of the Alternative Service Book. But the Report made no significant contribution, in this vital post-war period, to understanding how the Church might fulfil its responsibilities to itself and to the wider society.

12.2.4: The Chadwick Report, 1970

Nearly twenty years later, the fourth Church and State Report to date appeared – *Chadwick 1970*. This Archbishops' Commission was appointed to serve after a resolution of the Church Assembly in 1965 with the following terms of reference: 'to make recommendations as to the modifications in the constitutional relationship between Church and State which are desirable and practicable and in so doing to take account of current and future steps to promote greater unity between the Churches'.[51] The Commission received evidence from seventy-three witnesses (individuals and organisations) and was helped by five consultants from other Churches. The evidence of witnesses was not published. On the ecclesiastical and legal side, the Commission was dominated by persons who might have been expected not to arrive at conclusions radically dissimilar from those of *Moberley 1952*. Some of these persons, e.g. the then Bishop of Chester and the then Bishop of Leicester, are on record to that effect in other contexts.[52] There were two MPs,[53] three legal

[51] *Chadwick 1970*, p. ix.
[52] Bishop Gerald A. Ellison in *The Churchman's Duty* (London: Hodder and Stoughton, 1957) and Bishop Ronald R. Williams in *What's Right with the Church of England?*, (London: Lutterworth Press, 1966).
[53] D.W. Coe and W.R. van Straubenzee.

persons,[54] three women, and a future Secretary- General of the General Synod. There was no systematic theologian, if we reserve the more precise term 'ecclesiastical historian' for Professor Chadwick. Social policy interests were represented by Professor Kathleen Jones of York University.

After the brevity of *Moberley 1952*, Appendices reappeared in 1970 including a novel addition, namely the results of a study of existing material on religious belief and practice in England. Importantly, for the first time in the four Reports, there were dissentients three of whom objected comprehensively to the Report (Pitt, Cornwell and Coe). The terms of reference were more specific than those of 1917, 1935 or 1952 in *requiring* the Commission to deal with desirable and practicable modifications in the constitutional relationship between Church and State, and were innovative in explicitly requiring the Commission to take account of ecumenical matters.

Chadwick 1970 is, then, the first of the four Reports to have to deal publicly with major disagreements in its ranks. These differences surface in the body of the text as well as in the memoranda of dissent. The recommendations refer to 'what the majority of us think to be desirable and practicable in what we judge (so far as we are able) to be the present state of the public mind'.[55] This majority covers a spectrum including two main positions: those who do not want changes which end a national recognition of religion and who have little desire to extend the liberties of the Church, and those who do not want to end a national recognition of religion but want to adapt the laws, so that the recognition may be 'wider, and less exclusive, and more ecumenical'.

The general drift of the recommendations is in the direction of what may be termed 'the Scottish solution', in which the Church of Scotland's constitution has been ratified and confirmed, rather than conferred, by the State and where establish-

---

[54]If we add to the name of Hon. Mr. Justice Cumming-Bruce, Judge of the High Court, those of two of the assessors, namely D.M.M. Carey, Legal Secretary to the Archbishop of Canterbury, and Sir Harold Kent, Standing Counsel to the Church Assembly and General Synod (1964-72).

[55] *Chadwick 1970*, p. 67.

ment is compatible with complete spiritual autonomy. *Chadwick 1970* recommended, principally, that all matters of doctrine and worship should be subject to the *final* authority of the General Synod; that the Church should prescribe by Canon the forms of subscription to doctrine and should interpret by Canon the formularies of the Church; that a Committee be formed to present the Church's view when a Bishop is to be nominated; that leading members of other communions as well as Anglican bishops should sit in the House of Lords, and that no Church minister should be excluded from standing as a candidate for Parliament. This gradualist approach to change is well expressed in para. 46: 'there is a rub between the ancient historical polity and the new representative system [of synodical government] . . .The only way to prevent it from increasing, is to jettison, at least, one or two features of the ancient historical polity'.[56]

Chadwick 1970 is not an easy document with which to come to terms. It is written in a clipped, laconic style, free of high rhetoric, under great emotional self-control. It is eager to embrace all whom it can. It is devoted to sweet reasonableness, not wanting to cause or give offence. It carries lightly a good deal of historical learning and contemporary analysis. It seeks to be attentive to, and reflective of, the public mind in Church and society. But which public mind? It is sapient and man-of-the-world in its references to Parliament today. It gives the appearance of being fair-minded towards the dissentients within its ranks. It is a master of understatement and periphrasis; it sedulously avoids dogmatic pronouncements. It is an outstanding exercise in *diplomacy*. Yet these complimentary reactions provoked by the Report also, and at the same time, give cause for unease.

First, the predominant historical approach, as in 1917, 1935 and 1952, tends to presuppose that truth is to be found in the steady evolution of historical change. There is no real place for the irruption of discontinuity. Second, for the fourth time, and despite the material in paras. 25-28, there is little *theological* argument and certainly no clear and positive theological position reached in the main report except by implication. Third, as in

[56] P. 16.

the other three Reports, the more radical tradition of thought is not stated except by those who immediately or ultimately reject it (a point made by Ms. Pitt on page 69). Although I should have to engage in more detailed exegesis than is here possible to prove my point, I detect in the Report, in the last analysis, a less than ingenuous attitude to the dissenting opinions, which are presented just that bit too baldly, tending to convey the impression that these opinions are just that bit less rational and that bit more prone to 'enthusiasm' than those of the majority.

Fourth, the analysis of material on religious belief and practice in England, summarised in Appendix D amid a welter of statistics, undoubtedly, whether intentionally or not, conveys the impression that things are much better with the Established Church than the Jeremiahs are inclined to suppose. The writers of the Appendix choose to finish it with a reference to Bedouelle's 1968 book which is a 'remarkable account of the Church of England against the background of contemporary society'.[57] He argues, the writers quote, that England is not a secular society, but is rather implicitly Christian. The writers *could* have chosen a balancing quotation from, say, Bryan Wilson to end the Appendix. In the body of the Report, however, it is admitted that 'in the absence of agreement about the meaning, and even about the nature of the evidence, we have perforce relied on a number of impressionistic judgements'.[58] The question of data and trends is fudged and the predominantly conservative value-judgements of the Commission take their place. So there is no real attempt to grapple with the nature and effect of the changes in political, social and religious life over recent decades.

I turn now to the expressions of dissent. Ms. Valerie Pitt does not share the Commission's desire to preserve intact the legal apparatus of establishment and the historic forms of the Church-Crown-State relationship. Nor does she accept the assumptions upon which that desire rests. The Commission believes that 'the historic relationship of Church and people in England is still alive, if only as a sentiment inhibiting change, in

[57] P. 120.
[58] P. 6.

our society'. 'The Englishman's traditional indifference or antipathy to the Church's institutions, his habitual neglect of its common worship is, though regrettable, irrelevant'. 'The fact that [the Englishman]. . . expresses views totally at variance with any form of historic Christianity is a minor difficulty: what matters is the continuance and preservation of this "folk religion".'[59] Ms. Pitt, on the other hand, accepting that after so long the nation has taken some imprint in the forms of its life and its moral style from its association with the Church, nevertheless is not persuaded that what remains of 'this C. of E. idiom in our way of life represents a lively faith in the gospel or even that it is, any longer, a pastoral opportunity or an effective sentiment outside the Church's own institutions'.[60] This conclusion, for Ms. Pitt, is based on a difference of experience and theology. She does not meet these cultural Anglicans in the great conurbations. In any case, 'Christianity is not a folk or a tribal religion, it is not bred into us by the traditions of our ancestors. It is a gospel, a revealed religion, demanding an active and personal assent'. 'If we persist in this argument [that the link between Church and Crown must be retained for historical and cultural reasons] we may deepen and confirm the Englishman's habitual confusion of the Faith with a culture' and perhaps with a 'dying culture' at that. 'To assert that this popular *Weltanschauung* [namely "a cultural mix of ancestral attitudes"] is an "implicit Christianity" to be carefully safeguarded by the maintenance of the forms of Establishment is to forget the distinctive claims of the gospel. . .'[61]

With considerations such as these, Ms. Pitt goes on to propose the dismantling of the legal apparatus of the Royal Supremacy. But, Ms. Pitt claims, such an action will not of its own withdraw the Church from the national life or from its services to the community, for 'a church's national character is a matter of how it understands its churchly calling, and does not depend for its reality on the status which the national community gives it'[62] – a conclusion which Mr. Cornwell, in his dissent,

[59] P. 72.
[60] P. 73.
[61] Pp. 72-74
[62] P. 78.

shares. Mr. Cornwell also accords special prominence to the view that 'national recognition gives to the Church inappropriate prestige and dangerously masks realities', not least the reality that the Church of England is a minority group. Mr. Coe's dissent (he had joined the Commission as a believer in a modified form of establishment) covers similar ground, but gives special attention also to the ecumenical question which, he judges, will not be helped by the privileged position for the Church of England which the main body of the Report wants to maintain.

In this connection, in para. 11, the Report recalls the part of its terms of reference which required it to listen to, and respect, the wishes of other Churches. 'We have tried, and tried hard', the Report affirms, 'not to identify the interests of Christianity in England exclusively with the interests of the Church of England.'[63] Some useful and frank points are made in paras. 34-37 on 'The Needs of the Movement Towards Reunion', notably: 'the reality of the moment is that while the Church of England has a unique polity in its connexion with the State, it is the Churches generally which the State recognises'.[64] As the Report proceeds, however, consideration of the other Churches features less often and is a deal less positive (cf. paras. 62ff). The Report's first alternative proposal about the appointment of bishops (paras. 97-116) makes no reference to the other Churches. Whereas the second alternative proposal (paras. 121-133) observed that 'the Free Church representatives, whom we consulted, made it clear that their traditions could not tolerate such an arrangement as ours, and that they strongly dislike it'.[65] Thus, the part of the Prime Minister ought to cease, because among other things, 'reunion with anyone is impossible unless it ceases'. On the other hand, the Report recommended without division that other Church leaders should join Anglican

[63] P. 3.

[64] P. 12.

[65] P. 39. It is clear that I am not altogether happy with Paul A. Welsby's judgement in *A History of the Church of England 1945-1980* (Oxford: Oxford University Press, 1984), p. 220, that *Chadwick 1970* 'possessed an ecumenical and sociological awareness absent from previous reports on the subject'.

bishops in the House of Lords. Nevertheless, when the overall tenor and particular proposals of the Report are taken into account, it is clear that in fact the continuance of the present Church of England *sine die* is envisaged. There is no real sign of a desire for ecumenical rapprochement which other Churches might find encouraging. In this respect it is doubtful whether the Commission can really be held to have fulfilled one of its terms of reference.

12.3: Reflections on the Church and State Reports

Though spanning a period of over fifty years, including two world wars, the nuclear bomb and nuclear energy, the welfare state, large-scale immigration, the formation of the EEC, the advent of a multi-racial and multi-religious society, the Depression and contemporary unemployment, the technological revolution and the rise of the ecumenical movement, the four Reports are more notable for their similarities than for their differences. They are significantly alike in temper, method, material, aim, type of membership and underlying philosophy. Each of them has contained a sub-group of professional clergy and laity knowledgeable about the corridors and levers of power in respect of the machinery of Church, Parliament and Crown. Each Report has seen the issue of Church and State predominantly in historical-legal-constitutional terms, thus choosing to identify the well-springs of secular and Christian community with national structures and institutions.

There are a number of standpoints from which it would be useful to comment more broadly upon this set of reports. For example, we might try to judge just how much relative independence has, in fact, been achieved by the Church of England over this period. We might trace the increasing role of the laity. Or we might ask how far is, or ought to be, establishment a major issue today. These themes all deserve exploration. But, in the remainder of this essay, I want to examine a different theme, namely, what these four reports might reveal about the characteristic temper of the Church of

England, about its theological self-understanding and about its perception of the political realm.

All four reports in no small measure accept the historical Henrician and Elizabethan politico-religious settlements as somehow *theologically* normative as well. There is little disposition to submit those settlements to any serious critical analysis of a theological kind. From the outset, those settlements were such as firmly to subordinate Church to State and that position has not fundamentally changed. It is incorrect to say that Church and State are in equal partnership. But, while the main outline of this historical relationship is plain, the details are far from clear. 'The act of the state by which the Church was established was not one law but several. And those laws have been modified, repealed, re-enacted, amended, and altered by precedent, custom and convention until it is virtually impossible to know what the law is without litigation, lengthy enquiry or a process of trial and error.'[66] So, at the very heart of the relationship of Church and State in England, lies a *complex nexus* which cannot be easily grasped, which is not constructed on rational principles, but which is regularly invoked as the appropriate norm and starting point for all later considerations.

Part of that settlement included, at first, a harsh attitude to dissenters, and later a grudging tolerance which was not complete in its concessions until the 19th. Century. Thus, in the midst of this nexus is an ecumenical standing-apart and a grudging consent to other Churches which has found later expression in the Anglican-Methodist debacle and in the Covenant debates. It is characteristic of this nexus that, when the role or self-understanding of the Church is questioned, the response is by way of legal-constitutional adjustment of the received settlement. It is as if the primary churchly reality, the ecclesiastical essence, is to be located at that point. The Church's vital character is given to it by this quirky, contingent historical settlement, and by the fortunes of that settlement in English history since the 16th Century. This formation of theological principle by historical anomaly has had four effects.[67]

[66]Peter Hinchliff, *The One-Sided Reciprocity*, pp. 216ff.

[67] I have noted the powerful influence of historians on the four reports.

First, the Church has had to work out what is proper to itself and to the State in this one-sided reciprocity. The answer has been worked out in terms of the doctrine of 'spiritual independence'. On this principle, the Church accepts that, in all matters except forms of worship and doctrinal formulation, the Church is to be under the ultimate control of the State – that control expressed through Parliamentary approval of, and royal assent to, Church legislation. Thus, the word 'spiritual' is used to refer to two areas where the Church should be regarded as free to manage its own affairs, because worship and doctrine deal with transcendental realities which are not the business of the State. (The State has rightly called the Church's bluff in this respect on more than one occasion, and rightly so, because whatever other spiritual interests worship and doctrine represent, they also represent the power-politics of the Church, in which, in an established church, the State has a legitimate interest.) But the more important meaning of 'spiritual independence' should be not so much that of independence in certain areas categorised as 'spiritual', as of a *quality of the church's whole life giving it a critical and prophetic self-consciousness in relation to the totality of the national life in which it is involved.*

Second, in this confused, unprincipled nexus, the Church has had to work out, as the junior partner in the one-sided reciprocity, what its relationship should be towards the political life of the nation. The above discussion of the principle of 'spiritual independence' already hints that the Church must come to an unwritten agreement that, in return for freedom in the 'spiritual' areas, it accepts that politics, in the broad and narrower senses, is the responsibility of the State, while also accepting that, as the established Church, it somehow affirms the broad directions of politics. The nuances of this position have been well captured by G.S. Ecclestone:

'[The Church of England] nonetheless inherited from the past, and continued to maintain, a close institutional connexion with the state, typified in the presence of the bishops in the House of Lords.' '. . .a style of political involvement which is still characteristic of the Church of England. It is nonauthoritarian, seeking not so much to bind the state as to nudge it in particular directions by an appeal to a shared perception of what is desirable. It is predisposed to rely on the good faith and capacity of people in authority – ministers, civil servants, Members of Parliament – and to share their concern for the maintenance of order as an important feature of social life. Partly because of its long historical association with the legal and social structures of English life (themselves significantly influenced by a Christian past), it is disposed to emphasise and value the dimension of continuity in institutions and policies.' '. . .the absence of a single dominating philosophical or credal expression of Anglicanism . . . has meant that the Church of England has not been required by its theological self- understanding to think systematically about its place in society and the political dimension to its mission.' 'It cannot. . .be said that within the Church of England as a whole there is a sense of the need to look deeply at the rationale of its political involvement or to seek to understand what is happening in society.'[68]

As Ecclestone rightly notes, the approach of the Church of England to politics in the central nexus has been in terms of moral comment on certain areas, e.g. housing, which are believed to be less than political in the full sense, and more moral-pastoral, so that the basic political neutrality of the Church of England is not undermined.

Third, as we have seen, the confused and unprincipled central nexus counts against clear and decisive thinking about the Church. It has frequently been noted that, in the Church of England, initiatives have largely been taken by private individuals and by voluntary agencies. But then a conflict emerges between a voluntary or localised ecclesiastical response to a perceived need and the tendency at the central nexus to proceed by slow adjustment and piecemeal modification. For example, the rise of industrial mission was a late, small, but important voluntary response to some consequences of the Industrial Revolution which have radically transformed English life. But the attitudes which belong to the central nexus have not displayed any real sensitivity to the discontinuity brought about

[68]G.S. Ecclestone, *The Church of England and Politics* (GS 457, 1980), pp. 4–8.

by the Industrial Revolution and have, for the most part, massively affirmed the continuities, namely of ministry to the place of residence at the parish church. Sir Lewis Dibdin could not endure the proposal of *Selborne 1917* for working class electors selected by special means. The exclusive basis had to be parochial church councils.[69] Further, some of this hesitancy about industrial mission may lie in its being held to move the Church closer to the political realm, disturbing the balance referred to above.

Fourth, the Church and State reports reveal a distinctive way of working on the part of the Church of England when faced by certain problems. It involves the *reduction* of major theological, social or political issues to the manageable scale of domestic ecclesiastical-legal legislation taking up protracted periods of time in quasi-parliamentary procedures of labyrinthine complexity, passing up and down levels of consultative government more busily than the angels ascending and descending Jacob's ladder. This quite massive loss of proportion finds a *locus classicus* in Archbishop Fisher's presidential address to the Convocations in 1947 when he first spoke movingly of the needs of the nation, calling for political wisdom, spiritual integrity and economic efficiency, but then moved to the Church's response in its own life requiring as the 'first and most essential step' the reform of Canon Law, a process to which Fisher committed large amounts of the Church's time, energy and attention over several years.[70] The complexities of the central nexus as influencing the pattern of Church decision-making are reflected in the constitution of the Church Assembly, and even more of the General Synod whose Parliamentary procedures, severed from the constraints of pressure by political party and Cabinet, permit procedural self-indulgence and provoke incapacity for the making of decisions on a truly alarming scale. But at no point in, for example, *Selborne 1917*, were searching questions asked about the compatibility of these Church structures with criteria of Christian belief and practice. The legal-historical-constitutional hand has laid heavily upon these things. At times, an almost aesthetic delight in the means over against the ends is sensed.

[69] *Selborne 1917*, p. 68.
[70] See Welsby, *A History of the Church of England*, p. 41.

The temper of the Church and State Reports suggests a temper in the Church of England which seems to emerge again and again despite the efforts of individuals and voluntary groups to bring about a more clear-cut sense of decision and purpose. In *Christians and the State*, J.C. Bennett takes as a starting-point (very differently from the four reports), a theological principle, namely 'the way in which the Church exists to be invaded by that which comes from God'.[71] Bennett argues that to be open to such invasion, the Church should normally be separated from the State. Two of the reasons which Bennett gives in support of this position concern (1) that only thereby can the Church be sure of avoiding being used for the purposes of propaganda, and (2) that only thereby can the Christian body be clearly distinguishable from the national community. There are *obvious* examples of the Church being caught up on propaganda activities and in unsuitable effusions of national sentiment. But it is probably the less obvious instances which are more significant, instances where Christian thought and life accommodate themselves unconsciously and unthinkingly to attitudes of state which are actually far from the Christian mind.

What Ecclestone called the Church's lack of a sense of the need to look deeply at the rationale of its political involvement, and lack of willingness to seek to understand what is happening in society, leaves it highly vulnerable. Given the central nexus which I have illustrated from the Church and State Reports, I should have regarded it as altogether remarkable if the Church of England had *not* accepted as its own, for example, the general post-war policy of deterrence, nuclear armaments, NATO, etc., notwithstanding particular Church reports or groups which looked at these matters more critically. What is especially interesting about the 1983 debate about *The Church and the Bomb* is that Anglican Christians were thereby being asked to look afresh at fundamental theological attitudes to peace and war. That level of attention was not long sustained in the Church's public debate, the conversation quickly changing to the merits of particular secular policies and of particular political groupings. This shift of attention makes it difficult for the Church to

[71]J.C. Bennett, *Christians and the State* (New York: Scribners, 1958), p. 202.

address itself to the challenge of being 'invaded by that which comes from God'. The question which *should* have been addressed in that debate was rather about what Christians individually and collectively are obliged and constrained to be and to do, and to persuade others to be and to do, in obedience to the Christian vocation of peace-making. The temper of the Church of England, still caught up in what I have called the central nexus of Church and State, renders it apparently unable to hold fast to that kind of fundamental theological question. In matters of peace and war, of poverty and riches, and of relations with other countries, the Church of England (whatever its occasional rhetoric) still seems hypnotised by the history of its complex embeddedness in the State and still sufficiently bemused to think that it can exist apolitically amid political turbulence.

We can discern, therefore, an inherited tendency to accept the existing political arrangements as *defining* what ought to be the relationship between Church and State, an acceptance which inhibits serious questioning of the political process as such and of particular policies also. In this compromised position, for example, the Church has never really been *ready* in this century to think clearly and theologically about the results of applying criteria of the Just War to wars in which Britain has been involved. Charles Curran has noted a similar tendency in 20th. Century North American Catholicism.[72] This reserved attitude towards political realities is reflected in the sometimes expressed idea in the Church and State Reports that somehow the Queen as head of the Church should approve Church legislation without *any* kind of interference, check, or control by Parliament. Such a coronocentric notion should be anathema to the function of a constitutional monarch in a democratic society, yet it reflects a sentimental notion of monarchy, a lacklustre understanding of a national church, and a desire to retain the privileges and alleged benefits of establishment without any

[72] 'When will the theory of the Just War ever be used decisively to say No to our nation's policy?'. We can show 'historically how the just-war theory has almost inevitably been used to justify our wars', Charles E. Curran, *American Catholic Social Ethics* (Notre Dame and London: University of Notre Dame Press, 1982), p. 279.

accountability being involved. There is no need to deny that this muddled attitude towards the political realm in the central nexus is counter-balanced by all sorts of lively thinking and doing within different parts of the Church. But it still remains the case that these initiatives tend quickly to evaporate amid the muddy swamps of the central nexus, since no means exists to carry forward commitments to theological imperatives as continuing commitments rather than as a succession of diverse, pragmatic, hastily contrived reactions to the course of events.

12.4: Towards a New Church-State Relationship

The inauguration of synodical government in 1970, attended by high hopes, does not (I judge) appear to have yet affected the Church's self-understanding in any fundamental way. To the extent that the Church has, in fact, gained more independence from the State, it seems to have used that independence to increase its preoccupation with domestic matters, manifesting therein a poor record in actually making decisions. Is that increased independence freeing the Church to discover how to be a national church without the pseudo-apolitical stance of an *established* church? Some such development appears to be the hope of some in a new generation of Church leaders. But given the size and distribution of churches in England, is it sensible to talk of *the* or *a* national Church, except as the result of a major ecumenical regrouping? Or is the Church of England, enjoying its new measure of independence, steadily withdrawing from a commitment to the political realm and settling for a local ministry to those who show a preference for its ways of worship? Or, much more dangerously, is the Church of England still intent on owning the lost substance of Establishment, eager to retain a special place over against other English Christians as the National Church, but, in fact, content for the most part to accept a generally apolitical standpoint as one brand of 'spiritual preference' in a politically secular society?

To find a Christian way among these and other options demands much more basic theological thinking about the rationale of the Church's political involvement in society than the central nexus of Church and State has ever attempted or has wanted others to attempt, more basic thinking than any of the four Church and State Reports have managed to stimulate. History shows that the risk of the Church being the Church in little else but the name is real and ever-present. In one way and another, all the options which people seem to regard as available to the Church seem to presuppose one of two basic alternatives. They may assume a very tentative attitude towards politics, seeing it as something much narrower and more specialised than 'the sum total of principles, symbols, means and actions whereby Man endeavours to attain the *common* good of the *polis*'. Or they may argue a lusty denial of the political realm in some form of sectarian isolation. Certainly the Church and State Reports, with their misapplied notion of 'spiritual independence', imply the former attitude with all the hesitancy of crossing the boundary into politics proper which accompanies this point of view.

Panikkar, in his essay on 'Religion or Politics: The Western Dilemma',[73] is plainly of the opinion that both options represent an outmoded and obsolescent way of looking at the relation between religion and politics. Panikkar argues that 'we are approaching the close of the modern Western dichotomy between religion and politics, and we are coming near to a non-dualistic relation between the two'.[74] '. . . *Separation* between politics and religion is only understandable in the climate of dualistic thought, while *identification* is only understandable in a world of monism.' 'Religion has not to do with an eternal deprived of temporal roots, nor has politics to do with a temporal stripped of trans-temporal repercussions.'[75] Panikkar believes that at the present time, amid the decay of these false dualisms and monisms, new perceptions and experiences are stirring. 'We are discovering the sacred character of secular engagement and the political aspect of religious life.'[76] So the

[73] In eds., Peter H. Merkl and Ninian Smart, *Religion and Politics in the Modern World* (New York and London: New York University Press, 1983), pp. 44-60.
[74] Panikkar, pp. 46ff.
[75] Pp. 49ff.
[76] P. 52.

notions of 'politics' (meaning eternal and sacred affairs), are no longer valid. 'A religion for our times must be political, and thus cannot keep itself on the edge of problems of injustice, hunger, war, exploitation, the power of money, the function of the economy, armaments, ecological questions, demographic problems, etc.'[77] Thus, we have to ask a different question from the one asked by the West over many centuries. What is the relation between a religion which is not depoliticised and a politics which is not desacralised? This 'advaitic' relation between religion and politics, which issues in neither an established church nor in a sect, may be a helpful way in which to conceptualise some of the political stirrings currently in, and around the margins of, the Churches, for whose understanding and discriminating support we do not have at present adequate frameworks of thought. There is much in the interplay of politics and religion in contemporary Britain that deserves attention in Panikkar's scheme of things. It is even possible, if these stirrings gain momentum, that the Church and the churches could find themselves, with others, involved in the practical redefining of politics. But the four Church and State Reports were not in business for undertakings of that kind. One can only look out keenly and with interest for further signs of the Church's desire to struggle with the question of its basic Christian imperatives towards the political realm, that realm defined by itself and not simply by the State in a one-sided reciprocity.

[77] P. 55.

Chapter 13

THE ANGLICAN CHURCH AND THE SECULAR STATE

Raymond Plant

'Real Politics are the possession and distribution of power'
(Lady Montfort in Disraeli's *Endymion*)

'Not by might, not by power, but by my spirit says the
Lords of Hosts'
(Zachariah, Ch. 4, v. 6)

13.1: Introduction

The relationship between the Church and secular politics has
been brought into sharp public focus over the past few years.
The intervention in the debate about nuclear disarmament
provoked by the Board of Social Responsibility's report on *The
Church and the Bomb* and the subsequent debate at the General
Synod; the less than nationalistic features of the post-Falklands
Thanksgiving Service; and the growing preoccupation of the
Church with the poor and unemployed have been important in
bringing to attention the nature of the relationship between the
Church and politics – frequently to the annoyance of politicians.
Over the weekend of March 4–5 1984, for example, a Conserva-
tive MP, John Butcher, suggested that the Church should give
up politics for Lent and concentrate on its real mission saving
souls and filling pews.

There have also been more subtle, intellectual influences at
work in seeking to revise the question of the relationship
between the Church and State. Edward Norman's Reith
Lectures on *Christianity and the World Order* were bitingly critical
of what he saw as the Church's unreflective endorsement of the
political preferences of middle class *bien pensant* liberals. In this
he echoed some of the writings of Enoch Powell who has also
sought to question the political role of the Church by denying,
in collections of sermons such as *Wrestling with the Angel*, that

the message of Christ has any social and political import. Norman and Powell are, in their turn, part of a tradition of British thought on these matters which, until lately, has been rather submerged by a more liberal, affirmative view of the Church's social and political role, but in a tradition ably resurrected by Powell and Norman and very well chronicled, so far as the twentieth century is concerned, in Maurice Cowling's *Religion and Public Doctrine in Modern England*. Clearly, there is a lively debate here and in this chapter I shall try, as a political theorist and a rather hesitant Christian with an amateur interest in theology, to clarify some of the points at issue and to make some recommendations about how the Church should proceed in thinking about its political and social responsibilities assuming *pace* Norman, Powell and Cowling that it has some.

It would, of course, be a major error to think that the issues raised during the last few years and alluded to above, mark only the beginning of this debate. The nature of the relationship between the Church and the political world has always been a major concern of theologians and, for that matter, many secular theorists. Among theologians, one only has to think about the work of St. Augustine, whose *De Civitate Dei* articulates a systematic account of the relationship between Christianity and the political world in its doctrine of the two loves of the twin cities and the Christian's allegiance to the city of God; of St. Thomas with his subtle theories in *Summa Contra Gentiles*; of Calvin with his politically important doctrine of the priesthood of all believers; of Hooker's *Laws of Ecclesiastical Polity*; of Keble with his assize sermon on *National Apostasy* and, indeed, the Tractarian movement in general; of Bonhoeffer at an abstract level in *Sanctorum Communio* and in a tragically practical way *No Rusty Swords*; of William Temple in *Christianity and the Social Order*; and of the neo-Hegelian Henry Scott Holland, editor of *The Commonwealth* from its inception. Thus, the issue did not arise yesterday – there is a tradition of thought here which cannot be neglected in any systematic attempt to grapple with the problem.

Among more secular political theorists, too, there has been a recurring interest in the role of the Church and religion in the polity. Marsilius, Rousseau, Hobbes, Locke, Hegel and T.H.

Green stand out as thinkers who have been centrally concerned with the issue of the relation between politics and religion and, in the case of Hobbes, Rousseau and Hegel, with the potentially divisive effects on the political culture of a society, of a Church and a religion which embodies Aquinas's doctrine that 'man does not belong to the political community with all that he has, not with all that he is'.

At the level of practice, too, the witness of individual Christians against what they have taken to be deformations of political power have been a powerful element in Christian history. St. Ambrose, for example, refused to celebrate mass in the presence of the Emperor Theodosius after his implication in the massacre of Thessalonica. The history of such witness against political oppression both within one's own society and in others, has been a central and ineradicable feature of the Christian tradition. Canon Collins, Michael Scott, Fr. Huddleston and Dean Gonville-Ffrench-Bytagh are only recent examples of this tradition.

13.2:   Different Understandings of Church and Politics

The relationship between the Church and the world of secular politics is a very deep issue which cannot be settled by glibly quoting the words of Jesus about rendering unto Caesar the things that are Caesar's and unto God the things that are God's just because the passage does not tell us what things are to be taken as the things of Caesar. The world of political issues and political ethics is not just self-evident. Even if we accept the passage at its face value, we need some theologically based conception of the nature and limits of political power and political things. For both the Church and for politics the issue is much deeper than this. The rise of Christian religion, with its claim to authority over the things of God – at least the moral and spiritual life of mankind, independent of the power of the State, is a very profound development in Western thought and experience. In contrast to, say, the folk religion of the Greek city-state where religious, moral and political authority were homogeneous, the exercise of moral authority by the Christian

Church is always going to raise questions about the nature and extent of political authority which, because its extent is always in flux, is always going to have to be rethought. The growth of the role of the State and the growing politicisation of spheres of life which in earlier generations would have been thought to be independent and autonomous spheres of civil society, means that the Church is continually presented with changing conceptions of the realm of Caesar and the idea that the mere invocation of this biblical passage settles anything at all on its own is intellectually disingenuous.

In trying to come to grips with this question, I want to distinguish several distinct approaches to the issue. I am not suggesting that they have been held in a wholly pure and coherent form by any Christian thinker but they are useful analytical devices for dealing with a complex issue with nearly two thousand years of history behind it. The first position is what might be called the 'Christian Nation' or 'Christendom' approach. It assumes that the Church both has a duty, and is in a position, to articulate a fully developed political theology which will embody the demands of Christian thought and ethics in the sphere of politics. It is then the Church's task to try to struggle to gain general acceptance for this view within the polity so that political activity, both in terms of ends and means, is predicated upon Christian principles and Christian authority. The basis of such a Christian polity would be either the teaching of the Bible, or a theologically derived conception of natural laws, or the Christian tradition or, more usually, some mixture of them.

The second view would be almost the reverse of this, namely that the Church should recognise that it is only one institution among many others in a pluralistic society and while it should seek to exercise spiritual authority over its members, this is only in the sphere of private and religious morality. In a pluralist society, the Church cannot claim any authority in the sphere of political morality. In politics, Christian citizens must exercise their civic responsibilities independently of the authority of the Church.

In between these two positions is the 'Secularist' view that the Church has to examine secular political doctrines typically dealing with human rights, social justice, poverty, just war doctrines, etc. and to endorse those elements which appear to be most congenial to the Christian position. In this way, the Church is then in the position of supplying motivation for secular political doctrines rather than operating on the basis of a political theology of its own.

The final 'Conservative' view is that of Norman, Powell and Cowling et al., that the Church has nothing to do with the governance of society because its theology is concerned with personal morality and personal salvation rather than with the fate of a collectivity. I shall now turn to the discussion of these viewpoints in turn.

13.3: The Christendom View

The 'Christian Nation' or Christendom view has its roots in the history of Christianity in the West, particularly during the mediaeval period when there was no real conception of the distinction between Church and State. They were rather seen as aspects of a single whole, even by critics of the Church such as Marsilius of Padua. Church and society were inextricably bound together and the authority of the Church and the separate spheres of political authority were not very clearly defined.

In modern times, this distinction has been more clearly drawn, although in the case of the Anglican Church with its entrenched position within the polity as the established Church and with representation in the governance of the State in the House of Lords, the line is obviously fuzzy. Those who seek to argue for the revitalisation of the 'Christian Nation' approach argue that it is the duty of the Church to develop its own distinctive corporate view about political issues and to try to get this accepted as authoritative in politics. The argument here is that the Church is inextricably bound up with the State as a matter of fact. It is involved, by its liturgy, in the celebration of coronations, royal weddings, prayer in the House of Commons before the beginning of business, in the Remembrance Service at the Cenotaph, at Mayoral ceremonies, in securing and celebrating the legitimacy of institutions of the State and their continuity.

Granted this fact, the Church should seek to exercise substantive moral authority within the polity within which it is legally established, and it is to do this by trying to develop a political theology. As Professor Mascall argues in *Man: His Origin and Destiny*:

'The Christian answer to a state of affairs in which man finds himself under domination of the beings that ought to be subject to him is that he can only recover his true lordship if he places himself deliberately under the Lordship of God. This does not mean just the practice of individual religion, though that is quite indispensible; it means the deliberate ordering of human society in the light of the truths of the Christian faith. . . it means that theology must govern politics, politics must govern economics and economics must govern finance.'[1]

There are perhaps two forms which this argument can take. The first, more minimal version, would start from the fact of establishment and then go on to argue that this gives the Church a privileged place in the polity and therefore that the Church should use this unique position to give a moral lead on questions of the day. The very fact of the Church's establishment on this view gives it a role to speak to the nation on behalf of Christian moral claims.

A more complex argument would not start from the fact of the Church's position but would, on the contrary, argue that this position is itself in need of some theological justification. On this view, the Church would need a theology of social institutions, and of itself as such an institution and in its relation to the State. In this sense, the Church would have to develop a social and political theology and this would have at least two purposes. One would be to provide a theological account of the nature of the Church as an institution, and of the State and its institutions, whose legitimacy the Church, as the established Church, has a part in securing. To be so implicated in the structure and legitimacy of the State without having some theological justification for it, accepting it as just a bare fact

[1] E. Mascall, *Man: His Origin and Destiny*, (Westminster: Dacre Press, 1940), p. 75.

about the constitution of the Church, would seem to an observer to be a major intellectual and moral failing on the part of the Church. The second purpose of such a political theology would presuppose the first but go beyond it and concern itself not just with the theology of the Church as an institution in relation to the State but also with developing a theological position in relation to other political issues – justice, law, poverty, distribution, citizenship, foreign policy, etc. It is certainly political theology in its broader sense that Mascall endorses in the quotation cited earlier.

The term 'political theology' is treated with a good deal of caution in some quarters because, in the modern world, it has become closely associated with political radicalism particularly in the work of South American 'liberation theology' and in the writings of Jurgen Moltman which is heavily indebted to the writings of Ernst Bloch, the Marxist philosopher. However, there is no reason why this should be so. It is arguable that there is nothing in the nature of political theology which necessarily allies it to radicalism. Essentially, such a theology would operate with the doctrine of God and man in relation to God, the distinctive capacities and powers with which humans are endowed, the nature of human sociability and the ends of human life. It would then utilise these insights to theorise about political issues and have things to say about the nature of the State and its purposes, its relation to civil society, the rights and duties of individuals within it, the nature of justice and the role of law. On the face of it, if Christian theology has a theory of man or human nature, it is difficult to see how such a theory could be developed without having a view about the institutions, both social and political, within which the human personality is nurtured. It would also presumably entail a view about the nature of those institutions within which human beings might flourish and realise their God-given capacities and those institutions which tend to impede such individual development.

In this sense, most systematic theologies have had a political ideology and, as I have said, it is difficult to see how it could be avoided. The only way in which it could be avoided, and indeed regarded as intrinsically connected with radicalism, would be to argue that the sphere of human morality is, in fact, limited to personal morality and that in some sense political and economic activity is an arena to which moral categories do not apply. However, it is very difficult to see how this could be so. For example, even the most ardent defender of free markets unconstrained in their outcomes by moral criteria such as distributive justice has to draw upon moral categories in at least two ways. His defence of free markets is usually in terms of moral characteristics such as individual freedom and, in addition, however implicitly, they will have to rely on certain moral characteristics in persons to underpin market activities. Thus, integrity, promise-keeping and truth-telling seem to be inescapable moral foundations of markets and, in this sense, there is a sphere of public morality in even the most liberal economic market.

On the view being examined, therefore, the Church has a role in trying to articulate a distinctive and corporate view about the nature of morality and this will, in turn, be founded upon an explicit moral and political theology which will say something about basic political and social relationships. The sources of such a political and social theology would lie in Biblical theology, natural law or the tradition of the Church.

However, it is here that the major difficulty arises. The corporate political witness of the Church has to be based upon a theology but, of course, in the same way as theologians disagree about the way we should conceptualise the nature of God and man's relation to God, there are likely to be consequential disagreements over a social and political theology. This, of course, is paralleled in the field of political philosophy where even a single ideological stance such as liberalism has a number of competing and frequently exclusive theoretical underpinnings.

Even in those cases in theology where agreement seems most likely, as, for example, in the case of the moral equality of individuals as equal in the sight of God, this agreement is too general to secure any specific political outcome. In his book *The Church of God*, Donald Mackinnon argues as follows:

'. . .the coming of Jesus reveals to man his eternal destiny. His end is achieved not within but outside the ebb and flow of temporal history. Judgement, mercy, redemption, these fundamental words of the Christian Gospel are at the very basis of human rights. . .It is the act of God in Christ which reveals to man his inalienable dignity.'[2]

There are, of course, very few Christians who would disagree with these sentiments but the price of agreement is almost total vacuity. The idea of inalienable dignity rules very little out of the social and political realm. What sort of rights does this dignity underwrite, the negative rights not to be killed, tortured, interfered with, exploited; or positive rights to resources of various kinds – economic, educational, recreational, etc.? Or do the inherent dignity of the person and the rights derived from the principle only require that he should be treated with respect – but what is it to respect another person and what institutions are most comparable with this? Or does it mean that each person's interests ought to be taken into account in making social and political arrangements? But then what are interests? Are they linked to wants or needs; is the individual the final authority on what his interests are, and what about children, the mentally handicapped, the very old?

The problem here is paralleled in political theory. At one level it is possible to produce wholly descriptive definitions of basic concepts over which there would be a wide measure of agreement, for example that 'democracy is rule by the people'. Few would disagree with this but it is wholly unspecific in content and would apply to a very wide range of political arrangements. The price of agreement, in short, is vacuity. It is only when we try to spell out what body the 'people' is and how this rule is to be realised that we begin to say something specific. But this then becomes the first area within which disagreement arises. As Professor Preston argues in the context of Protestant social and political theology:

'The most common tactic. . .is to stick to agreed moral generalities or principles, which cannot be disputed because they

[2] D.M. MacKinnon, *The Church of God* (Westminster: Dacre Press, 1940), p. 102.

have no specific content. Preachers often do this and so do church statements.'[3]

In his view it is necessary for the Church to try to develop middle range moral and political principles which will be specific enough to be a general guide to public policy, but not themselves constituting a set of policies.

There seems to be a genuine need for this. Too often the Church's political pronouncements connect together the understandings of a particular policy or attitude and a very vague and general principle and assume that the connection between the two is clear. More often than not it is far from clear and one does need to know the intermediate principles which connect the general and the particular. Without these intermediate steps, the social and political theologian will be open to Enoch Powell's claim that there are no 'logical bridges. . .across the gulf between the assertions of Christianity and the conduct of the world's business'.

However, if political theology is to be taken seriously, two things seem to be required. The first is that the construction of these mediating principles is likely to be a very contested business. As I have already argued, if it remains at the level of general principle, social and political theology will be consensual but at the price of platitude. On the other hand, if social and political theologians are to build a more specific doctrine, they must recognise that it will be much less secure and this leads on to the second point. While remaining at the level of pious generality, the Church can carry its flock with it, despite the differences in politics between individual Christians, and this consensus is a major aspect of whatever authority the Church's statements on social and political issues have. The more specific the Church gets, the more contestable within the Church will its specific social doctrines be and, therefore, less authoritative for its members.

This is clearly the central dilemma for a 'Christian Nation' approach to Anglican social and political thought. The ultimate aim of such an approach, as indicated by the quotation from

[3] R.H. Preston, *Church and Society in the Late Twentieth Century: The Economic and Political Task*, (London: SCM Press, 1983), p. 142.

Mascall cited earlier, is the transformation of society by Christian principles so that these principles will apply not just to personal morality but also to the conduct of the affairs of the nation. However, as I have suggested, the more specific the principles are, and they have to be if they are to permeate the Christian Nation, the less authoritative they will be even for Christians. If the Church cannot speak authoritatively and consensually (within its own boundaries) on political affairs, connecting up particular issues with general principles rather than merely jumping from one to the other, then the 'Christian Nation' approach to social and political issues is, in all senses of the phrase, a pious hope.

However, the dilemmas, which I regard as intrinsic to the 'Christian Nation' approach, lead naturally to the next position to be discussed. If the Church is caught on the dilemma I have indicated, of having very little ability to speak with authority about social and political affairs either because its pronouncements are too general to mean very much, or too specific to be authoritative within the Church, then this does raise the question of whether the Church can play a role in politics at all in a pluralistic society.

13.4: The Pluralistic View

One figure who argued that it could not, that in a plural society the Church could not hope to speak in a convincing political tone, was J.N. Figgis, the Mirfield monk and historian of political thought, who died in 1919. Figgis was preoccupied with the nature of the authority of the Anglican Church in a pluralistic society. His argument was put in terms of the independence of the Church from political authority in matters of faith and doctrine. The freedom of the Church in relation to its own life and doctrine required the Church to concede certain freedom to other groups in society, and the State should not, therefore, seek to pursue a Christian policy in regard to its citizens. The argument for freedom cuts both ways:

'We cannot claim liberty for ourselves, while at the same time proposing to deny it to others. If we cry "hands off" to the civil power, in regard to such matters as marriage, doctrine, ritual, the conditions of communion within the Church – and it is the necessary condition of a free religious society that it should regulate these matters – then we must give up attempting to dictate the policy of the State in regard to the whole mass of its citizens.'[4]

In other words, the idea of the 'Christian Nation' has to be abandoned. The Church has to have the freedom from the State to act with authority over its own members in matters of liturgy, sacrament and private morality, but the Church in turn has no role to play on the broader political scene, for example in trying to secure marriage laws which would encapsulate a Christian doctrine of marriage.

In Figgis's view, it was, of course, right that the Church should decide how its own sacrament of marriage was to be administered and to choose to forbid its own members to remarry in Church after divorce, but that is the extent of its authority both actual and legitimate. Naturally, Christians are citizens with political interests and while, of course, one's religious convictions may play a role in the exercise of citizenship, this should not really be seen as Christian citizenship because the citizen of the modern State has to be aware that there are many who do not share his religious and moral beliefs and it would then be wrong for him to vote for policies which were designed to impose on the State some specifically Christian conception of the good.

In this sense, Figgis has produced a doctrine of the Church and a political theology which fit most clearly into a liberal society. Many contemporary liberal political theorists have argued that the State should be neutral over conceptions of 'the good'. The State cannot treat its citizens as equals if it prefers the imposition of one conception of 'the good' over others, granted that citizens will differ over their views about the good life. Rather, the State should seek to secure that framework of law and institutions within which individuals can pursue their own conception of 'the good', whether this is an individual good or

[4] J.N. Figgis, *Churches in the Modern State* (London: Longmans, Green, 1913), p. 112.

one to be pursued through a voluntary group. For some, this will mean joining Churches which are the vehicles for their particular conception of what 'the good' for man consists in. However, it would be quite wrong for the Church, as in the 'Christian Nation' approach, to try to secure specifically Christian legislation in a free and heterogeneous society. Figgis was a very strong pluralist who held that human goods were best pursued within groups which should have the highest degree of freedom between them, although within such voluntary groups, moral teaching and moral authority could be very strong.

The version of the liberal State, and the role which the Church has within it, is based on the idea that the State is neutral between substantive political goods, these being realised in individual group life with the highest degree of toleration between groups. As such, it stands in very sharp contrast to the 'Christian Nation' approach.

There are, however, a number of questions to be addressed by this approach, some of which go right to the heart both of the nature of Christian ethics and the political morality of the liberal state. From the Christian view, this theory invites us to draw a very rigid distinction between public and private morality with the very clear assumption that the moral life of the Christian can be realised in a wholly private context, with his family, within his Church and in private action towards other individuals within the society, for example in acts of private charity. The Christian ethic thus makes no demands on public action within the State, as, if they do, they are likely to be achievable by the cooperation of individuals who may differ over their fundamental beliefs and without appeal to a specific Christian motivation.

Take, for example, something like the establishment of a State system of blood donation. I may believe as a matter of Christian morality that I should give blood, but equally others may have similarly strong convictions about this based upon quite different beliefs. Cooperation in trying to bring pressure to bear to set up such a service can be achieved without having to predicate the service on a *particular* set of moral imperatives. By the same token, as a Christian, I may have a belief about my duties to the poor but again cooperation in achieving adequate resources to deal with poverty could be achieved in a comparable way without the policy being regarded as specifically Christian. Indeed, in a morally pluralistic society, it may well be counter-productive to try to base the development of a public policy on religious grounds because this may not facilitate cooperation with others. However, this is to concede that what are seen to be the desired outcomes of Christian ethics can be achieved without Christian doctrine and that, in fact, in the public realm, doctrine may militate against the possibility of the desired outcome.

The abstract question at issue here is that whether, in a plural society, some shared public morality may be necessary to underpin particular policies, assuming that, if it is, it can be agreed by the groups which compose a plural society independently of the theoretical view held by these different groups. However, this may just be wishful thinking in hard cases, the most obvious of which is abortion. Can the Christian accept, for example, abortion at more or less any stage of pregnancy on demand on the ground that while members of the Church would not themselves want this, they should be tolerant of those groups in society which may see this as part of the conception of 'the good', as clearly some feminists see it in connection with their views about the right to determine what should happen to their own bodies. It is cases like this that the distinction between public and private morality begins to look less secure. Should the Church be happy to tolerate what from some points of view might be regarded as murder, merely because, from another point of view of those undertaking the action, it is not.

Figgis rather assumes without really any argument that, in so far as a liberal State requires a public morality, it will be fairly minimal and that right-thinking citizens could come to agree on what it was, independent of their own particular moral and metaphysical outlooks. However, public policy, when it deals with the extremities of human life shows, I think, that this hope may be illusory. The idea that the State should be held together only by the cement of mutual tolerance is a fine ideal but it does not seem clear that the nature of Christian morality may well require that certain things should not be tolerated however sincerely some may feel that their actions are an intrinsic part of their conception of 'the good'. Of course, it is always open to the Church to condemn such actions as sinful but there are cases where the Christian citizen may want to argue they should be a crime too.

In this sense, political liberals such as Figgis may not have taken their thinking about secularisation and pluralism far enough. He rather assumes a framework of moral agreement between plural groups which, while not necessarily resting on Christian morality, is at least consistent with it. However, this may no longer be true and, in so far as it is not, his easy distinction between a private morality which I adopt as a Christian and the public morality I adopt as a citizen may be inadequate.

It is also important to realise that the neutral State is, in any case, an illusion not just because any State is going to need some minimal public morality to keep it running and secure loyalty to it, but for the deeper reason that the very idea of neutrality which is supposed to be indifferent to conceptions of 'the good' in fact favours private conceptions of 'the good' which are, not surprisingly, endorsed by liberals. The neutral State is incompatible with most views of the good life which require some communal realisation. So, for example, some forms of traditional conservatism should require a high degree of moral integration, shared tradition and patriotism to articulate it, and socialism, in whatever form, more obviously requires a more communal form of realisation. In this sense, the 'Christian Nation' approach would be rather like these two political ideologies, finding itself in the position of requiring some corporate and communal realisation; whereas the Figgis approach is obviously not apolitical, despite its protestations, because it produces a moral and theological doctrine which is not only consistent with the liberal State, but an endorsement of it. It is quite central to this view that the Christian life does not require a corporate and communal expression going beyond what can be attained within the Church as one more voluntary group or partial community with others in society.

13.5:   The Secularist View

The third alternative to be discussed falls somewhere between the 'Christian Nation' view and the pluralism of Figgis. It is the view characteristic of a good deal of the modern social and political stances of the Church that it is to provide some kind of underpinning to political principles which are arrived at on secular grounds. Whereas the 'Christian Nation' point of view sought to derive political and social imperatives from a theology and a theological anthropology, the tendency in the present view is to assimilate the Church's teaching on social and political issues to a set of secular principles such as social justice, human rights and liberty without really attempting in any very thorough-going way to derive these principles from an elaborated theological position.

Perhaps an example from my own recent experience will illustrate this. In 1981-2, I chaired a British Council of Churches' working party on poverty in the United Kingdom. Our task was not so much to produce yet more facts and figures about poverty so much as to discuss the Christian response to poverty. The issue of poverty and the moral claims of the poor go right to the heart of a good many of the central questions in social and political theory, questions such as what do we mean by social justice, needs and the moral claims that needs embody, the nature of the responsibility which we have to other individuals in our society, whether the relief of poverty is best tackled by state-organised strategies or by an 'echelon advance', allowing, according to the theories of Hayek and Friedman, the free market to increase wealth for the rich and poor, a more effective measure in their view than illusory collective schemes in the interests of social justice.

This issue also, of course, leads fairly naturally to considering the question of the relation between poverty and inequality. When I tried to grapple with these issues, two things became apparent. One was the great amount of work to be found in the social sciences and in political and social theory on the empirical and normative issues here, and the very small amount of independent theological thinking that had been done by the Churches on these issues, despite the growing preoccupation of the Church with just this sort of thing. Despite my own inclination to want to approach the problem from the theological end and to set the Christian view of poverty in the context of a political theology, this proved impossible and I was left with trying to look at modern social and political theory to see what could be reasonably regarded as generally consistent with the rather vague formulations of the Church in this area.

One example would be to look at the work of the American political philosopher, John Rawls. His book *A Theory of Justice* is concerned with the worst off members of society in the sense that one of the two principles of justice he advances is that the unequal distribution of primary goods such as income is only legitimate if it benefits the worst off. This conclusion is derived from an argument about what individuals who were mutually disinterested would regard as a fair distribution of goods if they did not know in advance whether they would lose or gain as the result of the principles they accepted. In some sense, parts of Rawls' theory are congenial to the current Christian concern with the worst off and what is taken to be the injustice of their position. Other parts of Rawls' view are uncongenial, for example his individualism and his limited view of altruism. However, there is nothing within the Church's own social and political theology which approaches the complexity and power of a theoretical statement of this sort, and in the absence of a fully developed social and political theology, one is left making rather *ad hoc* adjustments to prevailing secular theories in this field.

However, the peculiarity of this procedure is as obvious as it is currently unavoidable. It is not clear what the Church is adding, for example, to a theory of redistributive justice of its own, and one is left with the despair of feeling that one is looking for the odd bit of theological backing for one's political preferences which are held on quite other grounds. And, of course, it would be open to the conservative to do the same. In addition, one has to recognise that such secular political theories as one suggests for theological endorsement, are not themselves capable of being held as ultimate and objective truths about political life.

It is the difficulty embedded in these two points, the Christian assimilation of political principles derived on other grounds and the endless debatability of these doctrines, that leads us to the last of the four alternatives which I noted earlier, the view closely associated with Enoch Powell and Edward Norman, that the Christian Gospel is intrinsically apolitical and that the search for a political theology is an illusion.

13.6:   The Conservative View

This final alternative is to endorse more vehemently Figgis's distinction between public and private morality and to claim, as in their rather different ways both Enoch Powell and Edward Norman do, that Christianity is essentially about personal morality and personal salvation and has no, and ought to have no, explicitly articulated political theology. In Powell's view, this has nothing specifically to do with secularisation and the growth of a plural society. On the contrary, Powell wishes to insist on this point, made in the earlier section on the Christian Nation, that there is no logical bridge between Christ's teaching and the business of politics. Earlier, I suggested that, while the gap exists, it could perhaps be closed by the development of mediating principles, although these would have the effect of reducing their agreed and authoritative status within the Church. However, Powell wants to deny that these mediating links can be developed. Christ's teaching is wholly supernatural and we should not read any specific social and political commitments into the Church's actions in regard to the poor or the sick:

'You said that Christ's mission was directed to the poor....you instanced various healing actions; the opening of the eyes of the blind, the unstopping of the ears of the deaf, etc. Having noticed that, you omitted something else which Jesus did but which is not within the scope of the National Health Service – the raising of the dead. What I am saying is that Christ's mission to the blind, the poor, the deaf, and all the rest is only another part of his mission to raise the dead; that as the raising of the dead is supernatural – is religious if you like – so also is the rest of the healing ministry of Christ and we are not imitating Christ or fulfilling his commandments, when we are engaged in healing any more than when we are engaged in banking.'[5]

It is part of Powell's argument that we shall look in vain to the Gospels themselves for prescriptions about our social and political life and that whatever there is in the Gospels in the way of general prescription is both indefinite and frequently paradoxical:

'The refusal to answer the question "what shall I do?" is essential to Christianity. In the face of its doctrines incarnation, crucifixion, resurrection, redemption, judgement – the question "what then shall we do?" is not so much superfluous as uncomprehending. Yet the refusal to answer is almost intolerable to men and women, in the way that looking straight into the light of the sun is intolerable. Right from the beginning people set to work to fill what they took to be a void or an omission. We have seen how in Luke the narrative of the baptist was supplied with a few handy questions and answers; and the Gospels, as they have reached us, bear traces of the determination to satisfy the demand for some good plain rules of conduct. Much more often, however, it is we ourselves who, by dint of refusing to read what the Gospels actually say, have obtained the answer which Jesus refused to give but which we are set upon finding.'[6]

Central to the Christian Gospel, then, is not a social and political doctrine but a challenge to individuals to struggle with the paradoxes at the heart of Christianity and to live their lives in the light of what they can make of them.

Alongside this argument stands another which Edward Norman has developed very forcefully over the past decade; that is that when the Church has allied itself with particular forms of political activity, it has never really taken into account the

---

[5] J.E. Powell, *Wrestling with the Angel* (London: Sheldon Press, 1977), p. 132.
[6] J.E. Powell, *No Easy Answers* (London: Sheldon Press, 1973), p. 84.

fragility and relativity of political principles and the movements associated with them. Contemporary *bien pensant* liberalism, with its concern for human rights, social justice, redistribution, poverty and race relations, cannot be taken as the enduring and sole distillation of Christian political theology:

'To those who are sceptical of all versions of Christian politics, including conservative ones – and this is my own position – the present identification of Christianity with western bourgeois liberalism seems an unnecessary consecration of a highly relative and unstable set of values, the more unsatisfactory because it is generally done unconsciously. Liberalism actually occupies a very narrow band on the spectrum of political theories. To regard it as the distillation of Christian wisdom, as the contemporary repository of a timeless faith, is, to say the least, a short term view.'[7]

Norman goes on to give a sociological account of how and why this endorsement of liberal ideology has occurred, an account, the form of which clearly denies that it is the result of a clear and unavoidable theological imperative:

'Related by class and cultural preference to the educated elites whose endorsement of liberal values they so faithfully reproduce, the leaders of the western churches seem completely unaware of how partial their political vision actually is.'[8]

There are two aspects to Norman's argument but, in his view, the failure to attend to them leads to the same danger. The first is the now familiar one: that there is no direct way to pass from the teachings of Christ to political ideology and action derived therefrom; the other is to emphasise the relativity and contestability of political doctrines with the consequence that if Christianity is identified with a current modish ideology such as modern liberalism, the faith whose objects and nature, in his view, stand outside of history, will become implicated in the fate of a political creed which may wane. All such creeds wax and

[7] E. Norman, *Christianity and World Order* (London: Oxford University Press, 1979), pp. 7–8.
[8] *Ibid.*

wane because, again in Norman's view, they are ultimately grounded in human preferences and do not record objective truths about inescapable necessities of human nature and the circumstances of human life. The Church is, therefore, taking a tremendous risk in allying itself with a particular political creed, a risk which in the nature of the faith it should not take.

Indeed, Norman wants to press the point that the Biblical evidence of God's action in history in relation to human values reveals not only a God who is transcendent and beyond identification with the historical process but is also in some sense indifferent to passing phases of human motivation and the expression of these in corporate values of all kinds:

'The most urgent task of Christianity in our day is to rediscover that sense of historical relativism, before the faith itself is absorbed by a single historical interpretation. It is to return to the version of history actually recorded in the scriptures. For there we find, certainly, very particular contexts for the dealings of God with men. But the God who appears is always depicted as objectively separate from the world of human values. He is the Lord of History, whose will is not explained within generalised models of historical causation. . .It is an account of the rise and fall of religions and peoples: all showing God's disregard of men's sense of the permanence of values.'[9]

Certainly, in his attempt to bring the Church face to face with the relativity of political values, Norman is echoing sentiments which would be agreed by many secular political theorists. Since the decline of Hegelianism and Intuitionism in the early years of this century, a constant theme of social and political theory has been whether it is possible to ground social and political judgements in anything other than the preferences of individuals. Once the preferences have been articulated, we can then reason about the means to realise the values based upon such preferences, but, on this view, reason is not capable of prescribing ends. A consequence of this has been the view that if political principles are derived from a set of normative preferences and attitudes, then it is not possible to give objective

[9] *Ibid.*, p. 83.

definitions of political concepts such as state, rights, authority, power, community, etc. The meanings of these terms are open-textured, or 'essentially contestable', their meanings being fixed, when and if they are, not by objective truths about the basis of political life but by the explicit preferences of human agents, or the inexplicit and unconscious preferences embodied in particular political traditions and practices.

On such a view, the idea that the Church could ally itself with a body of political principles based upon wholly neutral and rational grounds is an illusion. All the Church would be doing would be to supply a motivational backup for a particular set of highly contingent preferences. Norman is clearly right in arguing that the Church, in so far as it derived its political attitudes from the secular world, has failed to come to grips with this issue. Of course, the force of this argument would be lessened if the Church grounded its political doctrines in a fully worked out political theology but Norman's other argument is that this is impossible.

However, the point about morality and preferences would apply with equal force to issues of personal morality and the concepts which we use to think about it. Christian attitudes to personal morality in the spheres of sex, marriage and family life, too, could be seen as falling foul of both of Norman's strictures. It is certainly unclear to me how one can drawn a sharp line between social and political morality on the one hand and personal morality on the other. If it is somehow in the nature of the former to be contestable and for there to be no logical bridge between Christian doctrine and such values, then these two points ought to apply to the same degree to matters of private morality. Most Christians, I suspect, would find this conclusion very difficult to accept.

In addition, it could be argued that, without further elaboration, Norman's depiction of God as the Lord of History and his endorsement of a strong form of historical relativism sit together rather strangely. A vehement degree of relativism such as Norman defends seems, on the face of it, to be incompatible with the idea of moral and spiritual progress within history. If one set of values is as good as another in the social and political world and, as I have argued, on this view for the world of private morality too, and if they cannot be grounded in anything other than the shifting sands of human preferences, then we lose any ability to make judgements about progress in history. This form of nihilism may be all very well for the secular relativist but it is not clear how God as the Lord of History fits into this picture. If God as the Lord of History is also the judge of human action in history, this would seem to imply the idea of a right and a wrong way of doing things – standards which may not be given to us in any clear way but which we must struggle continually with our limited capacities to understand and implement in our lives, both personal and corporate. If, as an agent, however lowly, in the historical process I cannot know or begin to know whether anything that I do is in accordance with the will of God, then this makes the life of Christian discipleship very indeterminate.

While existentialists have always assumed that the non-existence of God makes everything possible, Powell and Norman seem to assume equally that it is not possible to give any *Christian* reasons for action in the public sphere and I have suggested, by parity of reasoning, in the private sphere as well. I suspect what is in play here, despite Norman's disavowal of any Christian political morality, is the conservative view that the public realm is a sphere to which moral categories do not apply. For example, in the sphere of the distribution of economic rewards, the outcomes of uncoerced transaction in markets should be accepted as in principle unprincipled. But this is itself a highly disputed political stance.

13.7: Some Concluding Remarks

Politics is an inescapable form of human life, and one which attempts to deal with the circumstances of our created condition – diverse interests, limited altruism, scarce resources, etc., and as such it has a profound effect upon human flourishing for good or ill and the realisation of those distinctively human capacities which make man in the image of God. However, until the Church is more intellectually serious about its involvement in politics and tries to link its political and social ethics into a more developed theological understanding of man as a political animal, its claims to be taken seriously in politics will founder. We live in a world of ideologies, of visions of the good society and the good for man, which in this century have received considerable and sophisticated theoretical elaboration. Until the Church takes its task of developing a political theology in the light of its own understanding of God and the God-given circumstances of human life more seriously and not just fall into the embrace of one or other of these secular moralities, then its forays into politics are going to seem as rootless and naive as its critics take them to be.

INDEX